Between Philosophy and Politics

# Between Philosophy and Politics

## *The Alienation of Political Theory*

JOHN G. GUNNELL

*The University of Massachusetts Press*

*Amherst 1986*

Copyright © 1986 by The University of Massachusetts Press
All rights reserved
Printed in the United States of America
LC 85-14106
ISBN 0-87023-497-8 (cloth); 498-6 (paper)

Designed by Barbara Werden
Set in Linotron Sabon by G & S Typesetters, Inc.
Printed and bound by Cushing-Malloy, Inc.

*Library of Congress Cataloging-in-Publication Data*

Gunnell, John G.
  Between philosophy and politics.

  Bibliography: p.
  Includes index.
  1. Political science—Philosophy.   I. Title.
JA71.G86   1986     320'.01     85-14106
ISBN 0-87023-497-8 (alk. paper)
ISBN 0-87023-498-6 (pbk.: alk. paper)

*To Pam and Jenni—who know the difference between theory and practice.*

# Contents

# *Preface*

THIS WORK is a synthesis, clarification, and elaboration of a number of arguments, mostly critical, that I have made about the field of academic political theory and its relationship to philosophy and politics. These arguments have been the subject of considerable controversy and misunderstanding, and a principal purpose here is at least to make clear what is being said and to articulate unambiguously the themes that connect my criticisms of such ostensibly disparate enterprises as behavioral political science and the study of the history of political theory. More than one person has been quick to point out that my own work has been implicated in the very problems that I address, but I have no wish to avoid certain dimensions of this paradox or to suggest that my animadversions do not entail self-criticism. My arguments are deeply rooted in the dialectic of the discourse of academic political theory, and the criticisms are internal. I do not, however, wish to disguise the fact that I have a profound and serious quarrel with much of the work that constitutes the political theory "establishment." Although this quarrel is essentially one involving the substantive character of the field, it also relates to matters of style. Political theory has, I believe, become an increasingly effete but pretentious activity whose self-image and claims about what it does and would do are conspicuously out of phase with its actual practice. For an activity so avowedly committed to reflection, criticism, and political transformation, it seems peculiarly resistant to authentic self-examination and actual involvement in the uncertainties of existential political action, even within the cloisters of the academy where it enjoys the potential privileges of citizenship.

There are some debts that I am enthusiastic about acknowledging. Richard Martin, the editor at the University of Massachusetts Press, played a large part in the conception of this project, and he nurtured it with patience and encouragement as well as a rare understanding of the substance of the work.

The association with my peers and teachers at the University of California at Berkeley during the early 1960s remains a formative influence and one that I increasingly nostalgically savor. Norman Jacobson's ideas continue to echo in my work in many ways, and he taught me that, of all things, political theory is not immune from having to take account of itself. Although some may not think my disagreements with Sheldon Wolin are negligible, it should be obvious that I have rotated around his intellectual compass. Since 1964, Paul Kress and I have been engaged in a constant conversation, and Gene Poschman has been a source of insight since the day he came upon me lost in the stacks looking for something called the *Congressional Record*. I acknowledge their ideas the way Woody Guthrie acknowledged folk tunes.

I, like many others, have for some time benefited from George Kateb's keen intellect and generous spirit, and it is a pleasure to be able to say so in something of a public manner. During the past few years, John Nelson and Ira Strauber have done much to make me aware of what I have said and what I have done by saying it. They have helped me sustain a belief in the significance of my arguments, while never relenting in their criticism.

Martin Edelman has chaired my department with wisdom and charity during the past two years and has done much to sustain and reconstitute the atmosphere that has, over the years and on the whole, made the State University of New York at Albany a place of felicity. Two graduate students, Christopher Robinson and Karen Sotherland, gave the draft of the manuscript a detailed reading and offered valuable suggestions for revision.

Dede Gunnell's support during this sometimes confining project has far exceeded the demands of mere justice.

Between Philosophy and Politics

# Introduction

*The beginning is more than half the work.*
PLATO

THIS BOOK is a general critique of academic political theory. The focus is on political theory, philosophy, politics and, particularly, the relationships among them. It is what should be called, I suppose, a deconstructive effort, because the purpose is basically one of destroying a number of myths that not only pervade the literature of academic political theory but have in large measure come to define it. Although in the final chapters I attempt to point beyond these myths and indicate the possibilities of political theory, my purpose is primarily to bring political theory face to face with itself and demythologize the enterprise.

These myths include the beliefs that the canon of classic texts from at least Plato to Marx constitutes an actual historical tradition that explains the present; that epistemology reveals the nature of scientific and social scientific explanation and provides the foundation of scientific inquiry and knowledge; that philosophy and political theory can discover and articulate transcendental grounds of political judgment; that politics is something more than a conventional form of human action or has some essential character that explains it and endows it with value; and that academic discourse about politics is equivalent to political discourse. It is the concatenation of these myths that has caused what I will refer to as the alienation of political theory.

This alienation has several analytically distinguishable dimensions, but it is basically a function of political theory's dependence on various forms of philosophical and metatheoretical discourse and its failure to come to grips with its actual relationship to politics. To explain this situation would be in part simply to relate the history of academic political theory, which is a task that I have attempted to take on, in a preliminary way, in another context (1983b). What such an investigation reveals is that the images of political theory of and by which we are now possessed are basically inventions of the discourse of academic political theory, particularly as it has evolved within American political science. As both a mode and an object of inquiry, political theory is less the world-historical phenomenon in terms of which the field attempts to understand itself than an idea that has evolved within that field. But no matter how intelligible the situation may be when viewed historically in a disciplinary and professional context, it is in part the manifestation of an underlying paradox, or confusion, involving the very idea of political knowledge. To some extent this paradox characterizes the social sciences in general, but it is, for various reasons, more poignantly evident in the case of political theory.

The nature of this problem will become clear, I hope, in the course of this book, but the basic difficulty involves a failure to deal adequately with the difference between knowledge *in* politics and knowledge *about* politics and with the question of the authority of the latter in relationship to the former. The social sciences and social theory in general must grapple with the dilemma that their claims to knowledge imply an end in action that they are seldom in a position to pursue. In the case of political theory, understood as either science or wisdom, academic estrangement has not been suffered lightly, but the problem has seldom been confronted authentically.

Unlike other social sciences, the heroes and putative founders of political theory, and political science as well, have not, for the most part, been individuals who can be remotely construed, with historical warrant, as significantly connected with the field. Although contemporary sociology might reasonably count Max Weber and Emile Durkheim among its ancestors, political theory's choice of someone like Aristotle is largely romantic. And although Plato, Machiavelli, Locke, and Marx may not have been statesmen or even necessarily successful intellectuals, theirs was more a world of action than one of professional scholarship. No matter how diverse the activities of those individuals who have conventionally been designated as the classic political theorists may appear when scrutinized in detail, it is safe to say that there is, on the whole, a great distance between those activities and modern academic disciplines. And although it may be possible, at some level of abstraction, to distinguish, analytically or functionally, certain similarities in concern and endeavor between contemporary political theory as an academic field and these historical paradigms, such assimilation is fundamentally distortive. Political theory has at times projected its own academic enterprise on its adopted ancestors and at other times cast its identity in the image of its epic view of the classic pantheon, but in both cases it has characteristically mythologized both its subject matter and its own activity.

Political theorists have by no means always accepted the classic canon as a positive model. Sometimes, as in the case of behavioralism in political science, they have defined their enterprise in terms of a contrast with what has generally been understood as the great tradition of political theory, or, at least, they have understood themselves as surpassing or perfecting that tradition. When the classics have not been the basic focus of the perennial identity crisis of the field, science has been the benchmark—in terms of either emulation or rejection. But the images of science have been equally distorted. The persistent tendency to believe that political theory was, or could be, like scientific theory has been grounded in a series of philosophical myths about science and scientific inquiry. It is just such myths that have produced the various dimensions of the alienation of political theory.

First, and most importantly, there is an alienation from politics as an object of inquiry. This is a consequence of political theory's uncritical appropriation of, and absorption in, various metatheoretical or philosophical tropes. Much of political theory addresses not what might be called the particularities of politics but rather philosophical images of politics, and it seeks to define and resolve political issues as well as the issue of its relationship to politics in metatheoretical terms. Claims about politics are displaced by allusions, often spurious, to politics. Neither actual political objects nor the ontological (or theoretical) character of such objects has been the subject of recent political theory.

Second, but closely related to the first problem, is an alienation from the study of politics or a loss of theoretical autonomy resulting from the dependence of political theory on other fields. The literature of political theory has, in many instances, become little more than a repetition of arguments derived from the philosophy of science or social science, metaethics, hermeneutics, phenomenology, analytical philosophy and conceptual analysis, existentialism, structuralism, history. There is little consideration of their intrinsic validity, their applicability to political inquiry, or the problem of moving from philosophical claims about inquiry to prescriptions for its practice.

Third, political theory has become alienated from itself in that its self-image and self-ascribed divisions (historical, normative, empirical, critical, formal, etc.) are less aspects of some integrated and autonomous activity or elements of an evolving practice than categories derived from various metatheoretical realms of discourse. And, fourth, it has become alienated from itself not only through its loss of independent identity but in its estrangement from the very species of activity to which it aspires. Theorizing has become detached from actual practices of knowledge and given way to metatheorizing about objects that are largely philosophical inventions.

Although this study is not primarily historical, it is premised on certain historical or quasi-historical claims which will be made explicit but which cannot be fully documented in this context. One such claim, already alluded to, is that political theory is not the world-historical activity that it is often assumed to be. The assumption that it is or has been such an activity is largely a consequence of the reification and projection into the past and future of mythical and metatheoretical images of the enterprise. As something other than a category for distinguishing, at some level of abstraction, certain things that have a family resemblance, functional equivalence, or stipulative similarity, "political theory" and "political philosophy" refer simply to the activity and product of an academic discipline.

Although it is tempting to slip into a metaphor suggesting that political theory has *become* alienated, it may be more accurate to say that it was always alienated. There never was any such existentially autonomous activity that can be historically distinguished as standing in or beside politics. Political theory and its history are a phenomenon of approximately the last century, and it is an academic phenomenon. Although this distance from politics that is a function of political theory as an academic enterprise is not in itself invidious, the failure to recognize and confront the reality of this distancing has become the source of egregious alienation and bad faith.

Another historical assumption is that the alienation of political theory is in part a consequence of the fact that the transcendental and epistemological traditions in philosophy upon which much of political theory has drawn are themselves alienated enterprises. The contemporary dilemma of political theory has arisen as much through the acquisition of characteristics of these intellectual styles as from the circumstances of its own activity. Furthermore, although political theory is in an important sense an invention of political and social science, these disciplines are, in an equally important sense, an invention of philosophy. It is a great mistake to assume that the historical relationship between philosophy and natural science is an adequate model for understanding the relationship between philosophy and social science.

It should be clear at this point that when I speak of "political theory" I am referring not to the mythical images that populate the literature and are the object of my deconstructive efforts but rather to the academic discourse that has generated those images. Neither am I talking about some categorical such as "reflection on politics" or simply about theory as opposed to practice. My subject is the literature of the conventional enterprise of political theory in political science and the wider self-ascribed interdisciplinary field of political theory and political philosophy.

When speaking of philosophy, I am speaking not about a generic category such as reflective or self-conscious thought but, primarily, about professional academic philosophical literature and specific historical traditions in this field. I am concerned particularly with certain epistemological, logical, and methodological arguments that have tended to dominate much of the literature of philosophy and that have influenced political theory, but I also include, for example, certain transcendental claims such as those involved in various notions of natural law.

My reference for "politics" is equally specific, but, for the most part, I will not be talking about particular historical forms of politics except to indicate that most of political theory does not address these particularities. In the later sections of the book, I will talk about politics as a kind of object and attempt to speak theoretically, in a legislated but fully explicated sense of the term, about politics and the kind of issues that I believe a theory of politics should address. My argument, somewhat paradoxically, will be that there can be no theory of politics per se, because political objects are only a species or mode of human action. There can be no generic theory of politics any more (or less) than there can be a theory of religion, science, and art or of Christianity, biology, and cubism.

My use of these terms, then, is not categorical or analytical in any a priori sense. To the extent to which I employ the terms categorically or generically, I assume that they represent empirical or existential divisions that persist conventionally within the contexts I am discussing. In making distinctions among political theory, philosophy, and politics, I am not assuming any particular set of relationships or lack of relationships. My assumption is that these are distinct practices —whatever the specific lines of demarcation and penumbral areas might be at any time or place. I want to take care not to project specific boundaries and configurations into universals and not to distort specific instances by the imposition of such universals and the baggage that they may happen to carry.

I find this approach relatively unproblematical, but certain conceptual confusions may intrude. One such confusion has thoroughly infiltrated the language of political theory. This involves not only the failure to distinguish categorical or generic uses of terms such as "politics" from uses that specify or describe particular practices and historically persistent forms of practice but also a failure to admit or recognize any such distinction in principle. Another confusion involves a neglect of the difference between distinctions and relations.

To claim, for example, as I will, that it is important to make distinctions among political theory, philosophy, and politics is not to suggest that there are not, or should not be, relationships among them. To acknowledge the distinction is in fact the precondition of making any claims about such connections. And to make an argument about relations of a particular and historical kind is not to suggest identity. In order to make this point less abstract and to guard against the misinterpretation of subsequent arguments, I will indicate one area to which the point applies.

I will be arguing that there is a tendency in various areas of political theory to conflate academic and political discourse simply because the former is about—or may intuitively be believed to have even an indirect impact on—the latter or because the language of the latter may be shared with the former. My point is not that there are no possibilities for important and fruitful relationships among political theory, philosophy, and politics but rather that these relationships have often been misunderstood and misconceived and that the distinction has been systematically blurred. My purpose is to explore the nexus and engage in some straight thinking about what political theory is and what it might be. There are, however, some concerns about this kind of undertaking that I share with those who might depreciate it, and, even at the risk of appearing apologetic or defensive, I will address some of these issues.

This could be construed as largely a negative venture, and although the argument will take a more positive turn toward the end of the work, I would not bridle at that characterization. I believe that much of political theory, particularly in the last twenty-five years, has become narcissistic and that it must be confronted with the reality of its condition and particularly with its status as an academic enterprise. My argument is not simply that what is required is a clearing operation which, when accomplished, will allow us to move forward to great achievements of social knowledge and political transformation. Political theory has condemned itself to irrelevance by harboring visions of knowledge beyond its capacity and pretensions to a concern about political change that far exceeds the practical commitments of its practitioners.

Political theory speaks of scientific knowledge comparable to natural science and engineering; of knowledge of the meaning of history and the human condition; of transcendental grounds of political values; of the reflective grasp of the structural and ideological constraints of modernity and the discovery of the means and ends of human emancipation; of achieving at last a truly historical understanding of the past of our present that will also clarify in general the relationship between thought and action; of recovering from the classics a philosophical understanding of the nature of political things that will be a key to some measure of political salvation; of producing political education that appreciates the past and saves the future by speaking truth to power and raising the consciousness of the potentially and rightfully powerful; of supplying the logic and substance of sound normative judgments about public policy choices; and so on. Such claims are not merely rhetorical lapses in an otherwise rational enterprise. They are the illusions and delusions of an enterprise that has become alienated and inauthentic.

Some of the founders of the myths that dominate the field, Charles Merriam and his idea of scientific theory, for example, came to philosophy in the midst of social crisis and with political purpose. Some, like Leo Strauss, who emigrated to the United States in the 1930s may have found in political theory a kind of symbolic action born from political alienation, but for most the symbolism has been unreflectively learned and practiced in a world far removed from political life and even political passion. My argument is not necessarily that political theory should shrink its vision or be satisfied with the crabbed life of a scholarly underlaborer, but as long as it is content to remain basically an academic enterprise, it must confront the question of its relationship to political life and the condition of ambiguity into which it has drifted in its relationship to both philosophy and politics.

But, one might ask, is not such an undertaking a metatheoretical critique of metatheory that serves to perpetuate the problem, the apotheosis of narcissism, the epitome of what is being called into question? This may be the case, but the difficulties of political theory must be met on their own ground. Although political theory responds quickly, almost automatically, to changes in philosophical fashion and general academic ambience as well as consistently, but more slowly, to changes in political climate, this environment has very little critical impact. Isaiah Berlin once claimed that political theory would not perish, could not die, as long as there were value judgments to be made in a world of plural ends (1962), but this was to confuse the genus with the species or the function with the structure. Political theory will not die as long as it maintains itself as an academic institution, and effective criticism, and change, can come only from within that institution.

To destroy the myths that have become definitive of political theory is not to destroy the institution and realm of discourse but to transform it. The ends of that transformation are, from my perspective, relatively concrete. The primary goal is to direct efforts toward what I consider to be substantive theory as opposed to metatheoretical claims about theory and theorizing. Substantive theory involves, first of all, claims and arguments about the character of political (and social) phenomena. To explain, describe, evaluate, or perform some other act with regard to political phenomena presupposes some detailed explication of the constitution of those phenomena and something that is more than an abstract metatheoretical proposition. Such an undertaking, however, is only to some degree analytically separable from particular substantive claims about politics.

It is one of the philosophical myths of political theory, in both political science and the wider field, that theory is some sort of special element or product in the practices of knowledge that is more than pragmatically distinguishable from the corpus of specific claims and conventions that make up those practices. But what we might analytically extract as theory is embedded in those concrete substantive claims. An end to the alienation of political theory would ultimately entail theory engaging the particularity of politics in more than a cursory manner. Today substantive theory, to the extent that it exists, appears largely, and strangely, in the inverted role of justifying and illustrating the metatheoretical arguments that have become the core of the enterprise.

The practice of substantive theory would eventually force political theory to confront what its alienated versions have attempted to reduce to a philosophical issue, that is, the problem of the relationship between political theory and politics. It would be presumptuous to believe that there is some specific and definitive answer to this question, because to some degree it involves the whole issue of the place of the university in society. I would hope for little more than the opening of dialogue on this matter and an end to the evasion of the issue by feigning parallels between political theorists and natural scientists, revolutionary intellectuals, prophets, and other unlikely models.

I do, at least for the sake of nostalgia, want to suggest that political theory has a certain promise for moving about in the demimondes between academia and politics and between philosophy and social science. Both its mythical prototypes (Plato and Machiavelli, for example) and its actual ancestors (John Stuart Mill and Charles Merriam) sought political change through philosophy, the academy, or some transpolitical realm of discourse, and a realistic understanding of their endeavors may still be instructive in many ways. In the present situation, political theory is in some measure at least potentially free from many of the dogmas and narrow perspectives of both philosophy and social science. If unburdened of the myths that tend to condemn it to self-delusion, it could play an effective but yet undefined role of critical mediation between philosophy and politics and between the university and society.

Whether or not political theory, as a distinct field and enterprise, has any such future, the critique of political theory amounts to more than the formally tertiary activity of talking about those who claim to talk about political talk. The persistent myth that academic, and often highly philosophically mediated, claims about politics are in some fundamental way identical with practical or political claims conveniently absolves the political theorist from really confronting the relationship between theory and practice. But it requires no survey research to ascertain that in contemporary Western and non-Western societies social science and the humanities are a significant form of political education and that their claims infiltrate social thought and action.

Although it is important not to exaggerate this role of political theory and raise it to cosmic proportions, political theory is at the very least implicated in the teaching of the teachers who contribute to molding political perceptions, and its impact on various dimensions of social knowledge is not without practical consequence. The critique of social science and political theory could, consequently, be construed in a limited way as a critique of politics, but there is less room for disputing that it is a critique of a structure of knowledge that has a significant relationship to politics, the university, and other social institutions. One of the problems with political theory today, however, is that it has largely withdrawn from a critique of political science.

Chapter 1 presents, in synoptic form, the general argument of the book. Chapters 2 and 3 pursue, respectively and in detail, the ideas of political theory as science and tradition that have exercised such a significant hold over the field. Chapters 4 and 5 explore in a broader and more discursive manner the state of contemporary academic political theory with an emphasis on its metatheoretical propensities. Chapter 6 attempts to present the rudiments of a theory of action that would illustrate the demand for substantive theory that informs the earlier and critical chapters.

# 1

## *The Alienation of Political Theory*

Philosophy and the study of the real world are related to one another like masturbation and sexual love.

KARL MARX

MORE THAN thirty years ago, Alfred Cobban (1953) charged that the Western tradition of political theory, a tradition concerned with ethical issues, had ceased to develop and had entered a period of decline. Cobban's argument was only one of many claims about the decline of political theory that appeared in the 1950s, and the idea of political theory as it is understood today was in large measure invented during the course of these discussions. Cobban, like many of the period, argued that the immediate cause of the retreat from questions of what "ought to be" was the impact of the "modes of thought" characteristic of science and history, that is, value freedom and relativism, but he believed that the underlying source of the problem was the circumstance in which political theory had become "disengaged from political facts" and "practice" and had "become instead an academic discipline" (rep. 1969:298–99).

Cobban's analysis of political theory was perceptive, but it also involved a fundamental mistake that was made by almost all those engaged in these debates about the decline of political theory. It was the assumption that the canon of classic texts that had become part of the curriculum of political studies in the university represented an actual historical tradition whose latest phase was academic political theory, including the study of those texts. Arguments about decline begged the fundamental issue. There was no doubt that there was an academic tradition of political theory, but the notion that it was the decline of a greater tradition reaching from Plato to recent years was a pervasive myth. It is difficult to be sure just how literally someone like Cobban intended this connection, but it is clear that the idea of the historical integrity of the tradition gained increasing importance during the next decade.

Although Cobban did not correctly understand the genesis of the situation, he recognized the dilemma of political theory as an academic discipline. And, even as an academic discipline, it was by the 1950s becoming increasingly alienated from direct engagement with issues in political practice and from contact with political facts. The question of the extent to which political theory had concerned itself with ethical issues was more moot, for many during this period would claim that it was precisely an excessive emphasis on such matters that was the problem. The behavioralist account of the decline of political theory also recognized a detachment of political theory from political reality. This account, which began to develop during this period, was also historically questionable, and its diagnosis and recommendations were significantly different from those of individuals such as Cobban. It claimed that science offered a way of re-engaging political facts and creating an identity for political theory.

Even if the self-image of political theory in the past had, in retrospect, not always been very plausible, its failure, beginning in the 1950s, to face up to what it was and might be was nothing short of prodigious. And in seeking an identity it increasingly lost its intellectual autonomy. Although certain elements, under siege within the discipline of political science, would by the 1970s achieve a large measure of professional independence as an interdisciplinary field, political theory increasingly became little more than variations on metatheoretical themes in philosophy and philosophical history. By the 1980s, not only was political theory thoroughly estranged from its object, politics, but its components, both inside and outside political science, had become dispersed and even incapable of meaningful debate.

The alienation of political theory had its immediate origins in the controversy that arose in the midst of the behavioral revolution in political science. Although it is difficult, and artificial, to make a sharp distinction between the pre- and post-1950 eras, the division is a somewhat indigenous one, and the continuities as well as the transformations are worth noting. It is most important to understand the nature of the behavioral revolution and its relationship to the earlier history of political science, because this information is not readily accessible in the rhetoric of either the revolutionaries or the counterrevolutionaries.

It would be a mistake to impose too programmatic and schematic an image on these events associated with the behavioral revolution. The participants were far from fully able to articulate the circumstances in which they were involved, and the various positions were more diverse and complex than they often seem in retrospect. But, despite many appearances to the contrary, the behavioral revolution was a conservative revolution. This is not to say that it did not fundamentally change the character of political science or that it did not institute new research programs, but it was fought in defense of old ideals and traditional, if unrealized, goals in both politics and social science. As in many conservative revolutions, however, the enemy was not accurately specified, but revolution required something definite to be overthrown.

If one is familiar with the history of American political science prior to 1940 (see Ricci, 1984; Seidelman, 1985), the behavioral attack on historical or "traditional" political theory is not comprehensible on its face. It might be suggested that, because the revolutionaries needed something to revolt against, the history of political theory seemed most alien to the scientific goals of behavioralism. There is also the less cynical and more historically sensitive thesis that change within the discipline had always been advanced in the name of theory. Because the history of political theory largely occupied the subfield and held the title, it became the focus of criticism. And matters like the typical postwar emphasis on science and the need to demonstrate "scientificness" in order to secure research funding, the failure of previous phases of the discipline to achieve its scientific vision, the dominance of positivism and scientism in the other social sciences and in philosophy, and the retreat from practical concerns in favor of pure science are all relevant. Yet even the composite of all these factors does not provide an adequate explanation for exactly what happened in political theory.

The fact that most of the pivotal figures in the behavioral movement had been trained as traditional political theorists might be taken as an anomaly, but it is part of the explanation and touches a matter that goes deeper than their conventional occupation with theoretical issues. Prior to 1940 there is very little to indicate any tension between science and history in American political science. Political theory had characteristically been understood as including the history of political theory, which was in turn represented largely as the progressive history of political science and democratic values. And, despite some variation in the terms employed, political science and political theory were assumed to consist of both empirical and normative propositions about politics and government.

From the paradigm-setting texts of William Dunning (1902–20) to the protobehavioral arguments of Charles Merriam (1925) to George Sabine's influential history of political theory (1937), the scientific and political ideology of the discipline had remained remarkably uniform. Despite some exceptions, the discipline was generally politically conservative although maybe at times intellectually radical in its dreams of an instrumental social science allied with a national state for the solution of social and political problems. Its propensities were distinctly pragmatic and grounded in a belief in the complementarity, if not outright identity, of scientific and liberal democratic values, along with a constant aversion to the taint of what it took to be speculative philosophy and metaphysics and their political and ideological counterparts. The history of political theory was understood as demonstrating all this and, particularly in the 1930s, offered a vehicle for democratic self-consciousness in the face of alien political challenges from both the left and right.

From 1900 to 1945 there was hardly a major figure in political theory, or political science, who was not involved in both the history of political theory and the advancement of political science as a science, and one would look in vain for any significant tension between these notions of theory. This was in part because "theory," "theorist," and "theorizing" were concepts that had been consistently understood in a rather functional manner. Political theories, in both political science and political life, were ideas about the state, whether descriptive, causal, or prescriptive and evaluative, as opposed to facts and institutions. They were, particularly as an aspect of political science, mental constructs for organizing and manipulating, both intellectually and practically, the mass of data that social scientists and statesmen confronted in the social and political world.

There are a variety of historical reasons why the profession of political science was born with a subfield called "political theory," but it was not because "theory" and its cognates had any very definite or specific meaning when the American Political Science Association was founded (1903). In some respects the history of the subfield is the history of the attempt to give "theory" meaning. It is the history of its reification. Even through the 1940s the term was largely used in a functional or categorical sense. Its reification was basically a product of the debates about theory that began in the 1950s. But the fundamental interpretative question remains—What was the root of the conflict within political theory and between political theory and political science?

The problem stemmed from the intrusion of ideas promulgated by the German émigrés of the 1930s. These individuals included Leo Strauss, Hannah Arendt, Theodor Adorno, Eric Voegelin, Franz Neuman, Arnold Brecht, Herbert Marcuse, Max Horkheimer. Although often not yet in published form, these ideas had begun, during the 1940s, to have a significant impact on the profession and discipline of political science and particularly on the discourse of political theory.

These thinkers appeared, at least from the American perspective, to be political theorists, but their ideas had been formed in the context of German philosophy and the practical experience of totalitarianism. Whether left or right in their ideological leanings, many of these individuals represented a position and orientation that threatened some of the basic premises of American political science and political theory.

American political science had been heavily influenced by German thought during its formative period in the late 1800s as well as during the first two decades of the twentieth century, and political science (and political theory) was in many respects Hegelian and Comtean in its early years. However, the general reaction against "speculative" philosophy that characterized the early 1900s had succeeded in thoroughly "Americanizing" these ideas both politically and philosophically. The world-historical visions of the third great wave of German influence were not easily assimilated in either style or substance. Although there were many specific problems stemming from the attachment of these thinkers to Marxism, certain theological doctrines, and other alien perspectives, a more basic and general difficulty was their historical pessimism and their depreciation of both liberalism and science.

The perspective introduced by Voegelin, Strauss, Arendt, and Marcuse entailed the idea that the history of politics and political theory in the West, at least in recent times, was one of decline. This notion was tied to a critique of both liberalism and science. Liberalism was construed in one way or another as decadent, as the historical threshold of fascism and nazism, and the facade of socially repressive forces. Science, scientific philosophy, and technology were conceived in similar manner, and social science was often understood as their most heinous manifestation. Science was the instrument of political oppression and the enemy of humanism.

There were numerous other antithetical elements in these new themes in political theory, but maybe most important was the resurgence of what in the earlier years would have been called "speculative" political philosophy. Although it might not be difficult to perceive the cosmos of normative givens inherent in American pragmatism and realism, American political scientists believed not only in separating facts and values but in the relativity of values and the danger in transcendental claims. The new wave of thought, however, maintained that value relativism and the separation of fact and value were both causes and symptoms of a crisis of modernity. Almost without exception, these thinkers sought, either in history or outside it, a source of transcendental judgment for the critique of politics.

Other matters of dissonance might be detailed, but this should be sufficient to indicate that the European infusion of ideas in political theory, which began to take effect in the 1940s and was more fully visible by the 1950s, precipitated a crucial moment for the self-image of American political science. The idea of political theory as part of an empirical science of politics integrally related to the evolution of liberal thought and practice, an idea that had been at the core of American political science from its earliest beginnings, was in jeopardy. The consequence would be the end of the alliance between, if not the identity of, theory as history and theory as science and a proliferation of metatheoretical arguments in defense of each.

One would be forced to search very hard for any sophisticated and philosophically informed source of or reflection on notions about political theory as part of empirical political science before the 1950s. The basic claims about theory and science, even the language and phrasing of those claims, changed very little in the forty years from Merriam's announcement of, or call for, the creation of a systematic interdisciplinary causal "science of human behavior" (1925:11) to Easton's statement of the "behavioral credo" and the commitment to develop "a science of politics modeled after the methodological assumptions of the natural sciences" (1965a:8). What, increasingly, did change, however, was the relationship between philosophy and political science or between metatheoretical rhetoric and scientific practice.

It was a long time, not until well into the 1970s, before political scientists of the behavioral persuasion became fully aware of either the philosophical sources of their scientific identity or the existence of alternative images of science and social scientific explanation. But as early as 1950 Harold Lasswell, in one of the first attempts of the behavioral, or proto-behavioral, era to provide a theoretical "framework for political science," indicated that his efforts were informed by a "thorough-going empiricist philosophy of the sciences" based on "logical positivism, operationalism, and instrumentalism" (Lasswell and Kaplan, 1950:xiii, xiv). Even his collaboration on this work with the philosopher Abraham Kaplan indicated a new dimension or threshold in the relationship between political science and philosophy.

There is little evidence that would suggest that in the previous twenty years Lasswell had any very deep involvement with the philosophy of science. And his case was typical of the advocates of scientism. From the beginning, natural science had been a model, or contrast model, for the social sciences, and nowhere was this more true than in political science. What was also the case, however, was that social scientists, almost without exception and without regard to whether they wished to identify themselves with it or disassociate themselves from it, had no significant contact with or knowledge of the practices of natural science. Natural science was basically either a legitimating or a critical symbol mediated through various philosophical images.

It would require a detailed historical examination of particular cases to determine the extent to which the social sciences were influenced by philosophical accounts of science and the extent to which they employed such accounts rhetorically, either reflectively or unreflectively, for justification and criticism. The relationship was, however, an integral and complex one, and it is safe to say that eventually a change in the philosophical image of science would produce an identity crisis in the social sciences. In the history of American political science, the balance between influence and legitimation, to the extent that they can be analytically disentangled, has differed at various points.

Through 1950 there was little defection from the principle that natural science was a positive model. And, from the beginning of the discipline to the end of the behavioral era, the basic assumptions, on the part of both proponents and opponents of scientism, about the nature and demands of scientific method and explanation changed very little. Even the transition from Comtean and Spencerian images of science, dominant in the first two decades of the century, to those of logical positivism, beginning in the 1940s, did not significantly alter the basic ideas about the character of scientific inquiry. What did shift, overall, was the valence between influence and legitimation. It is necessary to exercise care in making this distinction, because even the rationalizing uses of the symbol of natural science indicate a form of influence to the degree that individuals are constrained and directed by the symbols available. But by the 1960s political scientists had become significantly more the instruments of their symbolism than in Merriam's era, despite the growth in their reflectiveness about the source.

For both internal and external reasons and audiences, Merriam had evoked and invoked the image of science for his enterprise. This was also largely true for the political scientists of the 1950s, but although Merriam, despite his lack of success in many respects, had little focused internal opposition to his program apart from critics who believed he was either too much or too little committed to practical goals, his successors believed that the survival of the traditional scientific image of political theory, as well as the basic goals of the discipline, was at risk. The symbol of science, by the 1950s, no longer commanded immediate and general respect. The historical situation seemed to signal increasing urgency about the need to realize the scientific potential of the discipline, but there was at the same time a challenge to the authority of both the general symbol of science and the specific image that had characterized political science.

It was in this context that political scientists entered into a critique of the study of the history of political theory and sought to develop a more articulate vision of their scientific commitments. Although numerous factors contributed to the resurgence of scientism that characterized the behavioral revolution, what has been neglected, and misunderstood, is the extent to which that recommitment was a reaction to the subversion of political science's scientific and political identity that was being mounted not only within the discipline but within what had traditionally been understood as its intellectual core—political theory.

It was also in this context, in part in response to the behavioral attack and in part simply because of the ideas represented in that movement, that the study of the history of political theory was transformed into a vehicle for the critique of what, by the 1960s, was becoming mainstream political science. Among the authors of this critique were both those, such as Strauss, who had begun to challenge the basic vision of liberal scientific progress and some of those more anomalously positioned individuals who had been simply "doing" the history of political theory in the usual American way. They found themselves, somewhat inexplicably, the target of their peers, with whom they thought they shared basic premises about the compatibility of history and science. The dialogue between these protagonists, which lasted well into the 1970s, and the waves of philosophical reflection about political theory which that dialogue in part engendered were the basic cause of the contemporary alienation of political theory. And it was not merely an alienation of the spirit. Both sides began to practice what they preached.

This was not the first time in the social sciences that a *Methodenstreit* had profound disciplinary and professional effects, but this conflict largely absorbed theoretical discussion in political science for a quarter of a century. It not only fundamentally shaped significant portions of political science, especially the subfield of political theory, but significantly contributed to the emergence of the wider field of political theory and philosophy which, despite later assumptions about its perennial character, was hardly differentiated and identifiable prior to the 1960s.

At its core, behavioralism or the behavioral movement, as something other than simply what political scientists did and came to do, was an amalgam of quasi-philosophical ideas about scientific explanation. Whether or not these ideas were reflectively instrumental, they served an ideological function within the discipline and produced a unifying force that had not been sustained in earlier years. The atmosphere of enthusiasm and the commitment to challenging what behavioralists characterized as the orthodoxy of historical and institutional analysis may have led some truly to believe in their extravagant claims about such matters as emulating the laws of physics. There is, however, reason to suggest that professional and disciplinary identity was the most significant goal.

Political science, more so than the other social sciences, was from its beginning more a holding company for some loosely related fields of inquiry and research programs than a discipline with a theoretical core. The behavioral "revolution" and the behavioral "mood" were in part manifestations of a continuing attempt to establish a scientific and disciplinary identity. One of the factors that contributed to the success of behavioralism was the sense of urgency created by both the real and perceived external context and the sense of lagging behind other fields in scientific accomplishment, but there were also important internal factors.

One of the forces that animated political theory, particularly the history of political theory, in the 1930s was the belief in the need to construct or, more accurately, make explicit and coherent a liberal democratic ideology that would be comparable to and confront the foreign ideologies on the left and right that theatened both political mind and space. Behavioralism was doing something on this order with regard to the discipline's scientific image, but the similarity is more than analogous. The 1950s were also a period of ideological consolidation. The extent to which the creation of value theory that would be equal to the times was part of the behavioral program is often forgotten in view of its dominant and subsequent emphasis on scientific method, but more important was the persistence of the faith in the complementarity of democracy and science that permeated the behavioral literature.

In the controversies of the 1960s over the political, and apolitical, role of the discipline, critics pointed to the extent to which behavioralism, in theory and practice, reflected and legitimated dominant liberal values. Doing science, and the particular kind of science that characterized behavioralism, was a kind of value theory. The doctrines of the priority of pure science and the separation of facts and values only appeared to be a contradiction of the professed concern with liberal democracy. The behavioral revolution was, then, a conservative one in several respects. Its basic goals and notions of science had defined the discipline from its inception, and in varying degrees of explicitness it was a defense of traditional liberalism and American institutions.

In many respects the behavioral revolution was a theoretical one—apart from the fact that, with regard to its scientific goals, it did not accomplish in practice what it claimed in theory. Not only were most of the major spokesmen by training political theorists, but the subfield of political theory was where the revolutionary and antirevolutionary debates largely took place. A transformation in theory and its uses was also to be the fulcrum for disciplinary change. But most important for the argument here is the fact that the behavioral movement, by the time this self-ascribed persuasion had become a disciplinary orthodoxy in the 1960s, produced an unprecedented metatheoretical self-consciousness that had a far-reaching impact on the practice of research as well as the evolution of images of political theory.

No matter what innovations behavioralism introduced into the research programs of political science or what changes it effected in the orientation of the discipline toward politics, it persisted in legitimating political inquiry in terms of the authority of its scientificness. And, as in previous periods (e.g., Merriam, 1925), the history of the discipline was represented as the story of the progress of science as conceived in the present and, particularly, as the growth of theory (e.g., Almond, 1966; Truman, 1965). Theory was understood as the hallmark of science. Although it would be appropriate to write the history of many fields of knowledge as the history of the evolution of theories about their object of research, it might be more reasonable to write the history of political science from the perspective of its theory of theory. What came to characterize the behavioral era, however, was the fact that these images of theory became less and less merely legitimating myths as scientific practice became increasingly an attempt to legitimate epistemological and methodological commitments.

David Easton's claim about the "decline" of political theory and the need for its reconstitution (1951; 1953) was characteristic (although maybe the paradigm case) of a number of attacks on what came to be understood by both its critics and its defenders as "traditional theory." This meant in effect the study of what had come to be understood as the "great tradition" from Plato to the present and the normative concerns that supposedly characterized that putative tradition. The terms of this critique had, in fact, been developing steadily during the past decade as both the new European influences on the subfield of political theory were felt and the various postwar factors pointing to a need to reassert and revise the scientific image of political science took shape.

Easton's argument, and it is important to note exactly what the argument claimed, was that the tradition that had begun with the Greeks had undergone "impoverishment" in the hands of historically oriented scholars such as George Sabine who had transformed it into a history of political ideas that both lacked relevance to contemporary values and contributed little to the task of developing "a generalized theory about the relations of facts" that could serve as the "theoretical organ" of a truly scientific study of politics. What was required was a "theoretical revolution" that both released political theory from parasitic historicism and transcended the "hyperfactualism" and "crude empiricism" of previous years.

The account provided by individuals such as Easton was in many respects quite accurate with regard to its description of the character and condition of political theory and political science, but it misrepresented the intentions, motives, and work of those, such as Sabine, whom it overtly criticized. Sabine's analysis of political theory (1939), for example, was not significantly different from Easton's. Although he wrote about the history of political theory, he did not depreciate the scientific study of politics or see anything but the compatibility, even identity, of the two enterprises. The criticism was directed at a genre that harbored the incipient critics of political science but in which they were still not highly visible. Although the historians of political theory—Strauss, Arendt, and Voegelin, for example—who came into prominence in the postwar years were in fact already antagonistic toward the values of American political science, the behavioral critique crystallized and galvanized hostile attitudes and precipitated a fundamental split within the field. It would be an exaggeration to say that the arguments that emerged from the literature of the history of political theory in the succeeding years were simply a response to that critique, but they were certainly in large measure shaped by it.

Just as behavioralists had attempted to redefine and demarcate political theory, the traditionalists, who now to some extent identified themselves in terms of those who criticized them, elaborated an alternative image of theory and its past and future that at least initially was more part of a defensive maneuver than anything having to do with the normal practice of research. Individuals such as Strauss set out to diagnose what they also called the "decline of political philosophy," but they described that decline in terms of assumptions at the core of behavioralism and the liberal values with which it was associated. Furthermore, the argument, sometimes explicit and sometimes implicit, was that both the historical approach and what was to be discovered or recalled by this approach were not only far from decadent but the key to solving the problem of decline.

What is most important with respect to the argument here is that this controversy, which developed during the 1950s and came to a head in the 1960s, was not, strictly speaking, a theoretical controversy at all. Although there were various dimensions of substantive theoretical conflict about politics and political phenomena embedded in the contending claims of behavioralism and those who became its institutional critics, the dispute was about, or at least was carried on in terms of metatheoretical arguments about, the nature of theory, the history of theory, and the character and purpose of theorizing. Eventually such arguments began in many respects to overshadow and direct inquiry in these respective subfields of political science and to provide the basis for a wider interdisciplinary field of political theory which largely grew out of this realm of discourse and began to take institutional form in the 1970s.

What came to distinguish the literature on the history of political theory by the early 1960s was an increased emphasis on *the* tradition as a distinct and meaningful object of inquiry. From the somewhat loose construction that had characterized the work of such individuals as Sabine, there emerged the notion of the classic texts as representations of elements in an organic historical development that explained a crisis in contemporary politics and political thought. This crisis usually in some way included the condition of contemporary political and social science. In varying ways and degrees, the work of Leo Strauss, Eric Voegelin, Hannah Arendt, Sheldon Wolin, and numerous other interpreters contributed to the constitution of a paradigm that provided both a subject matter and an approach to study and research.

Either explicitly or implicitly, the message was that the study of the history of political theory was not some antiquarian enterprise devoid of relevance for contemporary politics and political values but something crucial for their understanding and a form of political inquiry far more important than that represented by modern political and social science. The account of the tradition became an etiology of the devolution of Western politics and political thought that sharply contrasted with those histories of the evolution of liberalism that had rested easily alongside the faith in an empirical science of politics. These new accounts imposed a schematic and synoptic meaning on the history of political thought, which was conceived as a unity, marked by points of beginning, reversal, and end, and presented as an entity to which one could literally apply such attributes as decline and revival. The idea of the tradition, which in various forms had been part of the study of the history of political theory since its inception, was transformed into the myth of the tradition—an elaborate myth about both the subject matter and the activity of studying it.

This myth did not turn on any single proposition. It was a syndrome of assumptions shared by academic political theorists. Among those, such as Strauss and Voegelin, who contributed to the creation of this syndrome, the precise form and content of the argument, its intention, and its purpose varied a great deal, but there were many common features. In all cases, a retrospective, analytically constituted, or stipulative tradition was reified and treated as an actual historical tradition and recast as a dramatic story with pivotal scenes and protagonists. The development of the tradition was charted by tracing a movement from one paradigmatic text and author to another—from Plato to the present—with the implication that these works were both representations and explanations of the historical period to which they were related.

Despite the variations in the historical conditions of their production, the classic texts were presented as belonging to a common literary genre that was the product of a historically identifiable activity called political theory, which was in turn distinguished by a relatively consistent set of concerns. This "great dialogue," as it was often more than metaphorically represented, was offered as the principal context for understanding a classic text. But, at the same time, counting a work as part of the tradition was what distinguished it as a classic. Although the myth was in various ways widely shared among scholars of political theory who did not themselves undertake cosmic interpretations of Western political thought and whose work was much more narrowly focused, the paradigm cases were usually associated with interpretations of the tradition that sought to provide a pathology of modernity.

The study of past political ideas and the analysis of the classic canon became a vehicle for a therapeutic exercise in discovering the intellectual source of a modern crisis and recovering certain truths, or at least important insights, buried beneath the accretions of the tradition. It was an act of deconstruction and reconstruction. In many cases, the concern was to recover the very idea of the political and reestablish its worth in an age where it had become depreciated or absorbed in other categories.

This literature contributed to the creation of a whole mythology about political theory and politics. This mythology included the notions that contemporary academic political theory was the heir to the great tradition; that it was an epic world-historical enterprise; that it was the theoretical dimension of political life and that the relationship exemplified a categorical relationship between thought and action; that ideas in general were the determinative historical forces and that, historically, modern politics could be explained in terms of classic texts; that political theory in the past and present had access to transcendental truths about politics; and that politics was an object of transcendental knowledge. But, if these claims about the tradition and its study were extravagant, they were no more inflated than the behavioralist account of theory and its role in science.

When held up to examination, both the myth of the tradition and the behavioral vision of theory seem, today, hardly credible, but their residue still lays a dead hand on many aspects of the literature of political theory. The paradigmatic statements of the behavioral notion of theory, like those associated with the myth of the tradition, varied in their particulars and especially in the degree to which they were intended literally or employed rhetorically. The tension between "traditional" and "scientific" theory led to hyperbole on both sides. But there were some common core features of the behavioral conception of theory.

Just as the idea of the tradition, so long the property of academic political theory, had been the vague but conventionally, and ultimately intuitively, accepted foundation that made the elaboration of the myth of the tradition possible and effective, the basic elements of the behavioral image of science were already embedded in the discourse of the profession. These included the ideas that there was a methodological unity of science; that empirical science was verifiable in a way that evaluative claims were not; that natural science was a model to be emulated; that true science involved generalization; that the core of scientific explanation was theoretical organization of ontologically and cognitively autonomous facts; that facts were in some way given to immediate experience and were the basis of testing generalizations even though they gained scientific significance in terms of those generalizations; and that theories were basically instrumental constructs for describing and explaining data and constructs that must be operationally defined in terms of such data.

What in part distinguished behavioralism from earlier scientism in political science was, first, the extent to which it brought these notions together and elaborated them in a relatively detailed and coherent manner. Second, it drew consistently, although often indirectly, on the philosophy of science and especially on the dominant persuasion of logical positivism and logical empiricism. Third, it did not simply employ these ideas to legitimate its research programs but attempted to realize these philosophical images of science in practice and transform them into methodological norms.

There were a number of distinct problems with the behavioralist goal of a general deductive and predictive theory of politics modeled on the natural sciences. First of all, there was a failure to consider the inherent difference between philosophical methodology and philosophical analyses of the logic and epistemology of science on the one hand and methods or intradisciplinary forms of research practice on the other hand. Second, even this philosophical image of science was largely secondhand by the time it reached political science and had been mediated through various secondary and tertiary works in philosophy and social science. There is no indication that behavioralists, at least initially, had any detailed firsthand knowledge of the philosophy of science, let alone the practice of natural science. Third, the particular philosophical tradition to which political scientists attached themselves was one that had progressively developed in isolation from any close attention to the actual history and current practice of science. Fourth, this philosophical literature seldom concerned itself specifically with matters of social scientific inquiry. Finally, even the assumption of the unity of science and the paradigm status of natural science, which were at the very core of the behavioral program, were themselves philosophical doctrines propagated by logical positivism and logical empiricism.

It was not, however, simply the failure to consider these problems that led to the alienation of theory in political science. It was also the particular philosophical model of theory and scientific explanation that was adopted and the kind of "theory" that was constructed in light of it. This involved a notion of explanation as the subsumption of particular facts under theoretical generalizations and a conception of theories as mental constructs that served as instruments for the organization and investigation of facts. Like the myth of the great tradition, this view of theory and scientific explanation had roots in the history of American political science.

Political scientists had always exhibited a fundamental ambivalence about theory that behavioralism not only failed to resolve but, in the end, exacerbated. In the early years, political scientists had defined their commitment to science and empiricism in terms of a rejection of formalism and a search for realism that would avoid the dangers of distortion inherent in metaphysics and speculative a priori claims. This translated into a demand for grasping the actual facts, the unmediated and irreducible facts, of political reality; grounding concepts and knowledge in such observable facts; and making all claims subject to their authority. Yet it was recognized that the facts did not entirely speak for themselves, that science was a business of abstraction and generalization, and that under modern conditions of inquiry the sheer amount of factual information was overwhelming without some mode of selection and organization.

From the beginning, the solution to this dilemma moved in the direction of theoretical formalism and an instrumentalist conception of scientific theory that entailed an ontological distinction between theories and facts. Theories were understood as basically conceptual tools, in themselves neither intrinsically right nor wrong, for discovering, ordering, explaining, and predicting observed phenomena, and they were to be judged according to how well they performed these functions. This position reinforced, and was reinforced by, a broader instrumentalist perspective that viewed political science as a practical science in the service of the state and directed toward political and governmental reform. This technological conception of science and theory received philosophical encouragement and validation from several sources.

Comte's and Spencer's methodological positivism and technocratic vision informed much of early political science. Philosophers and social theorists such as Karl Pearson influenced or provided support for the position of individuals like Merriam. And the pragmatic realism of John Dewey, Arthur Bentley, and C. S. Peirce further contributed to this general outlook. This practical orientation of political science made the idea of theory as a heuristic seem reasonable, but it was also supported by a more general antitheoretical intellectual propensity rooted in a tendency to believe that the conventions of the American political experience and liberalism were in some basic sense given and universal. This made the goals of generalization and factual objectivity seem feasible.

When behavioralism set out to effect its theoretical revolution, it retained this instrumental view of theory, and the dominant philosophy of science provided a basis for confirming and refining it. The latter was particularly important, because the behavioral credo emphasized the priority and autonomy of "pure" science. Instrumentalism now required an epistemological legitimacy independent of pragmatic validity. It was in part for this reason that the behavioral vision of theory became increasingly tied to the logical positivist and logical empiricist tradition that began to emerge by the early 1940s in the United States in the work of such individuals as Rudolf Carnap and Otto Neurath. In this school, theories and theoretical concepts were understood as primarily supervenient intellectual constructions or initially empirically empty logical calculi that, while organizing and explaining the relationship between facts, gained cognitive meaning by definitional ties to primitive and incorrigible observational data. This view of theory and the attending deductive model of explanation had become, by the 1950s, the "received" or "orthodox" philosophical reconstruction of science, one that gained acceptance on both sides of the argument about whether the social sciences should appropriate the methods of natural science.

Logical positivism not only supported traditional views of scientific explanation in political science but provided a new basis for other generally accepted notions, such as the separation of facts and values and the emotive and unverifiable character of value judgments. But, again, what most distinguished the behavioral attachment to this philosophical position was the extent to which it launched a program of "theory construction" and research practice that reflected this analysis of theory and science.

Theoretical endeavors in political science during the 1960s were dominated by the idea of the "conceptual framework." Although some held to the assumption that theory would arise inductively from particular empirical studies, the greatest efforts were devoted to the development of "models," "approaches," "strategies" of inquiry, and various other conceptual or analytical frameworks that were viewed as either theories or prototheories. These reflected various metaphors and analogies, but above all, variations on the idea of politics and government as a "system" were what informed this work. There was much in the history of political science that supported this strategy of inquiry in addition to the general attachment to various forms of instrumentalism, but, as Lasswell had claimed in 1950, it clearly was influenced by the orthodox philosophical theory of theory.

The basic argument was that science consisted of a marriage of theory building and data collection and that theories were abstract and somewhat arbitrary conceptual schema to be imposed on various data bases and given empirical meaning by operational definitions. It was assumed that all encounters with the facts were filtered through conceptual lenses and that science was in part a matter of making these constructs explicit and tailoring them to perform the various tasks connected with the intersubjective selection, description, and explanation of political facts. Theories were conceived as frameworks that made systematic and coordinated research programs possible.

Apart from the problems of translating a philosophical theory of theory into scientific practice, this analysis of theory distorted the character of scientific theory and obscured the extent to which theory, in science or any practice of knowledge, involves substantive claims that are constitutive of the facts. Consequently, it inhibited authentic theoretical discussion about political phenomena. But this philosophical myth also carried with it a myth about politics that operated at several levels.

First of all, it reinforced the tendency to take the facts of American politics as more than conventional. In this conception of science, the observation language for reporting and describing facts was largely that of everyday life. This incorporated the ideology of American liberalism and rendered it theoretically impervious by attributing to it the quality of factual givenness and objectivity. Second, the conceptual frameworks, despite their abstractness and apparent remoteness from political phenomena, nearly always reflected the structure and process of American politics and introduced an ideological bias that undermined the very objectivity that they were supposedly designed to achieve. They thus either idolized the political facts they reflected or fundamentally distorted configurations of political phenomena by interpreting them in terms of categories that were ultimately derived from American politics.

By the end of the 1960s, political science had officially divided political theory into three parts—historical, normative, and empirical. Although what was designated by "normative" would become more tangible as the general interdisciplinary field of political theory developed during the next decade, it was at this point more a category (largely one half of the fact/ value distinction) in search of a subject and a respository for endeavors that did not fall easily into the categories of traditional and scientific theory. The tension between the history of political theory and theory as part of what by this time had become the behavioral orthodoxy had led to the differentiation of political theory and the relative autonomy of these poles with their respective images and myths of theory and theorizing. The tension had also begun to recede as behavioralism, once firmly established and identified as political science, found little need either to define itself or to defend itself in relation to the history of political theory and as the history of political theory began to focus on its own domain and internal problems.

In 1969 Sheldon Wolin undertook the most explicit justification yet of the "vocation" of political theory as one of "transmitting" theories from the past to the present in the face of the growing pervasiveness of what he characterized as the "methodism" of the behavioral movement and its "diffidence toward theory and history" as well as contemporary political problems. Wolin claimed that the "wisdom" or "tacit political knowledge" gained through studying the tradition was necessary not only for political education and practical political judgment but also for "scientific imagination" and a sense of scientific significance. He also argued for the preservation of the "vocation by which political theories are created" and which had been neglected by a discipline that was characterized by "complacency" in a time of political chaos and crisis.

Although individuals such as Strauss and Wolin might differ on a great many issues, their interpretation of the fate of political theory and its relationship to political science was indeed similar in its general character. Wolin spoke for a generation of political theorists and articulated a rationale that had been developing since the early 1950s when the enterprise of studying the history of political theory had been first called into question. But Wolin's statement was anticlimactic in the sense that it reflected a debate that was winding down. The center of the critique of behavioralism was already beginning to shift in terms of both vehicle and issues, the study of the history of political theory would be absorbed with different problems, and mainstream political science would redefine its basic mission. Wolin's eulogy, or elegy, for the vocation of political theory and Easton's call, in the same issue of the *American Political Science Review* (1969), for a "new revolution" in political science that would direct attention more explicitly to issues of public policy represented the effective termini of political theory's absorption in a debate between scientific and traditional theory. But the myths about scientific theory and the great tradition engendered by that debate did not recede, and from those myths sprang the alienation of political theory that would characterize the 1970s.

The 1970s were marked by an increasing philosophization of political theory across a number of fronts. This was in part a consequence of meta-theoretical involvements spawned by the conflict between scientific and traditional political theory. It was also in some measure a result of the influence of European thought introduced by the émigrés through the vehicle of the history of political theory. But it was in large part a product of the growing professionalization and disciplinization of the field. Political theory, as a distinct and self-conscious scholarly enterprise, had almost exclusively resided in political science, but the controversy of the 1960s, as well as new aspects of the literature, had made significant elements of political theory uncomfortable and anomalous in that setting. These elements would not disappear from political science, but by the early 1970s political theory within political science tended more and more to become a microcosm of the wider and largely interdisciplinary field.

Within mainstream political science, the emphasis on theory building abated as political science refashioned its image in terms of a commitment or, more accurately, recommitment to policy science that contrasted with the behavioral emphasis on pure science. There were many reasons for this policy turn, including changes in research funding as well as considerable internal criticism within the discipline, represented for example by the Caucus for a New Political Science, regarding both the lack of politically significant research and its subtle and not so subtle political biases. Easton's proclamation of the "new revolution" in which the principal concern, at least in the short run, would be with politically relevant research produced few changes in political scientists' assumptions about scientific inquiry, but the turn away from scientism as the source of primary identity blunted the criticism that had characteristically been leveled against behavioralism.

The critique of political science in the 1970s was less in terms of its commitment to science in general than in terms of its particular assumptions about the character and demands of scientific inquiry. These assumptions had seldom been challenged directly, and the same basic image of science was shared by both behavioralists and their critics. The latter conceded the definition of science to behavioralism and identified their concerns in terms often inimical to the very idea of science. By the late 1960s, however, the challenges within the philosophy of science that had been directed against the approach and doctrines of logical positivism had begun to spill over into discussions of political theory, and by the mid-1970s arguments revolving around the work of Thomas Kuhn and others were at the center of political theory in political science (see, e.g., Gunnell, 1969; 1975).

The dependence of the behaviorial image of science on the philosophy of science made it inevitable and necessary that a critique of behavioralism would involve itself with this literature. The critique exposed the unreflective dependence of the behavioral program on a particular philosophical reconstruction of the logic and epistemology of science, and it at least raised questions about the general problem of the relationship between philosophy and political theory. But it also had the effect of drawing the field of political theory deeper into a series of metatheoretical and methodological issues.

As critics probed deeper into the integrity of the behavioral image of science and became more engaged and fascinated with the dissident literature in the philosophy of science, behavioralists themselves became more self-conscious about the source of their ideas and mounted a defense through an elaboration of the counterrevolutionary arguments in the philosophy of science (see Miller, 1972). They also struggled to make the work of individuals like Kuhn compatible with their notions about science and their versions of the history of political science. More and more, both critics and defenders of behavioralism submitted to the authority of philosophy, and increasingly debates in political theory became the residue of philosophical arguments. This perpetuated the idea that political inquiry must rest on and proceed from a methodological and epistemological foundation, and such issues continued to displace substantive theoretical attention to politics and questions about the nature of political phenomena.

Often, however, political theorists did not even reach the primary literature of philosophy in joining these issues. What entered the field, beginning in the mid-1960s, was a series of mediational works that instructed political and social scientists about the nature and ways of science and either the symmetry or asymmetry between the logic of explanation in natural and social science (e.g., Kaplan, 1964). Often debates were conducted on the authority of this material. Also, the discussions were extended by the availability of a body of literature in the philosophy of social science that, like the more recent work in the philosophy of science, allowed the argument to proceed beyond the poles of science and humanism that had dominated earlier controversy.

The critique of behavioralism in terms of the philosophy of science was a somewhat negative undertaking in that it did not really provide any solutions or alternatives to the problems it surfaced. But this critique was paralleled and complemented by one drawing upon the literature in the postpositivist philosophy of social science (e.g., Gunnell, 1968). The work of Peter Winch in the Wittgensteinian tradition of linguistic and analytic philosophy and Alfred Schutz in Continental phenomenology, for example, not only challenged positivist claims about the unity of scientific method but elaborated features of a logic of social scientific explanation and concept formation which they argued was demanded by the particular nature of social phenomena. This work emphasized, like that of Weber, the intentional and purposive meaning of social action and the need for social scientific explanation to refer to that meaning and reconstruct the conventional context within which it was intelligible.

Although this literature made some general claims about the character of social phenomena, it nevertheless consisted primarily of metatheoretical arguments about the logic and epistemology of social scientific explanation. Political theorists employed these arguments in very much the same way that behavioralists, for example, had approached the claims of the philosophy of science—as if they constituted a form or method of inquiry and a way of doing social science. In some respects, however, the problem was accentuated in the case of the critics of orthodox social science. Although philosophical analyses both influenced behavioral inquiry and served to justify concrete research programs, the appropriation of new trends in the philosophy of social science produced only a philosophical *idea* of an alternative social science and the nature of theory.

By the mid-1970s it was not uncommon for these opposed philosophical images of social scientific explanation, the positivist and postpositivist, to be treated as if they were alternative modes or paradigms of inquiry or even types of theory. The various threads of the postpositivist philosophy of social science were represented as the "restructuring of social and political theory" (Bernstein, 1976). Inevitably, philosophers were quick to attempt to solve the problem by suggesting that these two broadly defined notions or classes of social scientific explanation might be viewed as incommensurable but complementary approaches that reflected different dimensions of, or perspectives on, social phenomena and different cognitive interests on the part of social science (Braybrooke, 1965; Von Wright, 1971). Many political theorists were quick to adopt some such reconciliatory position (e.g., Moon, 1975). Rather than methodology and epistemology keeping pace with the practice of social science and political theory, the latter were desperately attempting to keep up with developments in philosophy as theory, epistemology, methodology, and method were thoroughly conflated. Political theorists were, ironically, becoming increasingly imprisoned within the metatheoretical arguments to which they had repaired in search of identity and autonomy. There was good reason, by the late 1970s, to be "against epistemology" (Kress, 1979).

These excursions into the philosophy of social science were part of the growing body of literature that by the 1970s was no longer anchored in political science and its subfield of political theory. The 1968 edition of the

*International Encyclopedia of the Social Sciences* not only treated political theory as part of political science but gave it a place as an additional, separate, and equal topic where it was discussed as if it were an autonomous discipline with its own history, divisions, and issues. During the next decade, the critique of behavioralism would to some extent continue to bring those elements of the subfield of political theory that were an integral aspect of mainstream political science into contact with those that reflected the wider field of political theory. But the issue nexus progressively atrophied as behavioralism became identical with political science and the various and burgeoning elements of political theory developed autonomous concerns as part of the wider and separate field that had begun to develop its own organizational structures, journals, and other accoutrements of professionalism. Those elements of the subfield of political theory in political science that represented, writ small, the more general field of political theory were increasingly a tolerated but isolated outpost disjoined from the concerns of political science.

The intellectual alienation of political theory, conceived as part of the scientific study of politics, from political theory, conceived as an independent field of knowledge and inquiry, was objectified in the institutional distinction between political theory as a subfield of political science and as an independent field of study. It was also institutionalized in the "official" divisions of the subfield of political theory in political science. These divisions—normative, historical, and empirical—reflected the fact that there was no common structure, or even a set of issues, that constituted the identity of political theory. This situation, however, was increasingly welcomed, and a separatist mood was common among both mainstream political scientists and those in political science and other fields who labeled themselves political theorists. The displacement of the core of political theory from political science may have seemed to free it from an increasingly hostile context, but it also to a large degree deprived it of a field of action and cut it loose from any direct contact with politics and political inquiry. What most clearly distinguished the field of political theory was its philosophical self-image.

This was not merely a matter of political theory more closely identifying with what had often been understood as political philosophy, characteristically the preferred designation of those like Strauss who wished to differentiate their concerns from mainstream political science. The philosophization of political theory was a much more fundamental phenomenon. It involved a disengagement from any actual practices and problems of political inquiry, an appropriation of philosophical categories of analysis and philosophically defined political issues, and a general and often unreflective repetition of a range of metatheoretical arguments superficially transposed into claims about political matters and problems of political knowledge.

One important line of development in this general trend and in the eventual constitution of the wider field of political theory had begun to take shape in the late 1960s as political theorists attempted to give content to the nebulous category of normative political theory and to deal with the so-called fact/value issue. What is important to note is that from the outset this was largely a philosophical or metatheoretical issue defined by the categories of logical positivism. Although it might have been intuitively related to actual problems of political judgment and political inquiry, the connection was tenuous at best. The unexamined assumptions were, first, that there were real practical problems, in general, such as justifying evaluative claims, achieving objectivity, or solving the relationship between theory and practice—that is, that these were more than *classes* of problems or analytical categories. Second, it was assumed that to the extent to which such problem definitions could reasonably be construed as identifying actual issues, philosophical solutions were tantamount to, or the basis of, practical solutions.

Part of the perceived crisis of political theory, beginning in the 1950s, had been the fear on the part of some (and the hope on the part of others) that political philosophy, as a set of metaphysical and moral claims, was in trouble. Philosophers like T. D. Weldon (1953; 1956) argued that in effect much of traditional political philosophy had rested on the mistaken belief that moral and political principles were demonstrable in some rational fashion comparable to the claims of natural science. And behavioralists were making largely the same invidious distinction. This *philosophical* dilemma about the justification of normative claims brought on by positivism and its undercutting of the idea of grounded value judgments was translated into a belief that the "tradition has been broken" and that political philosophy, as a practical possibility, "is dead" (Laslett, 1956).

At least two mistakes were involved in the definition of the crisis of political theory. The first was to assume the identity of practical and philosophical problems, and the second was to assume the historical identity of the classic canon and contemporary academic political philosophy. Consequently, it was not surprising that the appearance of postpositivist work in metaethics and related literature dealing with political values and the analysis of political concepts seemed to signal the reincarnation of political philosophy and the possibility of normative political theory. Whatever practical or political counterpart these problems might have been construed as reflecting, they were philosophical problems, formulated in a philosophical context and admitting of only philosophical solutions.

By the late 1960s it was proclaimed that "political philosophy in the English-speaking world is alive again" (Laslett and Runciman, 1967) in the form of a subspecies of autonomous moral reasoning that stood in a complementary relationship to empirical social science. Postpositivist themes in metaethics as represented by the work of Stephen Toulmin (1950) and R. M. Hare (1952; 1963), led to the conclusion that political philosophy was possible and that intercourse between facts and values was not only permissible but inevitable and fecund. Furthermore, all empirical arguments were informed by value premises, and most normative claims required factually grounded "good" reasons.

In this line of argument, political theory both functionally and, by allusion, in the form of the great tradition was factored out into two logical types of claims. Although the normative side of the equation had been temporarily called into question by positivism, its revitalization meant that the constituent parts could now be reconstituted and find a home in academic political theory and that the tradition once broken could find new life in the complementary relationship between social science and political philosophy (Runciman, 1963). Postpositivist philosophy in the form of linguistic analysis also seemed to suggest that it was once again possible to "do" political philosophy through an analysis of political concepts and that this too indicated a return to the traditional concerns of political theory. In effect, a mythological tradition, forged in part in the image of academic political theory, was declared as born again in the form of this same academic enterprise.

If there was any one work that was understood as representing the epiphany of political theory, it was John Rawls's *Theory of Justice* (1971). This book, the commentaries it occasioned, and the type of literature that it contributed to generating were taken as confirming the guarded optimism of theory watchers who believed that the vital signs of political theory were stirring. Isaiah Berlin's faith in the perennial bloom of political theory and the impossibility of reducing such value judgments to matters of science and logic had been tempered by the admission that "no commanding work in political theory has appeared in the 20th century" (1962). Rawls was widely acclaimed as filling this void, and his work, as well as that of Robert Nozick (*Anarchy, State, and Utopia*, 1974), was hailed as having ushered in an "upswell of political and social theorizing and speculation" that confirmed that political theory "obviously flourishes, all over the English-speaking world and outside it too" (Laslett and Fishkin, 1979:2, 5).

That outside world entered the English-speaking world in a significant sense with the translation of Jürgen Habermas's *Knowledge and Human Interest* (1971). Although Marcuse's work, more than a quarter of a century after the publication of *Reason and Revolution* (1941), had gained prominence in the literature of political theory during the late 1960s, it was probably Habermas more than anyone else who brought the so-called school of critical theory, associated with individuals like Max Horkheimer and Theodor Adorno, into the mainstream of academic political theory. His work, along with that of philosophers like Rawls, was also one of the principal factors in the institutionalization of political theory as a separate field apart from political science and other specialized disciplines such as philosophy and history. It also exemplified the alienated state of political theory.

Whatever the past of critical theory may have been, whatever practical concerns and political experience that originally motivated its founders, this literature, and the works produced by the vast academic cottage industry devoted to repeating, summarizing, and commenting on it, had little to do with existential politics. This was particularly true in the United States where it most contributed to shaping academic political theory and in which it found a congenial but domesticated home. Despite Marcuse's appeal to radical thought in the late 1960s or the relevance some found in Habermas's critique of modern capitalism, the issues provoked by this literature involved primarily metatheoretical reflection on the idea of theory and the theoretical enterprise. Rather than encouraging substantive discussions of politics, it tended to become, in itself, the interpretative object and the focus of theoretical concern. But already the problems, solutions, and arguments that characterized this literature were essentially philosophical constructions with only an allusive, and often spurious, connection with political phenomena and their historical particularities.

First of all, this literature, much like the work associated with individuals such as Rawls, was in some respects a philosophized ideology, but even those ideological roots, the connections with Marxism in one case and liberalism in the other, had become severely attenuated as the arguments were submerged and constrained by academic philosophical discourse. In the work of Habermas, for example, critical theory became largely an eclectic metatheoretical composite of arguments and concepts from philosophy, hermeneutics, social science, linguistics, psychoanalysis, and other academic fields and subfields. The problems increasingly became ones of making these often incommensurable realms of discourse compatible and of shaping them into some rationalized structure of argument. To the extent that there was an involvement with substantive theoretical issues about the nature of political and social phenomena, it was, like much of the work in the philosophy of social science, largely in support of some metatheoretical arguments about theory and social scientific explanation.

Second, although much of the focus of critical theory was on the relationship between theory and practice, or the connection between philosophy and politics, the real dilemmas associated with this range of issues, which are at the core of the problem of the alienation of political theory, were transformed into metatheoretical questions and treated accordingly. The practical problem of the relationship between social science and society was approached as an academic issue.

Finally, what most of the arguments associated with critical theory ultimately sought, much like the literature associated with the myth of the tradition, was a rationalistic basis for the authority of philosophical and social scientific judgments about practical matters. This is an issue rooted in the very origins of modern social science, which, because of its understanding of itself as a normative and even transformational practice, has been a persistent theme in the literature of political theory. The assumption sometimes seems to have been that the demonstration of such a basis would solve the theory/practice problem, but at a minimum the concern was to establish that authority in principle. This ultimately means at least a flirtation, but usually an affair, with transcendentalism.

It is necessary at the outset to clarify, or at least make an initial move in the direction of clarifying, this point about the relationship between the alienation of political theory and the transcendental urge. There is a significant difference between what might be called *practical* and *metatheoretical* transcendentalism and *internal* and *external* standards of judgment. In any practice of knowledge, whether highly disciplined as in a branch of natural science or some less easily circumscribed aspect of political and moral life, the bases of judgment and criteria of knowledge claims, whether accepted scientific theories, moral beliefs, or other fundamental principles, are in an important sense transcendental. They define experience and govern meaning, and, whether explicit or tacitly embedded in the web of conventions that constitute a practice, they occupy a privileged position. This practical or internal transcendentalism is significantly different from the external or metatheoretical transcendentalism characteristic of many of those second-order enterprises that make various practices of knowledge an object of inquiry.

What has characterized much of epistemology, metaethics, the philosophy of science and philosophy of social science, and other such second-order fields is the notion that they can posit metatheoretical or transpractical standards of knowledge that are, or should be, in some way practically as well as philosophically authoritative and applicable. And in large measure the strategy of their position involves a conflation of the distinction between these two realms. At a later point I will explore in more detail the distorted character of this understanding of the relation between what I will designate as substantive, theoretical, or first-order practices on the one hand and philosophical, metatheoretical, and second-order activities on the other hand. But the basic argument will be that, both historically and conceptually, the latter are parasitic. Although they are free to describe, explain, and evaluate their objects of inquiry as they see fit, they have no special intellectual authority, and obviously no necessary practical authority, over first-order practices.

A fundamental dimension of the alienation of political theory derives from its failure to deal authentically with its second-order status, but the problem is exacerbated by the fact that most of the philosophical doctrines from which contemporary political theory gains sustenance are themselves the product of alienated intellectual enterprises. It is not surprising that political theory, seeking bases of authoritative claims about politics, should be drawn to metatheoretical transcendentalism, but the idea that such bases can be metatheoretically underwritten or destroyed, logically or in principle, simply ignores the existential relationships between political theory and political practice and renders political theory inauthentic.

In a contingent sense, metatheory may affect substantive practices of knowledge. This may be unlikely in modern settings where theoretically and metatheoretically based activities such as science and the philosophy of science are not only functionally but institutionally distinguished, but the persistent and often pernicious impact of philosophy on social science is a clear example to the contrary. The point is not that such influence is in some general sense improper but rather that metatheoretical claims have no presumptive authority, on the basis of their reflectiveness, objectivity, or rationality, over first-order practices. This includes the relationship between political theory and politics. Much of political theory, however, proceeds on precisely such an assumption and, in doing so, not only distorts its own activity but avoids the practical problem of its relationship to politics, which it characteristically conceives and resolves, in a circular way, in metatheoretical terms. But political theory is doubly alienated in that the claims of philosophical epistemology, metaethics, the philosophy of history, natural law, positivism, and various other arguments on which it has drawn in seeking identity and authority presume, often to themselves as well as others, to have access to transtheoretical and transpractical, universal, and self-validating sources of judgment that should command practical assent.

Such philosophical transcendentalism is at the core of critical theory and the search of individuals such as Habermas for the standards of rationality based on categories of knowledge and interest supposedly revealed in history or on the logical demands of human language and communication. But the transcendental illusion touches most of political theory in one form or another. Why this is the case is in one sense quite obvious. It is what is perceived as the problem of relativism.

This is a problem that has haunted political theory, and philosophy, for a long time, and there are some historical as well as structural reasons for its persistence. One of the historical reasons was the belief, or at least the claim, of many intellectuals, including the German émigrés, that philosophical relativism was implicated in the rise of totalitarianism. This was less a substantiated argument than a typical intellectualist prejudice regarding the efficacy of philosophy in the practical world, which implied that if there was a philosophical cause there was a philosophical solution. Structurally, the idea of a metatheoretical answer to the problem of relativism is crucial to the claim of political theory's authority over practical or political judgments. Although I will be more expansive about this issue at a later point, it is necessary to indicate immediately why it is an issue that cries out for dissolution. Those who worry about this problem are those who do not, or who for various reasons do not wish to, distinguish between relativism as a philosophical problem and as a practical problem. But in both cases it is a pseudoproblem.

The only thing that relativism could mean in any practical context is the absence of defined standards of judgment. When such standards do not exist, there is no general answer to the problem and certainly no philosophical answer. To a large extent, practices of knowledge and conventional practices such as politics are defined by the existence of such standards or by ways of resolving conflicts about standards. At best, relativism could be understood as referring to a category of problems. The idea of relativism itself as a practical dilemma is a philosophical fiction. But relativism is not even a genuine philosophical problem.

Relativism as a philosophical problem is simply the logical counterpart of metatheoretical transcendentalism, and both are merely the academic memories and abstracted summaries of real problems devoid of substantive criteria and context. A sincere philosophical relativist is either an individual who naively accepts this philosophical dilemma about a nonexistent issue in a nonexistent context but spurns the fictive transcendental solution or a person who has received this pejorative label for failing to accept the pseudoproblem that philosophy has generated and, consequently, for failing to solve it according to the rules of the game. Behind the game is either philosophy's claim to parity in the problem-solving market or, more characteristically, its baseless claim to logical and epistemological authority over the conventional activities that constitute its chosen object of analysis. Philosophy, however, has been somewhat successful, at least in such quarters as social science and political theory, in perpetuating and propagating the scam that practical claims must either be grounded in transcendental philosophical criteria or fall into the abyss of relativism.

Transcendentalism appeals to academic political theory for a number of reasons. Political theory wishes to cast itself in the mold of its own constructions of epic actors in the great tradition; it seeks political authority without engaging in political action and leaving the academy; it may, in some more sophisticated instances, believe in the necessity of practical or political transcendentalism and seek to keep the noble lie alive; it wants to find a basis for allaying its fears about its scientific and political virility; and it of course has conjured up alienated images of those real problems that in practical life demand solutions. But it seeks a chimera and, paradoxically, probably condemns itself to practical irrelevance. It is, nevertheless, the transcendental urge that animates many of the elements of political theory throughout the ideological and philosophical spectrum.

Because the problem of relativism and transcendentalism has in some respects been an import from the Continent, it is not entirely fair to evaluate much of European academic social thought, including projects such as that of critical theory, simply in terms of what is discussed here as academic political theory. Its indigenous circumstances are somewhat different from the principal universe of discourse under consideration both in terms of its relationship to politics and in terms of the intellectual context that governs its meaning and significance. To the extent that such a contrast is relevant, it points up the degree to which that universe is a peculiarly American, or maybe Anglo-American, invention and the manner in which European ideas have been transformed as they have been integrated into that complex.

By the middle of the 1970s, the cluster of issues that had given a certain measure of identity to political theory had been largely dissipated. Although the residue of those issues was visible in the various constituents of the field, the origins were often forgotten and the themes attenuated. One might speak of this period as one of differentiation or, somewhat more critically, as the "dispersion" of the field and its subject matter (Gunnell, 1983b) or, still more harshly as I have here, as part of the alienation of various elements of political theory from each other. But what is clear is that there was a disappearance of any issue center that brought these elements together in terms of either dialogue or debate.

Although political theory had gained autonomy as an independent field of study, its parts were largely colonies of various philosophical sovereignties, and, to the extent that they existed, controversies that might have given rise to creative and substantive theorizing were transformed into outposts of philosophical argument in such areas as the philosophy of social science. The enclaves were all represented and tolerated in an increasingly pluralistic atmosphere (e.g., Deutsch, 1971) in the subfield of political theory in political science, but they had little relevance to the main discipline which was increasingly concerned with consolidating the "new revolution" and ratifying the image of political science as a policy science (Eulau, 1973; Leiserson, 1975; Ranney, 1976). Not only was it less exercised about its scientific image, but some of the strongest proponents of behavioralism were even willing to reject much of the scientific platform that had distinguished the movement (Almond and Genco, 1977; Eulau, 1977). By the mid-1970s the discipline's emphasis on theory, which had characterized the 1960s, had largely disappeared, and any clear notion of the identity of theory and its place in the field was difficult to ascertain.

Assumptions about science and theory embedded in political science did not, however, change a great deal. One area in which they once again became highly visible was the increasingly distinct area of formal, positive, or social choice theory, which its advocates began to advance as the mainstream of scientific development and identified in terms of the same logical positivist models of science derived from the philosophy of science that had characterized the behavioral program (e.g., Riker, 1982*b*; 1983; Riker and Ordeshook, 1973). Despite concerns among some leading political scientists about the "paucity of theoretical concerns" (Wahlke, 1979) and the failure to recognize alternative theoretical perspectives (Lindblom, 1982), there was a return to the same arguments about scientific explanation that had been so severely criticized and had contributed to the poverty of substantive theory in the discipline. But there was now little reaction either in the literature of political science or in the wider field of political theory—a fact that attests to the absence of an issue center. Much like the myth of the tradition that was still very much alive in the Straussian project and other theoretical relicts, this image of theory not only survived but found vitality in isolation and the atmosphere of pure tolerance that came to characterize the late 1970s and early 1980s.

One of the basic elements in the wider field of political theory during the 1970s was the appearance of the "new" history of political theory. This development was in part the consequence of professional historians entering the field and the recognition that much of the practice of the history of political theory was not, by most conventional standards, really historical in terms of either purpose or approach. It was political and philosophical commentary. The new history claimed to offer a "truly" historical method for understanding the meaning of the classic texts and other material in the history of political ideas and for locating and tracing the "actual" historical traditions to which they belonged (Pocock, 1971; Skinner, 1969).

Although a considerable body of literature appeared that was associated with this approach, its status as a candidate for replacing the "old" history was far from clear. It promised to extract the study of the history of political theory from such alienating intellectual structures as those surrounding the idea of the great tradition and at least make the history of political ideas a real object of study. To some extent it accomplished this goal, but in other ways it contributed to the alienation of political theory by identifying its program in terms of metatheoretical images of historical explanation grounded in the postpositivist philosophy of science and, often, divorcing itself from any general concern with the field of political inquiry.

The real concerns of the new history, despite its emphasis on exegetical accuracy and the recovery of the authorial intention, had little to do with the interpretation of texts, and much of its concern about the non- or ahistorical character of previous work was actually a reflection of its unhappiness with a particular kind of historical analysis that was based on materialist or Marxist premises. The "new" history was in fact part or an extension of a well-established contextualist idealist historiographical tradition, and, apart from its substantive research contributions, what was new about it was basically its extended metatheoretical justification of its endeavor and the critique of what it took to be its rivals. Its actual theoretical assumptions were submerged and undeveloped, and what it proposed as a "method" was in fact a philosophical argument about historical explanation that generated another dimension of the *Methodenstreit* in the philosophy of social science and political theory.

To some extent, the methodological emphasis that became the hallmark of the new history was a function of its search for legitimation as a mode of doing the history of political theory, but metatheoretical reflection was also a consequence of the growing autonomy of the history of political theory and its disengagement both from the more political concerns that originally had motivated traditional scholarship and from the role of critic that it had played in political science. In any event, there was some irony in these trends, not the least of which was the fact that concerns about method came to the fore as the defining characteristic of the historical approach to political theory after two decades of historians of political theory attacking political science for its "methodism." There was also irony in the fact that, although behavioralists had attacked traditional scholarship for being too historical, the new historians now attacked it for being inadequately historical. But my concern is principally with the manner in which the debates on these issues exacerbated the alienation of political theory.

The discussion generated by the new history was not, for the most part, about competing historical claims or even about theoretical claims regarding the character of historical phenomena. Because one of the purposes of the new history had been to establish, or reestablish, the legitimacy of the study of the history of political theory on the basis of a metatheoretical warrant and to establish the historicity of a particular kind of historical practice, it was a methodological argument that most clearly defined this literature. It constituted neither a theory of the text or of social phenomena in general nor a method of historical inquiry, and the only ground on which the claims could be joined was metatheoretical. The result was to move discussions in the history of political theory into the realm of the philosophy of history, hermeneutics, and the philosophy of social science. Once again political theory became an extension of philosophical arguments that it seldom either critically examined or extended. As in other cases, political theory's search for identity and purpose ended in a loss of autonomy.

By the mid-1980s political theory, then, both in the discipline of political science and as a more general field, had settled into a number of relatively discrete enclaves governed by alien universes of discourse and had become estranged, through philosophical myths about theory, tradition, science, and politics, not only from the particularities of politics but from substantive theoretical analyses of the nature of political phenomena. It had largely become a series of metatheoretical claims about metatheoretical objects and issues; yet even the metatheoretical enterprises to which it attached itself were often unreflectively embraced and inauthentic in their own right. Even to say that political theory had devolved in a series of intellectual fads might not be to put too fine an edge on it.

What is often taken as the recent philosophical renaissance in political theory even evokes in some of its partisans "a nightmarish feeling that 'the literature' has taken off on an independent life of its own and now carries on like the broomstick bewitched by the sorcerer's apprentice" (Barry 1980). The image that comes to my mind is an old "Monty Python" skit, parodying television game shows, where the contestants, racing against a time clock, were set the task of summarizing Proust. As it turned out that no one could possibly win the game, the prize was awarded on the basis of purely subjective criteria. However this simile might best be applied to political theory, the enterprise often does seem like an arbitrary exercise in recapitulating the work of Rawls, Habermas, and the variety of cult figures from whom political theorists seek a basis for pursuing some less than well-defined, reflectively and autonomously chosen end in a series of games that go by the name of critical theory, formal theory, and the like.

Because there is hardly any decline and, in fact, maybe a "glut" (Barry, 1980) in the literary production of political theory and philosophy and the professional and scholarly activities that compose its various domains, there are encouraging signs for those who would measure the health of the field in terms of prolificacy and prolixity. For many this is an adequate measure of the "possibility" of the enterprise, and the pluralism and fertility of contemporary political theory and its institutional independence, both in and outside political science, are an indication that it has recaptured what many have believed to have been its "grand manner" of the past (e.g., Freeman and Robertson, 1980: 1, 11). I would suggest a different assessment of the current situation.

Whatever criticism one might offer with regard to political theory during the fifties and sixties and well into the seventies, there were general issues in and about the field that were joined. There was also a deeper sense of the problem of the relationship between political theory and politics. Many, in both mainstream political science and political theory, may applaud the separation of the two and the growth of pluralism, but there is now little in the way of common concern and controversy and little sense of what the identity of political theory is or might be. Political theory has largely withdrawn from a critique of modern political science except in the most abstract terms, and political science has little that could be identified as theoretical controversy in its literature. Similarly, one would be hard pressed to indicate problems that bring into contention the various elements of the wider field of political theory. The final word would seem to be that any significant dialogue has disappeared—both within political theory and between political theory and politics. The critique of political theory presented in the following chapters is intended as a move in the resumption of such a dialogue.

# 2
## *Theory and Science*

There were a lot of people there [MIT] who seemed to think that political science is, in fact, a science. . . . I don't have anything against any of them personally. Personally, they were fine. But it just became less fun.

TOM LEHRER

BY THE TIME that a comprehensive critique of the behavioral vision of science, from the standpoint of the philosophy of science, had appeared in the literature of political science (e.g., Gunnell, 1975), the "orthodox" or "received" view of theory and scientific explanation that had dominated the field for so long, and which had been associated primarily with the doctrines of logical positivism and logical empiricism, had all but been destroyed (for a detailed complete history and analysis, see Suppe, 1977). The issues joined in that philosophical revolution did not disappear, but they became increasingly technical and refined and, with few exceptions (e.g., Lakatos, 1970), of decreasing comprehensibility and interest to social scientists once the battle-front had receded from more general and popular issues in philosophy and the combatants had retreated to the trenches of professionalism. Kuhn's work, for example, before and after the famous book that seemed to provide social scientists with such a flexible instrument of critique and legitimation, was scarcely noticed.

The characteristic cultural lag in the relationship between philosophy and social science explains the fact that the critique of positivism in social science was just beginning to have a significant impact at the point at which it was, in effect, complete in philosophy, but issues in the philosophy of science had little subsequent impact on the principal discourse of social science. What was less obvious, however, was the extent to which the old image of theory remained embedded in the education and practice of political scientists. This indicates something of the complexity of the relationship between political science and the philosophy of science.

Although behavioralism, in both methodology and method or as image and program, was grounded in a particular philosophical persuasion, its actual acquaintance with that persuasion was slight. Even though the debates about positivism and the philosophy of science certainly elevated these issues to a new level of reflectiveness, in many respects they were really debates about the legitimacy of the behavioral enterprise and were carried on over the head of the practice of inquiry. To a large extent, the agenda of the critics, both those associated with the history of political theory and those armed with the philosophy of social science, was much more cosmic than a concern with the direction of political science. And the behavioralists were basically determined to underwrite their enterprise in philosophical terms and protect it from the new wave of philosophical criticism. The consequence was that the actual practice of political science was seldom either concretely engaged or altered. But the basic assumptions that informed the behavioral vision of science were nevertheless solidified and eventually to a large degree neglected as erstwhile critics, dismissing political science as unregenerate, passed on to increasingly meta-theoretically defined issues within the wider field of political theory.

The policy turn in political science, the weight of criticism regarding the orthodox image of science, the "success" of the behavioral revolution, and other factors all contributed to a retreat from the overt propagation of scientism in political science and even from the practice of theorizing that had most distinguished political science in the 1960s. By the late 1970s one might have asked, although few did, what had happened to the manifold "conceptual frameworks," such as the systems theory elaborated by Easton, and how many research programs were marked by the application of such constructs. What this situation disguised, however, was the extent to which the basic assumptions about science had remained unchanged and, to a large extent, unscathed.

At an earlier point, there had been a considerable gap between the rhetoric of behavioralism regarding scientific explanation and the actual conduct of research. By the 1970s many of those claims about scientific explanation, despite changing fads in research strategies, were deeply implicated in the practice of political science and the education of political science students, even when not explicitly enunciated and defended in the rhetoric of the field. This, to some extent, explains the resurgence of the orthodox image in the 1980s, particularly in such areas as what has come to be called positive or formal theory, but the matter is more complicated.

First, as already noted, the dispersion of political theory in the 1970s attenuated meaningful dialogue within the discipline. Political scientists felt little need to defend their enterprise, and many political theorists were willing to write off mainstream political science (e.g., Kateb, 1977). Second, as just indicated, the heated controversy about theory had been conducted largely in terms of competing philosophies of science and social science that rarely came to grips with concrete issues of inquiry. There were, expectedly, once again calls for synthesis and a mediation of competing perspectives (e.g., Bluhm, 1982; Moon, 1982), but these were also largely metatheoretical solutions to metatheoretically defined problems. Third, because there was little distinction, on either side of the debate, between philosophical images of science and scientific practice, the complex problems of the relationship between philosophy and political inquiry that were involved in the behavioral program and its conception of theory seldom were explicitly noted and addressed. Finally, the instrumentalist conception of theory, which dominated the field and which will be examined in more detail in this chapter, made it possible to jettison whole programs of theorizing, such as systems theory, without altering the basic notion of theory and mode of theoretical practice.

The irony was that, although the controversies about theory that had characterized the 1970s had atrophied, the roots of those controversies were very much alive, and the old ideas about theory continued to dominate the respective dispersed theoretical enclaves—only now often free from external as well as internal criticism. In political science today, there may not, for various reasons, be many who would attempt to legitimate their enterprise by reference to positivism, but the basic ideas remain very much the same. One recent commentator, for example, suggests that the failure of theory in political science has brought us "to the end of an era in political science, a slow whimpering end," and that this has much to do with the "definition of theory articulated by logical positivists and accepted by many scholars in the discipline" (Ostrom, 1982:11,13). But, characteristically, such claims fail both to confront in any detail the content of the positivist position and to depart from its notion of theory in any significant sense. Furthermore, many critics of positivism continue to equate this philosophy with a description of the practice of natural science and either simply argue for its limitations with regard to social science or defend the complementarity of naturalistic (positivistic) and more humanistic approaches.

The principal purpose here is to bring into relief the underlying problem: the poverty of theory that has resulted from the attachment, in principle and practice, to the orthodox philosophical image of theory and scientific explanation. And this in turn requires a demonstration of how that impoverishment flows from a failure to understand the relationship between philosophy and the practice of inquiry.

Although in some respects the discipline of political science has in recent years placed less emphasis on the development of general theories comparable to those of natural science, there has been, particularly with the differentiation of categories and subfields such as "empirical political theory," "methodology," and "positive political theory," a revitalized concern with such a project. This is hardly surprising. Not only did the basic dedication to this project and the same ideas about theory persist, but assumptions about theory in economics, from which much of the new wave of empirical theory borrows, have been based on the same positivist ideas about explanation and the same instrumentalist interpretation of scientific theory that characterized the behavioral movement. Although the concern with public policy initially may have involved decreased emphasis on general theory, the acceptance of the discipline of economics as a model of a successful policy science has in large measure been based on the authority of its theoretical core, and political science is once again very concerned with its status as a science externally as well as internally.

This concern also springs from the fact that the scientific hopes of the behavioral era were not fulfilled, even in the eyes of some of its major representatives (e.g., Wahlke, 1979). Some have realized the rhetorical character of many of the earlier claims about political science as a science and been content to pursue research programs that no longer required any special justification. Some, such as Gabriel Almond and Heinz Eulau, have quite explicitly disavowed the basic tenet of the behavioral credo and its philosophical justification involving the emulation of natural science. Although Almond did not acknowledge the critique of behavioralism that took place within the discipline in the 1970s, he was willing to concede most of the major points advanced in that critique and even to suggest that political scientists had been led astray by positivist philosophy.

Almond argued that political scientists had turned away from their "ontological base" and ignored approaches "appropriate to human and social reality" (Almond and Genco, 1977:522). Furthermore, the deductive or hypothetico-deductive model of scientific explanation, which was at the core of the behavioral vision, was, after all, an inappropriate paradigm. The "explanatory strategy of hard science had only a limited application to the social sciences," and the "search for regularities and lawful relationships" and the "enshrining of the notion of generalization" were a mistake (493). Eulau recognized how the behavioral claims about science and the ensuing cycle of criticism and justification had produced an "exaggerated, almost pathological, concern" with metatheory that culminated in "the curious notion that the philosophy of science is the high road to scientific knowledge, as if the business of the philosophy of science were science rather than philosophy" (1977:6).

Such sentiments were not, however, at least visibly, widespread. There was little in the way of reflective analysis of past commitments or consideration of the extent to which those commitments were still embedded in the discipline. Most political scientists simply stopped talking about the issue and concentrated on developing more sophisticated research methods and strategies that would be relevant to public policy. Warren Miller argued that such methods would lead to the unification of the discipline and that only temporary problems of personnel and funding stood in the way of bringing "political science into a new age of intellectual ferment and maturity" that would allow it to "make a massive contribution to the welfare of the nation while evolving into a conceptually coherent scholarly enterprise" (1981:14,15). This had been, at least since the formal beginning of the discipline, the basic but continually unfulfilled promise, but for some that promise required a more definite vision of science.

It is not an unrepresentative view that claimed that "the hoped for cumulation of knowledge into a coherent body of theory has not occurred" in a way that would provide a "basis of our discipline" (Ostrom, 1982:13). Neither the commitment to positivism nor the critique of that position yielded such a basis. Positivism, it is suggested, had led to an emphasis on quantification, description, and "data collection and analysis" rather than the "priority of theory" that could unify the discipline and direct empirical research by focusing on "the processes involved in the relevant world of inquiry" (Ostrom, 1982:13,14). The lament is basically the same as that voiced by Easton and others thirty years earlier.

Although there is today a definite uneasiness in the field of political science about the philosophical assumptions that had informed the behavioral vision of science and a general but somewhat vague recognition and acceptance of the critique of that position, notions of theory are still primarily informed by those assumptions. More importantly, the same problems regarding the relationship between the philosophy of science and the practice of political inquiry and the relationship between political theory and political phenomena remain. There is, for example, a willingness to accept the notion of the complementarity of various "theoretical" approaches to both normative and empirical studies and the nebulous idea that the various pursuits loosely identified as theory—from critical theory to social choice—can be somehow unified. But this eclectic position reflects more a confusion about these elements and their relationship to each other and to political science than any articulate notion of coherence. Political science has not faced up to the crisis of identity that was inherent in the critique of the philosophical foundations of behavioralism. It has either ignored that critique or attempted to integrate and absorb it, but it has not really confronted it.

From a philosophical standpoint, there was much that was wrong with the claims of logical positivism/empiricism that rendered it a questionable account of science, but this was only one difficulty, and one that was far from being solved by transfusions from the work of Kuhn and other critics. This only indicated the extent to which it was mistakenly assumed that the philosophy of science was essentially all of one piece in terms of both approach and argument and that its relationship to science was unproblematical. The second difficulty revolved around the fact that, even if the orthodox account of science was a philosophically adequate treatment of explanation in natural science, the question of its relevance as an explication of social scientific inquiry was consistently begged. But the most fundamental problem involved the failure to distinguish between philosophical claims, whatever their philosophical adequacy, about explanation and theory, on the one hand, and methods of inquiry and the practice of theory, on the other hand. It was the belief that there was no basic logical difference between the philosophy of science and scientific practice or between methodology and method and that philosophical models of explanation literally were, or could be the basis of, approaches to theory construction and empirical inquiry.

One of the consequences of this belief and the attempt to theorize according to such a philosophical mandate was a particular kind of theoretical activity. The attachment to the instrumentalist conception of scientific theory, which in various forms had consistently characterized the logical positivist/empiricist tradition, tended to obviate substantive theorizing and, in a peculiar way, both idolize *and* distort commonsense perceptions of politics and everyday modes of political activity. The conceptual frameworks imposed on the data rendered configurations of conventional political facts opaque, but at the same time the positivist notion of the factual "givenness" guaranteed that the substantive theoretical assumptions embodied in political conventions and institutions, as well as the "observation" statements of social science, were impervious to theoretical criticism. Furthermore, because behavioralism produced little in the way of an explicit theory of political phenomena, there was little overt theoretical conflict or genuine theoretical discussion within political science or between behavioralists and their critics. The implications of all this were conservative—both scientifically and ideologically. Because the consequences are very much still with us today, it is important to understand fully the philosophical roots of the problem.

In the relatively short history (maybe a century) of the philosophy of science as a distinct discipline, there have been considerable variation and ambiguity in its self-understanding of its relationship to science. Some of the differences between contemporary positions are, however, relatively clear. Though Karl Popper, for example, is adamant about the extent to which philosophical standards of critical rationalism did, can, and should contribute to the growth of scientific knowledge, others such as Kuhn conceive of the philosopher's role as more that of an underlaborer concerned less with normative claims than with explications of the history and current structure of scientific explanation (see Lakatos and Musgrave, 1970). Stephen Toulmin, for example, argues that philosophers are in no position to "dictate the principles to which scientists *ought* to conform in their theorizing," and to the extent to which they take on a prescriptive role, they should enter into dialogue "on equal terms with other participants" (1968:345).

Whatever the attitude of philosophers toward their subject matter, it is probably safe to say that, despite what might be taken to be some pointed exceptions, the philosophy of science, as an academic discipline, has had little impact on the practice of natural science. Furthermore, there are grounds for questioning the extent to which it has had much direct contact with science even as an object of inquiry. One of the principal claims of those such as Kuhn, Paul Feyerabend, Norwood Russell Hanson, and Michael Scriven who, beginning in the late 1950s, mounted the critique of the logical positivist/empiricist tradition was that it in fact paid little attention to the actual practice of science. The same claim could be made about John Stuart Mill and other early contributors to the philosophy of science. Probably for a long time the philosophy of science at least reacted in a significant way to changes in science and scientific theory, but although this never entirely ceased to be the case, it increasingly addressed philosophically constituted issues whose connection with actual scientific problems was tenuous.

Although the history of the relationship cannot be explored here, the social sciences, in their search for scientific identity, from their beginnings were profoundly influenced by philosophy in general and the philosophy of science in particular. Furthermore, although it would be reasonable to suggest that, historically, the philosophy of science originally evolved out of the practice of natural science, the social sciences in large measure evolved out of philosophy. And this patrimony explains in part the subsequent subservience of social science to philosophical authority. Although it may seem odd to suggest that behavioralists were both beholden to the philosophy of science and less than well acquainted with the field and the doctrines to which they subscribed, this was in fact the case. Behavioralism may have had little direct and detailed knowledge of this literature, but the basic image was mediated through secondary works in both philosophy and social science.

In addition to the genetic authority of philosophy over social science, one of the reasons that political science was unreflective about the relationship was that its use of philosophy was often as a rationalization either for advancing programs within the field or for presenting an image of the discipline to the external world. It was not the first time that a discipline became the prisoner of its rationalizations, but for a variety of reasons political science generally came to assume that the philosophy of science provided an unproblematical account of science and that there was an identity of philosophical models and scientific practice. These assumptions became more deeply embedded with the intellectual hegemony of logical positivism/empiricism by the 1940s, which was also the period in which, despite the more self-conscious statements of the next decade, the basic tenets of the behavioral movement were formulated (Gunnell, 1983b: 10–12). Although political scientists may have been less than thoroughly acquainted with the philosophical literature from which they sought sustenance and instruction, the normative cast of this literature served to reinforce the belief that this was not only an adequate image of science but a compendium of the principles of scientific method rather than a philosophical or methodological claim *about* such procedures. This was in part yet another indication of the derivative character of the knowledge of this material, but the philosophers of science and the authors of mediational works often wrote as if they were both describing the logic of the practice of natural science and instructing others in the practice of that logic.

The point is not to demonstrate simply that natural scientists were unaffected by philosophical images of science whereas political scientists were so constrained. One might suggest that what natural scientists know is the object of their knowledge and *how* to do science and that their knowledge *about* science is not particularly authoritative or reflective. Asking the average natural scientist about the nature of scientific method is not likely to produce an answer as sophisticated as that elicited from a philosopher or even a social scientist, because the latter, unlike the former, has usually been schooled in these matters. As Kuhn has observed, the textbook "image of science" that is accepted so widely "even by scientists themselves" (1970c: 1) is ultimately an attenuated philosophical one. What really separates natural science and social science in this respect is

the extent to which the latter has sought to transform that image
mode of scientific practice. Yet, whatever the disparate and often a
ous intentions of philosophers of science, there is little indication tha~ ~~~,
have conceived of themselves as providing guides to practical inquiry in
this sense.

Such firm partisans of logical empiricism as Herbert Feigl have stressed
that these philosophical claims were "never intended to be an account of
the origin and development of scientific theories" (1969:17), and Carl
Hempel, who probably more than anyone else was the author of current
images of the orthodox notion of scientific theory and explanation, has
stressed that "these models are not meant to describe how working scientists actually formulate their explanatory accounts" (1965:412). Within
the logical empiricist tradition, the question of the relationship between
scientific practice and philosophical reconstructions of the logic of that
practice has been far from a settled one, and there is considerable ambiguity in the work of individuals such as Hempel about the exact character of
the relationship. How, for example, philosophy can render a rational reconstruction of explanation in science without either analyzing in detail
the practice of explanation in science or evaluating those reconstructions
against empirical observations of that practice, which is largely the character of Hempel's claim (1965:424–28), is far from clear. What is clear is
that the philosophical accounts are not in either intention or fact descriptions of science and that in the work of someone like Hempel the concept
of scientific explanation is explicitly a very different thing from explanations in science. And the latter are explicitly rejected as criteria for assessing the validity of the former and as the basic objects of inquiry.

The normative character of the logical positivist/empiricist reconstructions of scientific explanation definitely muddies the issue of the relationship between philosophy and science, particularly because the matter was
neither settled nor fully clarified within that tradition. But, whatever the
philosophical approach, its philosophical adequacy, or its descriptive veri-
similitude, and whether reconstructionist, as in the case of positivism, or
contextualist, as in the case of the critics, philosophical theories of theory
are logically distinct from, and only contingently related to, the practice of
science. Although there may be all sorts of possible significant relationships between them, it would, out of hand, be as bizarre to think of such
philosophical claims as guides to scientific practice as it would be to think
of the philosophy of religion as the basis of religious practice. But, again,
despite all the other problems involved in the complex relationship between philosophy and social science, a large measure of responsibility for
the confusion lies with mediational literature that translated these philo-

sophical arguments into prescriptive maxims. These apologists for various philosophical doctrines and social scientific programs contributed significantly to the alienation of political theory in political science.

Much of this literature, authored by philosophers, was simply an almost catechismal summary and defense of the prevailing logical empiricist position and oriented toward an audience of social scientists and elementary students of the philosophy of social science (e.g., Brodbeck, 1968; Rudner, 1966). It was primarily concerned with propagating the philosophical thesis of the logical symmetry of natural and social scientific explanation, but it indicated little acquaintance with the practice of the particular social sciences—or with natural science for that matter. And it was often polemical and actively distortive of arguments (such as those of Max Weber and Peter Winch) that it took as examples of a contrary position. This literature, however, conformed to the predispositions of behavioralism and supported its purposes.

Some of the mediational material authored by political scientists appeared at the height of the spillover of arguments from the philosophy of science and were little more than an apology for the behavioral persuasion and an attempt to provide articulate support for its commitment to scientism (e.g., Gregor, 1971) in the face of growing criticism (e.g., Gunnell, 1968; 1969; 1975; Spragens, 1973). Although the critique of positivism in political science was necessary and, in view of the revolution in the philosophy of science itself, inevitable, it did contribute, like the mediational apologies for positivism, to the alienation of political theory and the displacement of theoretical issues by epistemological issues.

Much of the earlier literature in political science that attempted to deal philosophically with the character and demands of scientific explanation was nearly as naive about the problems of the relationship of philosophy to science and the vagaries of the philosophical enterprise as the working political scientists who allowed these images to hold them captive (e.g., Meehan, 1965; Van Dyke, 1960). Few went so far as to deal with the fact that when someone like Hempel spoke of scientific explanation he was explicitly talking about not only a philosophically constituted object but one that was not even intended, as distinguished, for example, from the claims of someone like Kuhn, primarily as a description or explication of the practice of science (Hempel, 1965:44). Even Abraham Kaplan, whose account stressed the "autonomy of inquiry" and the difference between philosophically "reconstructed logic" and the "logic-in-use" of working scientists, paradoxically offered up a synthetic philosophical methodology "to guide the behavioral scientist" (1964). Kaplan's treatise came closest to being the standard philosophical reference for social scientists on matters scientific, but his attempt to integrate the various doctrines in the philosophy of science and interpret them within the context of the American pragmatic tradition of social scientific inquiry probably did more to exacerbate than to solve the problem of the relationship between social science and philosophy.

Philosophers proclaimed the unity of scientific method, and political scientists accepted the basic idea as well as the particular definition of unity that was dominant in that philosophy. Political scientists rarely penetrated the philosophical discourse that produced these claims. What they extracted was an abstract formal notion of scientific explanation that was translated into a set of even more abstract explanatory principles. They characteristically understood their project as a "result of the impact of the natural sciences on the social sciences" (Kirkpatrick, 1962:14) or as a consequence of having "emulated the techniques of the students of physical nature" (Riker, 1962:3). The goal, even though a long way off in the view of most, was to "reach the state of maturity associated with the theory of physics" (Easton, 1953:58). There is no evidence that any of these claims derived from even a superficial acquaintance with the practice of natural science, and there is no indication that political scientists understood the differences between the particular formulations of the principal philosophical model that they accepted (e.g., Hempel, 1965; Nagel, 1961; Popper, 1961) or some of the crucial differences between those formulations and the more popularized renditions in the mediational literature.

What was extracted was typically a notion that scientific explanation was such that "from a few basic premises, empirically derived, it has proved possible to formulate deductively a whole body of intermediate theory and from this in turn, to predict the occurrence of empirical events" (Easton, 1953:58). The argument was that "in its ideal and most powerful form, a general theory achieves maximal value when it constitutes a deductive system of thought so that from a limited number of postulates, as assumptions and axioms, a whole body of empirically valid generalizations might be deduced in descending order of specificity" (Easton, 1966:9). This basic claim, poorly understood and explained, was at the core of the behavioral program. It included the assumptions that there was a unity of scientific logic; that natural science stood at the top of a hierarchy of sciences ordered by the extent to which they in practice exemplified that logic; that the logic involved the deductive subsumption of events under general laws or theories that were in turn deductively related; that such deductive explanations were at once causal and predictive in character; and that explanations that did not conform to this model were deficient.

The purpose here is not to undertake, or repeat, the extended philosophical critique of the deductive/nomological model and the approach to philosophy that gave rise to it (see Gunnell, 1975). As late as the early 1970s, political scientists still had only a vague idea of the origin, character, and criticisms of notions about the logic and epistemology of science that had come to constitute the "orthodox" view of theory and explanation (Feigl, 1969; 1970). The story of the rise and demise of logical positivism is today a rather familiar one (e.g., Achinstein and Barker, 1969). And the story of the war between those logical empiricists who clung to its legacy and those revolutionaries in the history and philosophy of science such as Kuhn who challenged the "received" image of theory has been carefully reconstructed (Suppe, 1977). The debate has wound down to skirmishes and technical issues far removed from the major concerns of social scientists. Nevertheless, the consciousness raising of political scientists about these matters largely ended in the mid-1970s, and, with the recession of internal criticism, not only did unreconstructed manifestations of these ideas continue to populate texts in the discipline but a kind of primitive positivism was reasserted, at least as a rhetorical framework, for advancing the cause of certain research programs such as those associated with formal theory.

There is no doubt that logical positivism and its philosophical tributaries maintained their vitality in the philosophy of science longer than in other areas of philosophy, and this fact is significant for understanding its impact on social science. Because its concerns were originally with science, and with scientizing philosophy, it tended to dominate the philosophical analysis of science, and its formulations came to represent science authoritatively even among philosophers. For many, especially in other fields, science, the philosophy of science, and positivism were largely undifferentiated concepts. Those in the social sciences and humanities who rejected a "scientific" approach were really rejecting the tenets of positivism, just as those who believed they were embracing the methods of science were actually subscribing to a particular set of philosophical doctrines. The actual practice of natural science and its comparability to social science were never actually confronted as genuine issues.

Even if positivism had not been philosophically dubious on a number of grounds, including both its approach to the analysis of science and the internal integrity of its claims, the notion that a practical program of science could be generated and evaluated on the basis of philosophical arguments was indefensible. Although few political scientists even began to come to grips with this assumption, it was implicit in many of their claims. William Riker, for example, argued that students of political behavior should "become students of the scientific method" and "examine the procedures of the physical sciences to abstract from them their techniques of success" (1962:7). But it is clear that what Riker and others referred to was in fact one dominant but eventually ravaged philosophical account of the logic of science. Riker suggested that "what social scientists have so greatly admired about the physical sciences is the fact that these latter actually measured up to our notion of what science should be," but he failed to address exactly how one would know what science "should be." Both the standard of measurement and the descripton of physical science were actually a philosophical reconstruction—and one that had little relationship to the practice of science.

Riker, like so many others of the period, offered the same formal précis of the deductive model of scientific explanations:

> they consist of a body of related verified generalizations which describe occurrences accurately enough to be used for prediction. Generalizations within each science are *related* because they are deduced from one set of axioms, which, though revised from time to time, are nevertheless a coherent theoretical model of motion. Generalizations are *verified* because, drawn as they are from a carefully constructed and precise theory, they have themselves been stated in a way that admits of verification by experiment, observation, and prediction. [1962:3−4]

Despite the devastating criticisms of this image of science that had developed by the early 1970s in both philosophy and social science, none of the principal exponents took the trouble to defend it philosophically or attempt to demonstrate either its descriptive accuracy with regard to natural science or its applicability to political inquiry. Individuals such as Riker stonewalled attempts at dialogue and justified their endeavors in terms of what they referred to as the "objectivist" philosophy of Nagel and Hempel as opposed to the "idealist interpretations of science" advanced by such critics as Kuhn (1977:16). The basic injunction that political scientists derived from this model of science, from Lasswell (Lasswell and Kaplan, 1950) to Riker, was to define their terms, generalize from their observations, test their generalizations by comparison with the facts, and thereby produce verified laws that would eventually constitute elements of a comprehensive theory of political behavior. Such claims at this level of abstraction were meaningless, apart from their rhetorical force, and only allusively connected to the research programs in political science.

Notwithstanding Riker's attempt to reconstruct the evolution of social choice theory during the past three decades in these terms and to identify this alleged development with "political theory," there is little to support such equations and even less to suggest that it bears any significant relationship to the growth of knowledge in natural science. His account (1983) basically neglects the real history of discourse about political theory since the beginning of the behavioral era, and he simply passes off challenges to his version of science as "efforts to turn political science into a belles-lettristic study" (1982*b*:753). In Riker's case, it may be questionable whether his claims should be taken as more than a defense of his particular research concerns, but a refusal to enter into genuine discussion of the merits of these arguments only exacerbates the alienation of political theory. His claims, however, do represent a pervasive mental set within the discipline that finds its structural counterpart in such current distinctions as that between "normative" and "empirical" theory.

Echoing the arguments of the 1950s, Riker anachronistically, counterfactually, and, one must assume (unless he is a modern Rip Van Winkle), somewhat disingenuously asserts that "in political science . . . the word 'theory' has come to refer primarily to moral philosophy" (1983:47). Although this was in fact never the case and could not even be remotely construed as such after the 1950s, Riker is intent on resurrecting the terms of the old debate. He wishes, he claims, "to use the word 'theory' as it is used in the other sciences," that is, to refer "to a set of deductively related sentences," but there is no reference at all to its actual use in the natural sciences. Riker asserts that economics is alone among the social sciences in creating such theory successfully, but he makes no attempt to demonstrate that this is the case. Finally, although he claims that the kind of work in which he has been involved represents a significant contribution to the development of this kind of theory in political science, he simply provides a capsulate history of social choice theory which he categorizes as the history of the development of "a deductive and testable theory about political events" and a set of propositions "to which 'theory' could be applied with etymological justification" (47). The claims in this argument are neither grounded nor connected.

One of the elements that Riker presents as part of this putative development is what he believes to be the progressive reformulaton of Duverger's law culminating in its incorporation into rational choice theory. This claim presents an interesting case for examining Riker's arguments about theory and science.

Like many political scientists who have invoked the authority of the philosophy of science, Riker's knowledge of the field is either slim or strategically deployed. He cites Karl Popper, for example, in support of his claim that propositions are "empirically verified" and his description of how a falsified proposition is replaced "with a revised one, which passes the test that the initial proposition failed" (1982*b*:753). Popper, however, has consistently rejected the notion of verification, which is basically a vestigial positivist concept. What Riker describes as proposition replacement and theory adjustment is essentially what Popper has criticized as the use of ad hoc hypotheses to sustain theories whose elements have been falsified. Riker presents his history of Duverger's law as an example of what Kuhn has called "normal science"—a notion that Popper has condemned as detrimental to the growth of scientific knowledge and that Kuhn advanced in the context of an argument about the logic of science that is antithetical to the basic assumptions informing Riker's claims about the "accumulation" of scientific knowledge demonstrated in his account of Duverger's hypothesis.

There is no way to pursue these issues. Riker merely drops these assertions about science and moves on to his story of how the "sentences" composing Duverger's law have now been transformed into something approximating the true sociological law that Duverger believed he had approached. There is no evidence that his claims are even consistent with the philosophy to which he is most beholden, let alone the actual practice of natural science. Riker's final revision of the law is as a "probabilistic" (as opposed to "deterministic" and "causal") claim that "plurality election rules bring about and maintain two-party competitions except in countries where (1) third parties nationally are continually one of two parties locally, and (2) one party among several is almost always the Condorcet winner in elections" (1982*b*:761).

It would be overkill to pursue the fact that this notion of a "probabilistic" law does not, on its face, conform to the formulations of Popper and Hempel or to any other standard treatment of the subject and that Riker does not even attempt to demonstrate any such congruence. He argues that the task of the next decade is to find an adequate theory to subsume the law, but he believes that it can be found in some aspect of "rational choice theory" involving the interplay between psychological and institutional characteristics and represented in claims like the following: "proportional representation and the second ballot runoff offer politicians an incentive for the formation of new parties and do not give them any disincentive" (759). *What is wrong with this picture?*

There would be limited purpose in repeating a technical philosophical critique of the covering-law model of explanation, for the related notions of explanation embraced by political scientists are only loosely reflective of such reconstructions. For the most part, only the crudest images have been derived from these excavations into the philosophy of science, and often the images do not accurately reflect the original formulations—which are themselves contentious. What political scientists have come away with are some abstract notions that explanation equals generalization and prediction, that empirical laws must be subsumed under theories, that deducibility and causality are symmetrical, that theories are verified by facts, and the like. Exactly how, or when, such maxims are exemplified in practice is even more vague. My concern here is not to demonstrate that Riker's substantive claims are incorrect or even that the kind of research he is involved with is inappropriate for political science. I simply want to destroy the belief that these claims bear any significant relationship to explanation in natural science and what might be construed as theories and laws in those fields. Only when this notion is disposed of can we begin to ask where theory is and should be in social science and what kinds of explanations are relevant with regard to the phenomena in question. It may very well be that social science should emulate natural science, but it is a mistake to believe that what Riker, for example, presents as a law is in fact an analogue of a claim in natural science.

One of the great myths that has been created by social science's attaching itself to the philosophy of science, or to the particular philosophy of science growing out of positivism, was not only that it must emulate natural science but that the world of science was intrinsically divided into the categories retailed by philosophy such as theory, law, and observation. Such terms and concepts do, of course, appear in scientific discourse but not in any very determinate manner and certainly not in any way lexically or conceptually equivalent to their philosophical uses. These are principally part of a philosophical language for talking about science, and they gain their meaning and relational significance in that context. They do not necessarily represent the structure of scientific practice in which the use of terms like "theory" and "law" vary considerably. It is possible, however, to say something about what is usually understood as a law in natural science and about how different it is from what political scientists represent as laws or protolaws as well as from many of the philosophical reconstructions of scientific laws.

One of the difficulties, which is surely attributable to the philosophy of science, is the emphasis on the semantic criteria for distinguishing laws and understanding the relationship among laws, theories, and observational claims. Philosophers of science have characteristically used statements of the "if . . . , then" and "all swans are white" variety to illustrate their analyses of scientific laws, and they have presented explanation as a deductive relationship between sentences. Social scientists have tended to believe that generalizations copying this logical form would yield analogous claims and that if they could construct syllogistic relationships between generalizations and observation statements they would have approximated scientific explanation. Brodbeck, for example, would have social scientists believe that "Earthquakes lead to misery and wreckage" has the status of scientific law (1968:371) and that subsuming a particular event under this generalization is a scientific explanation. This, however, is not at all the case, and it is just such an illusion of functional equivalency that has lulled political scientists into believing that scientific explanation could be methodologically achieved.

What Riker talks about as the development of Duverger's "law" might better be understood as the evolution of Duverger's "lore." It may be quite correct and/or useful, but it is much more on the order of an ideal typification drawn from historical experience or the type of claims made by natural historians (Beavers tend to build their dams across fast-flowing streams) than something on the order of a natural law. There are various ways that one might try to distinguish the claims that scientists usually take to be laws, but the logical or semantic form is not sufficient. What may be most clear about natural laws is what they are *not*. Riker characterizes Duverger's formulation as "entirely empirical, the record of observations" (1982*b*:761), but most of the claims that are usually taken as scientific laws are far from such summary, inductive, probabilistic claims. Even philosophers like Popper, to whom Riker seems to grant authority, explicitly reject such a characterization as well as the notion that the essence of explanation is to be found in deductive relations. For Popper, deductive relations are important only in the sense that falsified claims rebound via modus tollens on the theoretical premises from which they are derived (1961; 1962).

A law in science may function as an explanans subsuming various explananda, but the relationship is not simply a semantically deductive one, even though it could always be formally written in a way to meet this criterion, nor are all such subsumptions equivalent to the relationship between laws and observations in science. Despite what social scientific proponents of the hypothetico-deductive model would have us believe, abstracted summaries of empirical findings such as that adduced as Duverger's law are neither equivalent to natural laws nor a logical step in the creation of laws and theories.

The problem begins with the acceptance of the philosophical claim that scientific explanation, to be adequate (or, in the words of individuals such as Hempel, "complete"), requires laws. In the practice of science, adequacy and completeness are pragmatic and contextually determined matters, and the criteria differ considerably. Sometimes laws provide justifying grounds, and sometimes they do not. The emphasis on law in the belief that this is the hallmark of science has often diverted social science theory from fruitful inquiry and constrained its creativity. Particularly, this emphasis on formal, and at the same time questionable but unexamined, philosophical criteria has diverted attention away from substantive theories about the phenomena being explained and the criteria of adequate explanation entailed. But even if the question of law were at issue, it is neither a question of logical form and relations between sentences nor a matter of generalizing from observations. Most natural laws make claims about underlying processes and realities that belie commonsense observations and explain why things *appear* as they do. They are not summaries of regularities reported in an everyday observation language but rather claims about the character and scope of regularities that explain the nature of the regularities or their appearance. Laws are not empirical hypotheses but the framework for making and testing hypotheses.

Laws are common warrants for making claims and reaching conclusions in natural science and for evaluating claims and conclusions, but it is a mistake to think that they function like the premises in a formal deductive argument in which the conclusion is simply a semantic extrapolation. The validity of substantive scientific conclusions is not a species of validity in formal logic but a matter of the criteria within a particular scientific practice for connecting conclusions and warrants (laws, etc.) and qualifying the claim (probable, certain, etc.). Analytic arguments in formal logic have their own criteria of adequacy and rationality, but they are not the same as those used in making scientific arguments. The connection between laws and observations in science is never deductive in the analytic or syllogistic sense of that concept even though inferences are made in light of laws or in accordance with them (see, e.g., Toulmin, 1953; 1958).

What must be stressed here, however, is that Duverger's law, whatever its status as an explanatory warrant in political science, is not analogous to a law in natural science and it cannot claim any such authority even if that authority were appropriate. The attempt to claim such authority rests on the underlying but philosophically discredited notion of the unity and hierarchy of science and the correlative belief that scientific explanation is a transcendentally rational and philosophically determinate form of which particular practices of inquiry might more or less successfully partake. Such a notion is neither historically nor philosophically defensible. The concept of scientific explanation can at most be only part of a relatively abstract claim (historical, sociological, philosophical, etc.) about family resemblances (logical, epistemological, practical) among modes of scientific activity. It can hardly function, either philosophically or in scientific practice, as a basis for evaluating particular scientific claims and prescribing the form they should take. This does not mean that we cannot gain knowledge about what we regard as successful sciences. The difficulty is that our vision of those sciences has been distorted by philosophically mediated images that have obscured what is most important.

Neither the concept of explanation in general nor the concept of scientific explanation can be endowed with some transcontextual and transhistorical logical or epistemological content that provides a guide to scientific practice. Explanation, understanding, intelligibility, and the like are modal concepts that have a certain general force in our language but can be given full meaning only in terms of concrete, contextually relevant criteria of application. It is not a philosophical theory of science that defines scientific inquiry and makes it possible but, rather, scientific theories. About such theories we can philosophize in both a normative and an explanatory sense, but not without attention to what they are and the universes of discourse in which they appear.

It may be difficult to find equivalences—even between the natural sciences, let alone between the natural and social sciences—that we can speak of as theories, but in all these practices of inquiry there are or should be certain claims that are fundamental in the sense that they define the subject matter and explicate the *kinds* of phenomena that constitute the domain of facticity and provide the substantive criteria of adequate explanation. This, I will stipulate, is theory. One of the difficulties with political science is that these claims are deeply submerged in what is taken to be the theoretically neutral observation language of the discipline whereas the focus is on the generalizations that pass for laws and theories. But it has not only been the belief in the identity of explanation and generalization and other pieces of philosophical folklore associated with the deductive model that has inhibited theorizing and theoretical reflection.

Often associated with the deductive model is a particular epistemological claim about the nature of theories and their function and about the relationship between theories and facts. It would be difficult fully to account, historically, for the manner in which this theory of theories has come to influence political science. To some extent it has been a result of the impact of the philosophy of science and the mediational literature, and, as suggested earlier, it is in some respects a consequence of certain factors that shaped the evolution of political science in the United States. But it is closely associated with deep-seated assumptions in the disciplines of economics and sociology that political scientists have, from the beginning of the discipline (and in the work of individuals like Merriam) to the present, taken as the most advanced of the social sciences and as paradigms of method (e.g., Riker, 1962:6). At the core of this pervasive notion of theory is the idea that a theory is a model or instrumentally devised mental construct "that is a somewhat simplified version of what the real world to be described is believed to be like" (7). From such models are to be deduced, or otherwise generated, hypotheses that can be compared with the "real" world for purposes of verifying or amending the model.

These conceptual frameworks vary from so-called social choice theory and its models of rational behavior to the many forms of systems analysis that were so popular during the behavioral era and that set the generative form for what is today taken as theory in mainstream political science. As in the case of many of the empirical generalizations that have been offered up as bearing some analogy to natural science, they may be useful in many ways for describing political behavior and institutions. What is damaging is the presumption that theory and theorizing in natural science are something on this order and that in producing such schema we are creating the functional equivalent of scientific theory. This merely serves to alienate political science from substantive theoretical considerations, distance it from actual structures and processes of politics, and obscure the theoretical assumptions that are implicit in its supposedly incorrigible observation statements about the "real world." Political scientists have made their views about theory quite clear, but there are few if any instances of a reflective analysis and defense of the basic position or its philosophical ground. Probably the most explicit statement in social science is Milton Friedman's essay on the "methodology of positive economics" (1953).

Friedman argued that the goal of a "positive" social science is the development of "theories" or "hypotheses" that yield predictions. He claimed that theories constitute languages that have "no substantive content" and function basically "as a filing system for organizing empirical material and facilitating our understanding of it" (1953:7). On the basis of "factual evidence," we ascertain whether this system has "a meaningful empirical counterpart" and is "useful" for prediction, which is the essence of explanation and the criterion of validity. Not only is it unnecessary for a theory or its "assumptions" to be descriptively "realistic," but any significant theory that explains a great deal must be descriptively false. Theories are, in Friedman's view, instrumental constructs for ordering and "perceiving" facts in an "*as if*" fashion, which posit a "conceptual world" or model and provide "rules" for "specifying the correspondence between the variables or entities in the model and observable phenomena" (24). These instrumental constructs are somewhat arbitrary in the sense that they are, in principle and practice, alternative assumptions that could equally do the job. Choices are made on the basis of economy, precision, clarity, testability, and so forth, and because they are not realistic to begin with they are tested not by their descriptive realism or comparison with the world but by their predictive efficacy.

The reliance of this account on the logical positivist and "orthodox" theory of theory in philosophy is apparent, but before we examine this account and related notions of theory in political science in more detail it is worthwhile pointing to some problems in Friedman's argument. First, even though "facts" are understood as perceived in terms of a theory, in the sense of selected and ordered, there is a basic assumption that the "real world" and its facts are somehow "given," incorrigibly and immediately presented in experience, and ontologically distinct from theoretical constructs employed in explaining them. For Friedman, truth and realism are clearly functions of this experiential observation, and theories, as ideal typifications, cannnot be true or realistic or countermand commonsense perceptions of the real world. The theoretical or scientific conservatism of this position is obvious, and, parenthetically, although it cannot be explored in detail here, there is, as I have indicated earlier and as the example of Friedman indicates, more than an accidental relationship between this basic philosophical position, as well as the particular conceptual frameworks it has produced and legitimated, and political conservatism. Whether or not one finds this account of economics and social science persuasive, it has little to do with theory in natural science.

Theories in natural science are not realistic in the sense of corresponding to commonsense descriptions of the world. They might be construed as realistic rather because they are taken as real claims about the world that often contradict the appearances embraced by common sense. They are not simply, or at all, abstract typifications except in the sense that they are not particularistic descriptions, but to note that they are not descriptions does not entail the idea that they are not realistic claims about the structure of the universe. For those scientific claims that have not entered into our commonsense image of the world, it is a matter not of the theory being an appearance that explains the "real" world but of the illusory character of the commonsense world and its accidental properties. Friedman goes to great lengths in attempting to demonstrate how scientific theories are abstractions that never actually describe the world as it "is," but it would be much more accurate to say that those theories are claims about the way the world really is in the most fundamental sense—that is, in terms of its basic structural character. The notion that succeeding scientific theories are merely increasingly useful hypothetical constructs for explaining and predicting a given world is to depreciate the radical character of theoretical claims in science and unduly appreciate the manifold typifications that populate social science while at the same time disguising the theoretical and ideological assumptions embedded in its observation world.

The fit, for example, between Friedman's notion of theory and economic science and his ideas about public policy or between Riker's normative claims about politics and his theoretical position (1982*a*) is too obvious to be ignored. These models of human rationality and political institutions are basically abstracted versions of certain conventional social and political forms, and they bias the selection and interpretation of data accordingly. They are then often compared with the very world from which they have been abstracted, which in turn is presented not as a mere conventional construction of social behavior and its artifacts but as the data of observable reality for testing putatively universal propositions. "Theory" and "facts" converge to produce or reinforce the values inherent in particular forms of political and social life, or else such theories distort and obscure the actual modes of life by imposing alien constructions. Ideology hunting is not the concern here, but it must be noted that the orthodox notion of theory idolizes common sense and makes that version of reality theoretically privileged.

The argument cannot, however, be left at this level. It is necessary to look more closely at the philosophical claims behind theoretical instrumentalism and its manifestations in social and political science, even though the latter seldom reach the point of elucidating and defending those claims, claims that are both philosophically contentious and unpersuasive as a description of any scientific practice. Although the logical empiricist tradition increasingly qualified its notion of the relationship of theory to fact, the idea of the epistemological and ontological priority and givenness of the latter has persisted from the formulations of Ernst Mach, Moritz Schlick, Otto Neurath, and the early work of Rudolf Carnap through the more recent arguments of such individuals as Feigl, Nagel, and Hempel. And this view of theory has touched most other fields influenced by this tradition in the philosophy of science. Again, whatever one might think of this philosophical position, most of its primary advocates did not recommend it as a method of theory construction. Feigl, for example, has pointed out that "no philosopher of science in his right mind considers this sort of analysis as a recipe for the construction of theories" (1970:13), but mediated images of this formal analysis have been deployed in exactly that manner by social scientists.

According to the orthodox interpretation, a theory is composed of two fundamental parts. First, there is a set of basic assumptions cast as a logical system or calculus of axioms or postulates and other deductively related propositions. Second, the logical system is supplied, via semantic correspondence rules or bridging definitions, with an empirical interpretation that connects it with the facts of observation or familiar experience and that allows empirical claims to be derived as deduced consequences and tested. The language of theory and the language of observation are understood as sharply distinguished, with the latter primary, irreducible, incorrigible, and initially free from theoretical "contamination" (Nagel, 1961:7).

To understand this tradition in the philosophy of science, as well as the positions in social science that have been influenced by it, it is necessary to realize that from the beginning theories were a "problem" to be explained—or even explained away. The emphasis on the concept of theory, and an ostensible commitment to the primacy of theory in the scientific enterprise, was misleading, because theories were something to be accounted for within an analysis of science that viewed the activity as devoted to explaining the epistemologically prior facts of experience. The explanation of this philosophical prejudice against theoretical realism is complex, but several factors are worth mentioning.

In part, it derived from both the empiricist and the idealist origins of logical positivism. The former stressed the nominalistic character of facts, and the latter stressed the primacy of experience despite its sensationalist basis and the mental form imposed on it. In addition, much of the early work in this school of philosophy reflected a crisis in science around the turn of the century involving the breakdown of traditional mechanistic physics. Theory and the "facts" seemed to break apart. It was really a crisis in the scientific image of the universe or, in Kuhn's terms, a revolutionary moment in the transition between scientific paradigms, but this scientific crisis was translated into the philosophical problem of how to put theory and fact back together and at the same time maintain the idea of the primacy of empiricism and objectivity in science. Finally, the verificationist and atomistic philosophy of linguistic meaning that dominated the movement largely determined the structure of the analysis of theory and reinforced the depreciation of the theory.

Often it was a question of reducing theoretical concepts and claims to observational ones through operational definitions or some similar form of translation, but sometimes the analysis even led in the direction of the elimination, at least in principle, of the theoretical terms. This tradition consistently failed to find the language of observation (phenomenalism, physicalism, etc.) that could be the carrier of categorical and immediate knowledge, and neither it nor those it influenced were able to resolve what Hempel termed the "theoretician's dilemma" or the paradox involved in the idea of explaining facts by a "detour" through theories and at the same time making theoretical meaning dependent on facts. But it never let go of the basic ontological dichotomy and vision of science predicated upon it.

The theories of theory that appeared in this tradition were various forms of instrumentalism, pragmatism, conventionalism, constructionism, and fictionalism—all in varying ways and degrees devoted to explicating the function of theory in scientific explanation and grounding it in the linguistic protocols of so-called observed experience. The basic idea was that theories were analytical constructs that constituted economical formulations of the relationships between observable data and performed various other functions such as making generalization and prediction possible. Logical empiricism eventually gave up the more radical ideas of reductionism and admitted the underdetermination of theories by facts and the impossibility of anything beyond a partial interpretation in terms of observables. The rejection of the verificationist theory of meaning and related dogmas of empiricism have required an even greater reformulation of how theories gain cognitive meaning, but the definition of the problem and the basic assumptions about the structure of scientific theory have not been relinquished by those in this tradition such as Hempel and Nagel. And the important point is that the earlier formulations were the ones that informed the assumptions about theory in social science and the more primitive accounts that tended to dominate the mediational literature to which social scientists have had the most direct access.

Postpositivist work in the philosophy of science, influenced by the arguments of Kuhn, Feyerabend, and others, has fundamentally changed the theory of theory in the philosophy of science, but it is necessary to be wary about the significance of these arguments. The first reaction to Kuhn among political scientists was either to construct or to find "paradigms," but this involved the same basic mistake as that of those who had attempted to build and employ theories in accordance with the positivist interpretation of theory. We can learn from the philosophy of science, but it is necessary to be reflective and critical regarding such claims *about* science and the extent to which they offer guides to scientific practice.

Another, more intrinsic, difficulty with the "new" philosophy of science was that it frontally challenged the basic assumption of positivist/empiricist tradition regarding the relationship between theories and facts but in many respects remained trapped within the terms of the old framework. This was even the case with Popper, who long ago had vehemently rejected instrumentalism and verificationism in favor of theoretical realism and the position that theories are substantive claims or conjectures. Yet he still clung to a variation of the idea of truth as correspondence with theoretically independent facts (1972). Part of the problem derived from attempting to deal with the analysis of theory within the traditional categories, and it was a problem even in the case of those who argued against the commensurability of theories and against the idea of transtheoretical foundations of scientific knowledge.

What many have failed to understand is that arguments about science such as those of Kuhn cannot be separated from their approach to the philosophy of science. In the case of Kuhn, this involves the rejection of the idea that the discipline should be, and even realistically can be conceived as, devoted to articulating logical and epistemological standards of scientific assessment. This, for example, was really the crux of the disagreement between Kuhn and Popper (see Lakatos and Musgrave, 1970). Although the issue is of little significance to the natural sciences that have been little affected by such controversies, it is a matter of signal importance to the social sciences, which have attempted to seek methodological advice from philosophy. Kuhn's concern was to abolish the vestiges of the notion that there are philosophically discoverable universal standards of empirical knowledge and the logic of explanation. It is Kuhn's epistemological (or antiepistemological) argument rather than his "historical" claims that is crucial to his position, and that argument involves a different notion of the relationship between philosophy and science. It is precisely confusion about this relationship on which much of the controversy about Kuhn's work has revolved.

There is a rather constant refrain in the social sciences, which as usual is homologous with claims in philosophy, that Kuhn's work is in one way or another quite instructive but that it leaves us with no clear notion of scientific judgment and tends to undermine the idea of objectivity in science. In a word, the claim is that the position is relativistic and does not provide a basis for comparing scientific claims. The question that is begged in such an argument is whether there are any such *philosophical* bases and whether it can or should be the task of philosophy to seek them out. It fails to confront the more radical implications of Kuhn's argument regarding philosophy and its relationship to first-order fields of knowledge. The basic argument is evident in Wittgenstein as well as in the work of Peter Winch and Stephen Toulmin. More recently there have been other challenges on similar grounds to the very idea of philosophy, in the sense of formal logic and traditional epistemology, as a master science and the repository of the foundations of knowledge in general (Cavell, 1979; Rorty, 1979).

Kuhn's argument regarding paradigms and scientific change has gone through various stages of refinement (see, e.g., 1977), but the basic and relevant point was that paradigm shifts within science are revolutionary in that they constitute new matrices of scientific practice or forms of normal science and that at the core of such a paradigm shift is a new gestalt or set of exemplars which in effect offer a new view of reality and criteria for making and evaluating claims. Such changes happen in different ways at various times, and although new theories are always taken as better representations of reality, there is no external transparadigmatic philosophical basis for specifying how a theory is a "better representation of what nature is really like" or a "match" with "what is 'really there.'" Theories are what provide such criteria. There is "no theory-independent way to reconstruct phrases like 'really there,'" and "the notion of a match between the ontology of a theory and its 'real' counterpart in nature" is an illusion (Kuhn, 1970c: 206).

The point is not that science is not objective but that the meaning of "objectivity" or the criterion of its application is field-variant and context-dependent. What this means simply is that objectivity is a matter of scientific and not philosophical decision. It is not that Kuhn undermines the notion of objectivity in science but rather that he undermines the notion of the philosophical determination of objectivity. He attacked not the foundations of objectivity in science but only a particular *philosophical* claim about objectivity in science—a philosophical claim so entrenched that attacking it was taken by its exponents (e.g., Scheffler, 1967), and many others, as an attack on scientific knowledge and as a celebration of subjectivity. The failure in social science to distinguish clearly between philosophy and science is a mistake that began in philosophy itself. The stake that philosophy has in preserving its image as a master science and an authority regarding the logical and epistemological foundations of knowledge in general is great, and social science's, and political theory's, stake in believing and having others believe, in the accessibility of such privileged claims is equally great—although misguided.

The real difficulty with Kuhn's argument, as well as that of those who, like Feyerabend, have attacked what Wilfrid Sellars has called the "myth of the given" (1963 : 164), is, again, that such arguments often remain bound to the language of the orthodox position. This sometimes makes their point less than clear. In the case of the analysis of scientific theory, they seem to suggest at certain points that the problem is one of "reversing" the traditional notion of interpreting theories in terms of facts and demonstrating that facts are always "theory-laden." Although the meaning of the basic claim should be apparent, this manner of stating it gives far too much to the categories of the old dichotomy. It would be much better merely to emphasize what would seem to be the principal force of the claim. This is that "theory" and "fact" are terms that have only pragmatic meaning and boundaries within the practice of science and that at any time the "facts" of science are those claims that are in accord with the scientific image of the world, which in turn, one might say, is the sum of accepted scientific theories.

Even more directly and radically than Kuhn, Feyerabend attacked the "received" view of scientific theories and the notion of the autonomy of facts as well as the methodological rationalism of the philosophical tradition that produced these claims. He emphasized that what requires interpretation is not theory but observation and that neither in principal nor in practice can philosophy lay down rules of method for scientific practice. But, above all, Feyerabend stressed the extent to which the power of science rests on creativity and the violation of orthodoxy and rules of method (see 1964; 1965; 1970). Similar attacks on the "received" view and its approach were mounted by N. R. Hanson (1958; 1969; 1971), Michael Scriven (1958; 1959; 1962), Stephen Toulmin (1953; 1961; 1969), Peter Achinstein (1971), and Rom Harré (1970), but one of the most devastating analyses, although less noted in the social sciences, was Sellars's attack on philosophical claims about the foundations of knowledge.

If science is to be taken as a paradigm of empiricism and rationality, it is not because it possesses apodictic logic and transtheoretical epistemic foundations but because it is a self-correcting enterprise that, while sometimes dogmatic, "can put *any* claim in jeopardy" (Sellars, 1963 : 170). Not only are scientific theories ultimately incommensurable, in terms of fixed, universal, and authoritative standards in science and/or philosophy, but so are the scientific image of the world as a whole, on the one hand, and the ontology of the commonsense image of the world, on the other hand (172). The latter can hardly feature, as Brodbeck argues and most social scientists assume, as an authoritative language of observation for defining theoretical terms and testing theories. If theory explains the "facts" of commonsense perception, it does so by demonstrating or, maybe more accurately, convincing those concerned that these collective representations are illusions. The instrumentalist theory of theory is grounded on the "myth of the given," the myth of an autonomous observational framework free from theoretical criticism and reconstruction. When that myth falls, this "highly artifical and unrealistic picture of what scientists have actually done in the process of constructing theories" and all the talk about the schematic relationship between theories and facts and which belongs on top collapse (182).

If it is reasonable, analytically, to divide science into such categories as theory, law, and fact, it must be understood that such distinctions *are* analytical divisions between classes of claims that in the practice of science are only pragmatically distinguished, if distinguished at all. The relationship between the kind of claims that might be designated as theoretical (basic, universal, general, etc.) and those that are factual (specific, singular, contingent, etc.) is best understood as one involving the downward rather than upward movement of empirical meaning. Theories explain empirical laws by explaining why observables obey these laws just as the laws explain why things behave in the manner that they do. This usually involves a claim about what they really are. Theories perform many functions in science, but they cannot be understood as basically functional constructs. And their basic function is that they provide a claim about what exists, what kind of thing it is, and what form it takes.

By the early 1970s the fundamental critique of the logical positivist and logical empiricist analysis of theory in philosophy was largely complete, but the application of this analysis to the construction of theory and the defense of research programs in political science was just reaching its zenith. And it still remains the basis of the understanding of theory in empirical political science.

What came to be understood as the theoretical dimension of political science, and the core of theoretical revolution associated with behavioralism, consisted primarily of a variety of what were termed "analytical" or "conceptual" "frameworks," "orientations," "approaches," "models," "research designs," or "strategies of inquiry." For political scientists, as for those philosophers associated with the positivist tradition, the emphasis on theory was, however, somewhat misleading. Although a crucial element of the behavioral revolution was a rejection of historical particularism and various other forms of fact gathering that were taken as part of the early stages of empirical science, the new emphasis on theory did not diminish the idea of the authority of the "facts" as the object and benchmark of science or the idea of their "immaculate perception" (Hanson, 1969:77).

Like the logical empiricists from whom they drew support for their position, political scientists believed that, no matter how useful theories might be in thinking about facts, these facts at least presented themselves in some unproblematical manner and were or could be reported in an observation language that was independent of theory and theoretically incorrigible. Furthermore, it was assumed that theoretical constructs gained meaning through definition in this language and through what Feigl picturesquely described as the "upward seepage of the empirical juices" (1969:17). Although it might have been difficult to find within the practice of natural science an activity, and self-understanding of that activity, that looked much like the positivist/empiricist image of theorizing, both were isomorphically reflected in the behavioral vision of science. Here the philosophical theology about theories as ephemeral but useful "superlatives," appraised and defined by theoretically "uncontaminated" and "hard core" empirical "constants" (e.g., Feigl, 1970:7–8), became a practical faith.

Indeed, no one wanted to be associated with what Easton called "hyperfactualism," and everyone wanted to get on with emulating what was believed to be the theoretical advances characteristic of economics and sociology. But although "crude" or "rank, non-theoretical empiricism" (Almond, 1966:869) was definitely out and theory was understood as not only useful but necessary to the prediction and generalization required of a science, theories were viewed as instrumental and somewhat arbitrary constructs for finding one's way around and dealing with the ontologically distinct mass of information that was produced by modern research techniques. Theory and fact were understood as two quite universally distinct orders of things—the former mental and conventional and the latter material and experiential.

Critics of behavioralism were quick to respond to the problems involved in the imposition of these often ethnocentric and ideologically biased frameworks on various forms of political life, particularly in the area of comparative research. Here the dissonance between the frameworks, which were usually abstract versions of the American political system (e.g., Almond and Verba, 1963) and the political practices that were analyzed in these terms tended to be accentuated. But the more fundamental, yet less discussed, problem was the manner in which this notion of theory distanced inquiry from the particularities of the phenomena and from substantive theoretical questions about the character of the phenomena. There were also fundamental internal contradictions in the behavioral notion of theory just as there were in its philosophical counterpart.

In some respects, the parallel extended to matters of the approach to inquiry. The orthodox tradition in the philosophy of science eschewed contextual analysis and an exploration of the historical and contemporary conventions of the practice of science, which it approached in terms of an a priori philosophical framework. In a similar manner, behavioralism, at least in part because of its philosophical suppositions about scientific theory and inquiry, distanced itself from an internal analysis of political practices. Although one of the basic claims was that its theories offered an objective, or at least intersubjective, framework for analysis that forced principles of data selection and organization to the fore and allowed for comparability in research, such schemes were ultimately and necessarily distortive. Either these constructs were universalized typifications derived from a limited range of phenomena or they were so abstract and mechanistic that they failed to capture what was meaningful in understanding political behavior and institutions.

Given the basic idea of theory and explanation that was behind these endeavors, there was no way to avoid such difficulties. But to some degree the acceptance of this view of theory derived, as it did in the philosophy of science, from an underlying and profound fear and suspicion of theory as tainted by metaphysics and speculation. Theories seemed necessary for the goals of science, but they required definition and evaluation in terms of empirical "reality." What this entailed was a philosophical paradox, evident in such formulations as Hempel's account of the "theoretician's dilemma" (1965:189) and what was ultimately, even according to its own account, a social scientific oxymoron—"empirical theory."

It would be difficult to ascertain the exact extent to which the instrumentalist interpretation of theory informed theoretical practice as opposed to the extent to which it was employed as a rationalization of such practice. Yet the basic assumptions of that interpretation have been very apparent in the literature of mainstream political science and have been offered as either a method for "theory building" or as a justification for "theory construction." One of the principal attributes of this notion of theory is the technological orientation that presumes that theories are something to be "built" and applied to a prior and independently specifiable and determinate datum. This double-language conception of science, so characteristic of the positivist tradition, has dominated the discipline— the idea that there is "*an inherent gap*" between theory and fact that is grounded in "two distinct languages or ways of defining concepts," one in terms of theories and models and one in terms of the "real world" (Blalock, 1961:5—7). Theorizing and data collection, it is argued, can be independently undertaken and then "married" or conjoined by the sacrament of operational definition so that they can be brought into "creative juxtaposition" (Eulau, 1967:42; Riggs, 1964:401).

Textbooks and methodological essays have repeated précis of the hypothetico-deductive model and the "received" philosophy of theory with its emphasis on the reduction of theoretical concepts to observation predicates. "The operational definition," it is argued, "has become the hallmark of a 'hard science'" (Rapaport, 1966:6—9) and the manner in which meaning is bestowed. It is assumed that "theoretical concepts . . . all require operational definitions before their properties can scientifically be described and compared" (Alker, 1965:43). Herbert Simon, who since the 1940s has consistently propagated the positivist image of science, maintains that "scientific propositions" must be ultimately reducible to "statements about the observable world and the way in which it operates" (1947:248). Or, as Robert Merton suggests, theories have only "propaedeutic value" and are without empirical significance until joined to a "hard skeleton of fact" (1957: 13, 14). What is apparent in these formulations, which are generally representative of the literature of social science, is the assumption that the "observable world" and the language in which it is represented are in some fundamental (but nearly without exception unspecified) way unproblematical and given incorrigibly to immediate experience. Attempts to describe cogently this relationship between the two languages and liken it to natural science have, however, been elliptical and abortive.

Robert Dahl claims, with regard to one popular construct in political science, that "to call something a system is an abstract way (or . . . analytic way) of looking at concrete things. One should therefore be careful not to confuse the concrete thing with the analytic 'system.' A 'system' is merely an aspect of things abstracted from reality for purposes of analysis, like the circulatory system of a mammal or the personality system of a human being" (1963: 9). Dahl's argument is not simply that theories do not descriptively reproduce the world but that theories are ideal typifications. Such constructs might be important in social science, as Max Weber argued, but Dahl's point, contrary to Weber's thesis, is that there is symmetry between social and natural science with regard to the logic of theoretical concepts. Weber's claim was that, given the nature of social action (or his theoretical explication of it), ideal types are useful constructs that provide a mode of generalization appropriate to the social sciences, which are fundamentally historical or particularistic in character. Dahl, however, wishes to equate such abstractions with theory in natural science and, insofar as possible, detach them from historical particulars. But the idea that in biology the circulatory system is either understood or functions as only an analytical construct for understanding "real" biological facts indicates just how philosophically alienated from scientific inquiry political theory has become.

For the most part, proponents of the instrumentalist view of theory in social science have not even insisted that these constructs are, or should be, abstractions from descriptions of the aspects of the phenomena under investigation. The argument, sometimes relying on the common distinction in the positivist view of theory in philosophy of science between the context of discovery and the context of justification, is that these initially empirically empty schemes might come from anywhere. One arbitrarily creates models, so the typical story goes, and their validity is a matter of their utility in explaining and describing the "real" world and their correspondence with it. The paradox in this formulation is that it fails to confront the question of why theories are necessary if the real world is accessible as a means of judging theories or how, if theories are in some way necessary for knowledge of the world, they can be compared with that world. Nevertheless, the characteristic argument is that theory is a "tool" and "is not true or false, but can be more or less useful, depending on how well its explanatory capacity serves the purposes for which it is developed" (McDonald and Rosenau, 1968:317).

If there is any consistency in this position, any way to produce coherency among the claims that compose it, it resides in the notion that the "essential arbitrariness" (Holt and Richardson, 1970:24) of theoretical concepts is acceptable because theories are instruments for "relating and ordering" facts and "pertain wholly to mental operations" (McDonald and Rosenau, 1968:317). Although scientific claims require "verification by experiment, observation, and prediction" (Riker, 1962:4), empirical generalizations rather than theories are what are tested, because the latter are basically instrumentations. It would be difficult, however, in the face of any familiarity with the history and current practice of natural science, to sustain the notion that those claims usually identified as theories are merely assumed to be, or serve as, some sort of mnemonic device or heuristic analytical construct and that they are not constitutive of the propositions that are given the status of facts. Nevertheless, this continues to be the basic supposition of political scientists.

Whether or not theories in natural science can reasonably be construed as convenient fictions, it is convenient for political scientists to believe in the philosophical fiction that theories are only functional tools and that "the speculation of a Galileo, a Kepler, a Newton, or an Einstein" was "informed and controlled by a deep understanding of the hard empirical facts as they were known at the time" (Dahl, 1969:90). It would probably be more historically and conceptually accurate to say that the work of these individuals involved a direct challenge to such "facts." If scientific theories were simply ideal types and analytically useful constructs, the emulation of natural science would indeed be quite conceivable and something that might be accomplished, as Easton suggested, in a couple of decades of concentrated programmatic effort. To believe that theorizing in natural science is basically a technological project that can be methodologically carried out makes science seem accessible to everyone. Political scientists, failing in their attempt to cast themselves in the image of natural science, in effect found a philosophy that allowed them to see natural science in their own image.

If one disciplinary influence that reinforced and contributed to this notion of theory came from economics, another was situated in sociology, particularly in the work of Talcott Parsons and his structural/functional analysis of social systems. Not only did Parsons do much to popularize the concept of system that dominated the literature of political science during the height of the behavioral era, he also had a good deal to say about "the nature and conditions of empirical knowledge" (1970a:829). Parsons's analysis of these issues was considerably more sophisticated and reflective than that of most political theorists of the period. The volume *Toward a General Theory of Action* (Parsons and Shils, 1951) contains one of the most explicit and extended attempts to state the requirements of theorizing in the language of logical positivism and the allied doctrines of deductivism, operationalism, instrumentalism, and behaviorism (Sheldon, 1951:30–44). And his own claims about theory mirror these assumptions. For Parsons, the concept of a social system is "a theoretic device" (Parsons and Ackerman, 1966) and not part of a substantive claim about the nature of social reality.

Parsons's work provides a prominent example of how an emphasis on theory can be misleading. His work was certainly the paradigm case of theoretical sociology, and he was most often criticized for excessive speculation and attempts at "grand" theory. But, like many social scientists, his arguments were in many ways profoundly antitheoretical. The myth of the given and theoretical instrumentalism are at the core of his enterprise. There is, to be sure, a substantive theory of social action in Parsons's work, but it is largely a somewhat elliptical rendition of psychological behaviorism leavened by Weberian concepts. As in the case of behavioralism in political science, these theoretical assumptions become the submerged premises of the supposedly unproblematical observational framework, whereas the term "theory" is reserved to refer to the analytical manipulation of the phenomena.

Parsons defines his position as "analytical realism," which entails the notion that theories are neither "merely a reproduction of external reality" (naive realism) nor simply an "ideal order" (1949:28, 753; 1970a: 830). He argues that theories are analytical constructs to be employed in the investigation of the "external world of so-called empirical reality" but "that at least some of the general concepts of science are not fictional but adequately 'grasp' aspects of the objective external world" (1949:730, 753). The problem is how to make sense of such a formulation, and although he does a better job of it than most social scientists, he is already caught up in the characteristic paradoxes of positivist philosophy.

Like most social scientists, from Weber on, Parsons accepts the idea that conceptual schemes are inherently, and at least implicitly, inevitable aspects of perception—whether those of science or everyday life. As explicit scientific constructions, they provide an objective and systematic orientation toward data that aids in the discovery and exploration of facts.

But it is not simply that "all empirical observation is 'in terms of a conceptual scheme'" (1949:28, 30). Parsons goes so far as to note that factual knowledge is always propositional knowledge—a fact is a *proposition about* phenomena." The acceptance of this point potentially undermines the two-language view of science, but Parsons then goes on to speak of "phenomena themselves, which are concrete, really existent entities" against which the propositions of fact are to be tested; that is, "a fact is understood to be an 'empirically verifiable statement about phenomena in terms of a conceptual scheme'" (41). Either his account is contradictory or what is implied is some realm of nonpropositional knowledge that underlies all "theoretically" informed factual claims. The more generous interpretation grants consistency but brings us face to face with the myth of the given.

Theories, for Parsons, must ultimately be systems of propositions about facts (or factual propositions), and he argues that "it goes without saying that a theory to be sound must fit the facts" and be subject to "verification" by "observation of the facts" (1949:1, 6, 7; 1954:353, 365–66). This requires the familiar assumption about the reduction of theoretical concepts and the "elimination of all residual categories from science in favor of positively defined, empirically verifiable concepts," for only in this way can it be determined if "scientific theory 'works'" and is "not completely arbitrary but . . . adequately relevant to significant aspects of reality" (1949:17–19, 754). The basic logical positivist/empiricist scheme is accepted.

Parsons's concern was to establish "a general theory in the social sciences" that would have "three major functions": to codify "existing concrete knowledge," to "guide research," and to "control the biases of observation and interpretation." Such a theory would achieve "the long-term goal of scientific endeavor," which is complete deductive "empirical-theoretic systems" such as those associated with classical mechanics (Parsons and Shils, 1951:3, 49–51). A theory would be "a logical deductive system, with explicitly and formally stated axiomatic premises and, combined with appropriate minor premises, a set of deductions from them which fit empirically verifiable statements of fact." It would, however, be an analytical construct, not to be confused with "a concrete entity," for making intelligible an otherwise indeterminate "sea of facts" that constitute the "manifold of concrete reality," whose structure is not always "evident on the basis of the given data alone" (Parsons, 1970*a*:868, 839; 1970*b*:505).

The logical but problematical consequence of this image of theory, which Parsons, however, is eager to accept, is that "more than one distinguishable theoretical scheme applies to the same concrete set of phenomenon" (1970*b*: 507). It would be difficult, despite the arguments of some early positivists, to square such an account, philosophically or descriptively, with theory in natural science. Uninformed references by social scientists to wave and particle accounts of light and Heisenberg's uncertainty principle will not suffice. The claim might not be philosophically indefensible, but in light of recent work in the history and philosophy of science, it would require considerable elaboration. It is quite apparent, however, why such an assumption is attractive to social science. It is necessary in order to justify the theoretical pluralism and interdisciplinary borrowing that is characteristic of these fields and to rationalize the fact that no such "theory" has ever been, or could be, simply rejected as wrong. Theory is understood as a commodity or fungible product whose value fluctuates in the research market.

Parsons is not unaware of the paradoxes inherent in this formulation, but he does not do much about solving them. We cannot, he suggests, grasp reality without theory, but reality is to be the standard against which theory is judged. Theory ultimately distorts reality, but without theory reality is not comprehensible. For Parsons, theorizing becomes a kind of necessary but hubristic transgression that condemns us to see through a glass darkly. Theory is a detour but a necessary one. We can "*interact* with 'facts'" only in terms of "cognitive maps" or "orientational devices guiding conceptualization, research, and explanation," but we pay the Kantian price of never really knowing the world.

> We are not naive, we are not innocent; and "no fact is merely itself": a completely open mind is a completely empty one. There is a formative input to analysis, the components of which are not born *ex nihilo* in or of the moment of encounter with "facts"; rather, they are grounded in the orientation and frame of reference of the analyst. Indeed, in major part we create, we do not merely encounter, facticity. [Parsons and Ackerman, 1966: 24]

In the end, Parsons attempts to resolve the tension within this formulation by taking the position that ultimately even "*the facts of experience are myths*" and that theorizing does involve a kind of original sin that renders "no one entirely guiltless of the fallacy of misplaced concreteness" (25, 26).

The problem then becomes, for someone such as Parsons, to create an instrument that "escapes, as much as any analytical construct can, the negative consequences of mythologization" and that makes it possible to "slice up 'reality'" in a way that "mitigates" the inevitable distortions of theory. In order to grasp a fact, "we rip it from concrete *connectedness* and we pretend that it is a discrete particle." But "by ripping our 'facts' from their bed in connectedness we make them to some extent unreal" and distort them, because "*analytical thought itself is mythologization.*" It is a "*myth*, fiction," yet one that is necessary for knowledge (Parsons and Ackerman, 1966:25–28).

Parsons's tortuous analysis illustrates the difficulties of attempting to understand, let alone practice, theory in terms of a residue of ideas from logical positivism. In the end, both facts and theories are myths, and the reality that is supposed to underlie and verify both is inaccessible. Yet in many respects Parsons's arguments are more sensitive to the problems than those of most political scientists who have advanced similar notions.

Like Parsons, David Easton advocated a unified theory that would encompass "the whole field of inquiry" and be comparable to the "theory of motion in physics or of life in biology." One might very well ask if there actually are any such theories in natural science, but Easton does not believe that this could be accomplished immediately even though it should be the basic goal toward which the discipline of political science should move. Such a theory neither would nor could, in his view, emerge from the accumulation of facts and empirical generalizations. What is required is an "integrated conceptual framework at the highest level of abstraction" that would provide systematic "analytical tools" for the exploration of the "phenomenal world" and for making and testing generalizations (1965b: 8–12, 14, 29, 471). For Easton, the emphasis is on theorizing as the "construction" of instruments for giving "meaning, coherence, and direction" to research, instruments that would be judged in terms of their "utility in understanding phenomena." The extent to which Easton emphasizes the duality of theory and fact is evident in his insistence that "it is always possible to borrow the conceptual apparatus of other disciplines and apply them analogically to the data of a different field" (1953:52, 57; 1965a: 2, 4).

This assumption of the conceptual independence of theory and phenomena is apparent in Easton's characteristic image of the development of scientific method from "crude" empiricism and techniques of data collection to the sophisticated level of "concept formation and theory construction" that makes knowledge production and investigation more efficient (1965a: 17–18). This dualism is based not on a merely pragmatic distinction between theoretical and observational terms but rather on a basic ontological split between what he terms "empirical" and "symbolic" systems and the idea that "a political theory is but a symbolic system useful for understanding concrete or empirical political systems" (1965a: 5).

Although Easton does not make it explicit, the assumption seems to be that while the relationship between the language of theory and the language of observation is in various ways problematical, there is no problem about the relationship between the language of observation and "reality"—they are identical. What is simply given is the "empirical behavior which we observe and characterize as political life. These are the objects of observation, the things that, as students of politics, we would wish to understand and explain. We can speak of this phenomenal reality as the empirical and behaving system with respect to which we hope to develop some explanatory theory." The theoretical system, on the other hand, is "a set of ideas" or "a set of symbols through which we hope to identify, describe, delimit, and explain the behavior of the empirical system" (1965a: 26).

The question, and dilemma, that is apparent in such a formulation involves the nature of the incorrigible language of observation. If the world is given to us in immediate experience, in what sense does theory explain it? What was a conscious problem for the positivist philosophers and one they attempted to solve, ultimately unsuccessfully, becomes in the work of social scientists, a submerged and unexamined issue. The critical force of realism in early American political science, by the behavioral era, had been transformed, through the search for the empirical foundations of science, into the ontologization of appearances.

Easton emphasizes that "it is of the utmost importance to keep these two kinds of systems distinct," because the theoretical system is judged by the extent to which it "corresponds" to politics or the behaving system that it is "designed" to explain and that is its "point of reference." How, exactly, theoretical systems can be *designed* to correspond and refer to something and yet be necessary to apprehend and explain it is far from clear. The picture is complicated by the fact that though for Easton the empirical system is in an important sense given, "all systems are constructs of the mind." A system is "any aggregate of interactions that we choose to identify." It would seem that in the end, for Easton, theories can correspond to and be useful for explaining empirical systems because "both the behaving and the symbolic systems" are conceptual constructs. The empirical foundation in this view of explanation would appear to be the discrete "elements" of reality or "variables" out of which empirical systems are constituted and which in this sense render them more than merely symbolic systems (1965a: 26–27).

Easton urges giving up the idea "that political systems are given in nature," and he insists that such an idea has no "theoretically useful purpose," for "any set of political elements we wish to consider a system automatically becomes one." This argument reflects the philosophical idealism that was always inherent in the positivist analysis of theory, both in its notion of theories as mental constructs and in its notion of the identity of mind and experience. It also raises definite questions for the practice of social science, if it is assumed that inquiry is concerned with understanding "natural," that is, conventional, forms of political activity and not merely with relating, and predicting relationships between, arbitrarily chosen and defined variables. Easton goes even further than Parsons by suggesting that this approach can be taken "without violating the empirical data in any way" and insisting that whether a system is "given in nature or simply an arbitrary construct of the human mind is *operationally* a pointless and needless dichotomy" (1965a:29−31). Theory without guilt—or at least with absolution.

If, then, any of the given discrete variables that are supposedly given to experience can logically be conceived as an empirical system, even "a duckbilled platypus and the ace of spades," a question naturally arises about what systems political scientists would choose as objects of science and to which they would apply their symbolic theoretical systems. Easton's answer to this question is interesting. It amounts to saying that we do in fact select the systems that are given in convention and commonsense understanding and that constitute a kind of political nature. Such factors as "experience, insight, and past research" govern our selection and lead us to choose, as Easton did, a concept such as the authoritative allocation of values as definitive of politics. Thus "it might be meaningful to speak of political life as a natural system," because in practice it is neither "an arbitrary matter" nor a "matter of whim" but "what we know about political life through the study of history (past experience) and through the observation of ongoing systems (present experience)" (1965a:31−33, 48).

What this would mean in effect is that, from Easton's position, theory touches neither the constitution of specific variables nor the determination of empirical political systems. Commonsense perception, ideology, and the like lie at the foundation of empirical science. Not only are facts, as an order of existence, given to experience, but the historical forms of these facts have a fundamental immediacy and transparency. The question, then, is, Why do we need social science?

The real answer to this question lies buried in the past of political science where the assumption was that the social scientist, once freed from interest and ideology, could see the world as it was and that science was as much a matter of controlling and manipulating the world as understanding it. The failure of behavioralism to surface, and reflect on, that heritage and its determination, at the same time, to treat politics as simply an object of scientific knowledge produced paradoxes for which there were no satisfactory "scientific" answers.

Easton's approach is to suggest that everyday understanding is too unsystematic to meet the needs of science. Science is required because "the real world must be reduced and simplified in some way." Easton sees this as the task of theory, but the attempt to equate this with theory in natural science is dubious. One might believe that the enterprise of science is a kind of sophisticated and disciplined extension of everyday understanding, but it would be highly metaphorical to suggest that its specific theoretical claims about the world are only simplified reductions of common sense. Common sense and science are not only incommensurable but often in conflict. Easton's position implies that we already know the world. Otherwise, how could we simplify and reduce it? It is a position that reflects the legacy of a practical vision of political science where the concern was with changing a known political world—a concern that required selective and simplified perspectives relevant to the issues at hand. That vision was transformed by behavioralism into one of a pure or theoretical science, but the assumptions of an earlier generation continued to inform it. And there were no adequate "scientific" answers to the issues inherited by the discipline from its ancestors.

Easton argues that the evolution of the concept of system in political science has been analogous to the history of "the system called the atom" or "the idea of mass in physics," but this claim cannot withstand scrutiny. The history of the "atom" has been the history of atomic theory and the concomitant reconstitution of corresponding domains of physical fact. It is not the history of decisions regarding a relatively arbitrary symbolic system which was designed for dealing "in a unified way" with intuitively grasped arrangements of phenomenally given variables and which could be considered as *"neither true nor false"* but *"only more or less useful"* (1965a: 48, 32–34). This picture not only distorts natural science and makes it seem altogether too easy but alienates political inquiry both from a concern with its practical relationship to politics and from any theoretical understanding of its subject matter.

What is most theoretically problematical in Easton's scheme is exactly what he takes to be the givens of "phenomenal reality"—the "interactions among persons." And what are empirically or factually questionable are the conventional systems of politics that he understands as conveyed by common sense. It may be that what Easton speaks of as the "crude" "apperceptive mass" of human behavior is not an intelligible object or is too complex to deal with "in an undifferentiated and total way," but it is quite another thing to suggest that theory is only "a conceptual apparatus" or "tool to simplify reality." For Easton, theory is "analytical but nevertheless empirical" because it ultimately talks about "observable behavior" (1965a: 36–37, 44–45), but what makes the claims that are usually understood as theory in natural science empirical is that they provide the criteria for what exists as observable. The consequence of Easton's project is in principle, and has been in practice, the poverty of political theory.

Another extended representative excursion into the nature of theory during the heyday of the conceptual framework was the work of Karl Deutsch. Maybe more than anyone else, Deutsch, in defense of his "cybernetic model" of politics, propagated the idea of theory as an instrumental model and perpetuated the image of the history of science as an accumulation of empirical knowledge gained from progress in the construction of such models. He suggests, much like Easton, that the sciences pass through "philosophical" and "empirical" stages and that social science is at a point of developing "new symbolic models and/or strategies" that would define the enterprise (1963:3, 21). For Deutsch, theory construction is a kind of technological development that is prior to the research and data analysis that required such tools.

Scientific inquiry, he maintains, "is carried on by means of symbolic models" that are at least implicitly operative in all thinking, and the main task of theory in social science is to create explicit models that provide intersubjective frameworks for analyzing empirical facts. Typically, Deutsch takes the paradoxical position that there is no knowledge that is completely "objective," because it always is the product of a subjective orientation toward data that governs selection and organization. Virtual objectivity, or a practical facsimile of objectivity, is achieved by comparing our symbolic constructs with "the existing characteristics of the situation," just "as we match the distribution of symbols on a map against the distributions . . . on the landscape to be pictured" and by testing them in terms of "the practical requirements of the action for which the knowledge is to be used" (1963:4–6, 11–12).

The notion of objectivity developed by Deutsch is close to meaningless. He defines the concept of objectivity in terms of a situation for which there are no (even imaginable) criteria (the absence of a knowing subject and a framework of knowledge), suggests that it cannot be fully attained, and then argues that the degree to which it is possible can be ascertained by comparing explanatory and predictive claims with (objectively?) existing reality. Deutsch should not be criticized too severely for such conceptual problems, because in a more complex form they are prominent in philosophy, but they do indicate the degree to which social science has appropriated the abstract problems of philosophy and transformed them into practical, but equally insolvable, problems of inquiry. It is equally difficult to make sense of the garbled but nevertheless familiar account of inquiry that Deutsch presents in terms of his analogy between theories and "pictures, photographs, and maps," but, again, the assumptions are characteristically those of political scientists whatever the specific model they happen to embrace.

The scheme might be more plausible if the notion of model were not equated with theory, because it presupposes a kind of routine science in which theoretical questions have been settled and inquiry is a matter of exploring a presupposed realm of facts from various perspectives. Here the correspondence theory of truth and the idea of models as tools might make more sense. But, even on this basis, the concept of objectivity employed by individuals such as Deutsch is less than coherent. As for Parsons, theory necessarily seems to taint the data, but objectivity is not a meaningful concept unless it is possible to specify the criteria of its application. To say that theory prevents ultimate objectivity is to assume that theories are not claims about the world but rather devices for exploring a world that is given prior to theory. Theories appear as functionally necessary but epistemologically suspect. The paradox, again, is that the world is unknowable without models, yet their validity is a matter of correspondence with a world that is necessarily distorted by their application.

Lurking behind Deutsch's formulation is the counterpart, or reflection, of the positivist distinction between the contexts of discovery and justification. It is the idea that theories are basically a priori constructs of diverse and often subjective origin that receive empirical meaning and verifiable content through interpretation in terms of, and in comparison with, an external world. And this idea in turn is ultimately based on some version of the instrumentalist theory of theory, which Deutsch presents in its most radical form by stressing not only cognitive verification in terms of explanation and prediction but verification as manipulation and control. Drawing directly upon the positivist and logical empiricist claims about theory, he argues that

> together, a set of symbols and a set of rules may constitute what we may call a calculus, a logic, a game, or a model. . . . If this pattern and these laws resemble, to any relevant extent, any particular situa-

tion or class of situations in the outside world, then to that extent these outside situations can be "understood," that is, predicted—and perhaps even controlled—with aid of the model. Whether any such resemblance exists cannot be derived from the model, but only from the physical process of *verification*, that is, physical operations for matching some of the structure of the outside situation. [1963: 19–20]

In some respects, Deutsch's argument, which places considerable emphasis on pragmatic or manipulative testing of models, is more consistent than the more cognitive instrumentalism of Easton, but he consistently blurs the line between knowledge and control.

Given Deutsch's general formulation, it should be no surprise that he insists that all theoretical concepts be supplied with operational definitions. And his notion of theory as a cognitive map or photograph implies that theory is basically a perspective on an already known world, but one that must be simplified for certain purposes. A good theory is one that serves those purposes and various other instrumental epistemological functions such as organizing data. He even goes as far as to claim that a "theory is thus in principle an engine for the selection of information as well as its storage and retrieval, and for making predictions," and consequently should be judged by its "economy," "predictive performance," and "relevance" for doing what we want it to do (1963: 16–17; Deutsch and Rieselbach, 1965: 140). This might be a reasonable image of a computer, but it is questionable as a description of scientific theory.

By 1971 Deutsch, in the context of internal disciplinary criticism and in light of political science's reconstitution of its image in terms of public policy analysis, had broadened his view of theory a great deal to encompass much of what he had earlier relegated to the realm of political philosophy and distinguished from scientific theory. But he maintained his instrumentalist position, even in the course of adopting some ideas of Kuhn about scientific change. Whether theories are normative or empirical and whether they are used to produce "empirical knowledge," "pragmatic skills," or "wisdom," he insists that they are "orientations" that offer a "presentational image" of reality in the form of "an ensemble or configuration of interrelated propositions" that undergo revolutionary change when they no longer do the job for which they were created. The essence of theory remains a "coding" system or "a scheme for the orderly and efficient *storage and retrieval* of memories," the production of "*insight*, the organization and *strategic simplification* of knowledge," "*heuristics*" or "search devices for new observations, experiments and discoveries," and a basis for "self-critical cognition" that keeps us aware of "the assumptions and biases implicit in operations of verification and corroboration" (Deutsch, 1971: 11–16).

There is a way in which an examination of the incoherence involved in these assumptions points to a better understanding of theory. Once again, at the core of that incoherence is the begged question of how the world can be accessible only through theory and at the same the theory can be judged by its correspondence with that world. This paradox is evident in the attempt to explicate the nature of theory by reference to maps, lights, nets, different-colored lenses, grids, overlays, and other devices. One of the problems is that although these analogies may indicate some of the functions that theories perform in science they are also misleading in several respects.

First of all, although theories might be said to perform certain functions such as ordering data, they do a great deal more than this. They specify what data exist and what kind of things they "are" and, consequently, provide the basic criteria and conceptual context for making and assessing scientific claims. Second, although a theory might be understood as a model, it is not a model in the sense that social scientists tend to use that concept. Parsons, Easton, Deutsch, Riker, and others do not claim, and in fact consistently deny, that the structure of political reality actually conforms to their models, but in natural science a model that has the status of a theory or reflects a theory would be one that was understood as isomorphic with the basic character of the world. It would constitute a fundamental and substantive claim about that world. The models of the social scientist are at best ideal types and at worst arbitrary metaphors and similes designed to make some complex set of phenomena intelligible by thinking about it *as if* it were something else. Models in the latter sense might be useful in various respects, but they are not equivalent to theories in either character or function.

One way to deal with this issue is to pursue the notion of theory as a map. This analogy can be instructive, but social scientists seem to be as dim about maps as they are about theories. Maps, whether simple or detailed, are representations or models of what exists. Some may be designed for specific instrumental purposes and judged by the extent to which they correspond to a world we already know and do the job for which they were created, but they presuppose and embody geographical knowledge. Unlike the social scientist's vision of theory, we do not make maps arbitrarily, and they are the product rather than the starting point of inquiry and exploration. And maybe most important is the fact that maps are not universally applicable and interchangeable devices passed back and forth between the explorers of different territories or imposed on various data bases to determine how well they illuminate them. They are circumscribed and realistic claims.

The assumption of political scientists that there is more than a pragmatic distinction between theories and facts is not supported by an analogy with maps. A map is a symbolic construct, but it is not, except in specialized cases, conceptually autonomous and simply a figurative device for exploring and organizing an independently conceived and perceived realm of commonsense fact. There may be a disjunction between some formal cartographic conception of the universe and our commonsense perceptions, but, as with scientific theories, we usually will choose the former when the chips are down and would not assume that it is merely a tool for finding our way around in the "real" world. Most people take maps seriously, and when one map is rejected for another it is usually because it means a new vision of some segment of the world has been agreed upon—not because we have found a better instrument that in itself is neither valid nor invalid.

The characteristic argument that these conceptual frameworks and models are the basis of objectivity in social science is not sound. First of all, as in the case of Deutsch, there is the assumption that complete objectivity would require some kind of nonconceptual immediate perception, and then there is the conclusion that this is not in practice, or even in principle, possible because we always bring theories, concepts, and the like (which are equated with biases) to our observations. Thus objectivity and intersubjectivity are to be achieved in a diluted form by making our preconceptions systematic and explicit. This entire chain of reasoning is incoherent. It begins with an indefensible notion of objectivity and ends with a solution that denies its possibility.

The fundamental premise here is that there is a kind of nonpropositional or basic apprehension of what philosophers like Brodbeck speak of as the "facts of experience" or "differentiated slices of reality" that are reflected in "the language of commonsense" and "stand out, almost begging for names" (1968:4, 10−11). Theories and the concepts of science are considered to be of only instrumental value and imposed on facts for the purpose of generalization, prediction, and so forth. The particular variables can be objectively discerned, but the ordering schemes are conventional constructions. This has become a philosophically untenable notion, but it continues to inform social science.

What this means, in effect, is that theories are ultimately accepted as distortions and devalued as basic and realistic claims about the world. It is assumed that this situation can be mitigated in various ways (making theories public and explicit, for example), but the irony is that what is taken as objectivity is in principle ultimately denied to science. A further irony is that in practice objectivity does become impossible. The very mechanistic schemes and various other metaphors that social scientists have devised as explanatory theoretical models are so structurally biased, value-laden, and alien to both political phenomena in general and their particular instantiations that they tend, paradoxically, to distort and obscure what they are supposed to clarify and reveal.

The logical difficulties in some of these assumptions about facts and objectivity are evident. We have such concepts as fact, objectivity, and reality, but it is an egregious mistake to believe that such concepts refer to some specific realm of objects. They refer to a *class* of objects—the class posited by the propositions to which we subscribe for reasons that are authoritative in any conventional practice of knowledge at a particular time. It may be that when a set of entrenched beliefs or propositions is called into question it seems that the very idea of objective reality is being called into question, but that is just because we have come to identify the concept with its specific criteria of application. There is, however, more than a simple category mistake involved in this issue. Whatever the historical origins of philosophy's search for a basis for underwriting scientific knowledge, the persistence of the myth of the given and the instrumental interpretation of theory is now grounded in academic tradition, philosophical self-interest, and social scientific timidity.

I will have more to say about the issue of relativism and objectivity at a later point, because it is as much a concern of "normative" political theory as it is of empirical social science. What is worth repeating once more is that those philosophers and their social scientific fellow travelers (e.g., Landau, 1972) who attack Kuhn and others as relativists are responding to an attack not upon objectivity in science but upon their particular metatheoretical notion of objectivity. Philosophy did not establish the criteria of objectivity in science, and it cannot take them away. The relationships between science and philosophy are contingent, but even if the substance of an argument like Kuhn's should conceivably affect the practice of science, there is no good reason to believe that it would shake the faith of science in its claims to knowledge. Kuhn's arguments are about the character of what is taken to be knowledge in science and not about the validity of that knowledge or the truth of scientific claims. In the case of social science and its problems of scientific identity, it was attractive to believe that philosophy could underwrite science and supply doctrines that, if followed, could establish scientific legitimacy and success.

What Kuhn's arguments were directed toward was the great gap between the history and current practice of science on the one hand and the alienated philosophical conception of the enterprise on the other hand, and he attempted to produce a philosophical image that more accurately reflected that practice (1970*a*: 236). The philosophical orthodoxy had not been primarily concerned with such a goal, and there have been many who have questioned whether Kuhn attained it (e.g., Lakatos, 1970; Popper, 1970; Shapere, 1966; Toulmin, 1968; 1972). Whether or not, for example, his claims about scientific change are historically accurate and whether he is consistent in his use of "paradigm" are somewhat beside the point. It is in fact probably fair to say that the question of historical accuracy here is something of a red herring and that, like philosophers and historians of science before him, he projected an epistemology on the history of science. But it is probably also fair to acknowledge his point that his ventures into the history of science raised real questions about the content and approach of the orthodox philosophies and their legitimating accounts of science.

The real punch in Kuhn's argument, which was by far the least explicit element, struck at the assumption that philosophy, as practiced by traditional epistemology and methodology, could specify the foundations of scientific knowledge in some transcendental or transcontextual manner. The point was that the foundations of scientific knowledge resided in scientific theories. By implication, the traditional enterprise of academic philosophy was called into question as were certain notions in the social sciences that from their origins had reflected that traditional philosophical enterprise. This import of his argument was the underlying cause of the strong critical reaction as well as the eager reception, rather than simply the fact that he challenged an orthodox thesis in the philosophy of science. What Kuhn's argument implied was the *loss* of philosophy's special authority and the *possibility* of theoretical and methodological autonomy in the social sciences.

What is clear is that the collapse of the "given" is a crisis for both philosophy and social science, but those who viewed it, or represented it, as a crisis for science and its ideal of objectivity (Scheffler, 1967), as a movement toward "complete relativism" in science (Shapere, 1966), the reduction of science to "*mob psychology*" (Lakatos, 1970), the end of "rational discussion" in science (Popper, 1970), anarchy in scientific language (Brodbeck, 1968), the rejection of "empirical evidence" (Hempel, 1969), transformation of the idea of "truth" into "myth" (Nagel, 1971), and a retreat from moral and scientific objectivity in political theory were simply confusing their academic philosophical commitments with the foundations of the practices they studied. The only threat was to the integrity of a

particular philosophical approach and its reconstruction of scientific theory—and to the integrity of those elements of social science and political
theory that attempted to implement those notions or rationalize their activity in terms of them.

To raise questions about epistemological analyses regarding truth conditions in science in no way calls into question the truth value of scientific
claims. The rejection of philosophical transcendentalism and the idea of
the philosophy of science as a master science or the source of authority
regarding the conditions of scientific knowledge is not equivalent to a recommendation for irrationalism in science, and Kuhn has made this point
abundantly clear (1970*a*; 1970*b*; 1977). Part of the difficulty was simply
that with positivism and logical empiricism the philosophy of science had
a normative character that was less central in the work of the critics, and
the representatives of the former construed "relativism" as a normative as
well as an epistemological claim.

Kuhn's suggestion that the criteria of knowledge were relative to particular theories, paradigms and exemplars, and the general disciplinary
"matrix" was sometimes innocently construed by normatively inclined
philosophers and some social scientists as a *recommendation* for aban-
doning standards in science. This was, of course, grossly incorrect. After
all, Kuhn's work on scientific revolutions had begun as a recognition of the
"functions of dogma in science." Even Feyerabend's rejection of foundations and method and his call for "anarchy" in science were, despite his
violent break with Popper, still more an extension of Popper's critical rationalism and its efficacy regarding the growth of scientific knowledge
than a suggestion that science should not have standards of knowledge or
that it could be practiced without such standards. But most of the critical
reception was hardly so innocent. It was a direct response to a threat to
philosophy's self-image and those who had basked in its glow.

The theory/fact dichotomy had been severely qualified by most of its
major proponents, including Hempel, by the time the counterrevolutionary arguments in its defense had been articulated and had begun to enter
the discourse of political science (Miller, 1972). In philosophy it was more
a weakened protest than an argument that asserted, by the 1970s, that "it
is simply not true that all empirical knowledge is 'contaminated' by theories" (Feigl, 1970: 7–8). The strained attempts to resurrect some version
of the given once it had been exposed as a philosophical fiction were without significance, and the subsequent discussions became centered around
technical if not precious philosophical points that still suffered from the
intellectual burden of the old dichotomy but had little meaning for social
scientists.

Kuhn's basic point, as well as that of Feyerabend, was simply that the basis of scientific judgment is contextual and internal to scientific practice and that there are no relevant logical or epistemological "criteria of rationality which are independent of our understanding of the essentials of the scientific process" (1970b: 264). Scientific theories, not theories of scientific knowledge, are the foundations of knowledge in science. But this has not been an easy lesson for political science, and political theory in general, to learn.

It is one thing to accept as a regulative ideal the notion that theories are attempts to grasp reality or even instruments for understanding it and to think of the history of science as a progressive apprehension of the way the world is. But it is quite another thing to suggest that philosophy can point to a transtheoretical datum and language in which the world can be represented that are independent of particular theories and the basis, in practice, of their commensurability. Similarly, one might find it enlightening to accept philosophical maxims such as "Choose theories with the greatest empirical content" or "The greater the predictive power, the better the theory," but it is a mistake to think that the practice of science is grounded in such proverbs and maxims or that there are transcontextual criteria for fulfilling such standards, just as it is a mistake to think that we can become proficient in some specific practical endeavor simply by adhering to cautions such as not counting our chickens before they are hatched.

Relativism is a slippery concept. It seems much too easy to interpret the claim that observations in science are always relative to a theoretical context as advocating the notion that science is, and even should be, a matter of "dealer's choice." But no such extrapolation is warranted. What is clear is that the logical positivist/empiricist tradition in philosophy was, from the first, suspicious of the idea of theory and spent as much time explaining it away as explaining it. Political scientists who were influenced by this philosophy, in the sense of believing that it provided either a method of inquiry or a basis for rationalizing their enterprise, have accepted an impoverished notion of theory and its place in science, which has led them to overlook their existing theoretical assumptions and alienated them from creative theorizing. Aaron Wildavsky represents well mainstream political science's basic attitude toward theory when he suggests that, "after all, if things are just as they seem on the surface, who needs theorists?" (1979: 114).

# 3
## *Theory and Tradition*

In nothing do we see learned men more prone to untruth than in the
fabrication of Traditions.

NINTH CENTURY ISLAMIC SAYING

ALTHOUGH THE scientific image of theory that was advanced
by behavioralism was not countered by any exactly comparable notion of
political theory, there was enough thematic coherence among many of the
principal responses to make it reasonable, although not entirely accurate,
to think of the debate in terms of a conflict between "scientific" and "traditional" political theory. The critique of behavioralism in the 1950s and
1960s was largely an undertaking that fell to those concerned with the
history of political theory. This is not surprising, for this endeavor was the
most immediate target of the behavioral revolution and its theoretical
purge. But it produced a somewhat distanced confrontation. Behavioralists did not look very carefully at what the study of the history of political theory was, and had been, all about, and the "historians" tended to
engage the behavioral claims to science on an equally abstract level that
was often quite far removed from what political scientists actually said
and did. Much of the criticism was related to the dangers of authoritarian
control that some believed were implicit in the behavioral notion of science or even the more general dangers of treating human beings as objects
of science and neglecting the normative dimensions of politics (e.g., Storing, 1962). As Norman Jacobson suggested (1958), the issues tended to be
removed to the plane of a vacuous, abstract, philosophical debate between
scientism and moralism.

There is reason to suggest that during these years the enterprises of orthodox political science and dissident political theory, and the critical exchanges between them, were in many important ways mutually determinative. Even though traditional political theory criticized what it took to be the circumscribed vision of science embraced by behavioralism and the unfortunate implications of its pursuit, it largely granted to behavioralism the internal integrity of that vision. And, similarly, the idea of the tradition that formed the core of the historical arguments was generally accepted by the behavioralists and never engaged in any significant manner. The result was that the character of both endeavors tended to remain largely self-defined with little direct critical exposure. To understand both behavioralism and the study of the history of political theory requires moving beyond their self-images and their criticisms of each other.

There is an important sense in which the modes of education and scholarship that came to be associated with the study of the history of political theory must be understood as expressing a kind of political argument—no matter how philosophically metamorphosed. One might very well claim that behavioralism reflected and reinforced certain ideological assumptions, particularly those of the American liberal consensus, just as it is quite clear that much of the literature connected with the history of political theory constituted and, in fact, grew out of a critique of liberalism that would have been incomprehensible to generations of American scholars before World War II. But in basic intention and purpose, for better or worse, the behavioral literature cannot principally be construed as consisting of political argument, even though there are many reasons for saying that it was, in effect, a kind of political discourse.

Writing about the history of political theory, and the definition of this activity, were, on the other hand, very much shaped by such self-conscious political intentions and purposes. One of the basic difficulties, however, was that this enterprise never adequately came to grips with the problems of the status of political commentary in an academic and often somewhat esoteric scholarly setting and with its relationship to public discourse. And the irony was that, though historians of political theory often criticized behavioralism for its political blindness and unconcern, there was a real sense in which behavioralism, despite its estranged image of theory, moved closer to the phenomena of politics and political language than those who created the myth of tradition in the course of their pursuit of politically meaningful philosophical history.

After World War II, the character of the study of the history of political theory was increasingly shaped by émigré scholars like Strauss, Voegelin, and Arendt. Although their work was adapted to, and adopted by, the

American version of the idea of the tradition exemplified by individuals such as Dunning and Sabine, they brought new content to the field as well as fundamentally different attitudes toward history, the status of political values, liberalism, and science. To some extent the split between behavioralism, as it increasingly came to constitute the mainstream of political science, and the history of political theory was in fact a split engendered less by a conflict between "traditional" and "scientific" theory than by the incompatibility of the indigenous and émigré perspectives. The founders of the behavioral revolution were nearly all originally trained as political theorists (in the historical sense) and were educated in the American idea of the tradition. It was in part the transformation of that earlier idea of the tradition into the myth of the tradition, or at least the particular "political" content of that myth, that required them to make a choice with which they previously had never been confronted—a choice between empirical political science and the history of political theory.

In speaking of the myth of the tradition, I am, initially, speaking less of a specific paradigm that was shared within a particular school of thought than of an intellectual syndrome, identified by certain family resemblances, in some of the influential and increasingly dominant literature of the field. Some common intellectual roots informed these resemblances and emanated both from the political and philosophical background of the refugees and from the history of American political science prior to World War II, which provided the basic tradition of discourse onto which their ideas were grafted. But it would be a mistake to suggest that the works of Strauss, Arendt, and Voegelin, which I want to look at in some detail, were simply variations on a basic and mutually accepted argument. By the 1960s at the latest, however, the work of these individuals, now fused with the idea of the tradition in American political science, had given rise to a paradigm that governed research and education.

When we turn from some of this formative literature to the more general practices of scholarship and teaching within the field of political theory that were in various ways influenced by it, the elements of a paradigm, or exemplars within a disciplinary matrix, in a Kuhnian sense, are much more apparent. Although that paradigm has recently become an object of reflection and critical scrutiny, it has left an indelible mark on the field of political theory both in and outside the discipline of political science. And, much like the behavioral image of science and theory, it is far from a matter of simply historical concern. Not only are some of its most systematically developed variations, such as those associated with Strauss and Voegelin, alive and well, but its more general residue is widely evident in the language and assumptions of contemporary academic political theory, including much that has very little directly to do with the history of political thought. Even those who reject it have been significantly influenced by it in a number of ways, including the degree to which they have shaped their enterprises in opposition.

My concern here is not primarily with the evolution of the idea of the tradition and the myth of the tradition in the field of political theory (see Gunnell, 1979*b*). Neither do I wish to dwell, in this context, on the many interesting issues an acquaintance with that development suggests—for example, the extent to which the contemporary discourse of political theory and the conflict between political theory and mainstream political science have their roots in a post-World War II debate over liberalism (see Gunnell, 1983*b*). My concern is essentially to make clear exactly what the myth of the tradition is and the manner in which the assumptions that constitute that myth have contributed to the poverty of theory and to a neglect, if not a fundamental distortion, of our understanding of the relationship between academic political theory and politics. No matter what might be construed as its positive attributes, role, and consequences—and I am more than willing to admit that they were significant—its hold over the image and practice of political theory must be critically examined.

The difficulty with criticizing the myth of the tradition is that any such criticism is likely to be construed too broadly and as an attack on the very idea of the study of the history of political theory and on the idea that there is educational and scholarly value in thinking about the classic texts. Another problem is that such criticism is often taken as an implicit attack on the various political and academic concerns of those who generated and propagated this myth. The problem is that this myth, like the myth of theory in the philosophy of science and political science, has become such an integral aspect of the field that to call it into question is often viewed as calling the very enterprise of the history of political theory, if not political theory as a whole, into question. There is, of course, a certain sense in which this is correct, because to reflect on this myth does demand a fundamental rethinking of an enterprise that has in many respects come dangerously close to falling into a state of systematic self-delusion.

It is as important to make clear what the myth is *not* as it is to make clear what it is. It is not simply the claim that there is in some general sense a Western tradition of politics and political ideas that exists as a kind of seamless web of thought and action and that is the effective history within which we stand. Such a claim is almost a truism, and one could really not study it as historical totality any more, or less, than one could study Western civilization as a whole. It is also not merely the claim that there are, within this intellectual construct that we might think of as the history of political thought, various actual traditions of politics and political think-ing that in many respects might be self-ascribed and conventionally pre-constituted. It is not simply to note that the authors of the classic texts in various ways and degrees talked to and about each other. And it is cer-tainly not just the notion that we might reasonably, according to various criteria, analytically constitute and speak of traditions based on simi-larities of problems and concerns reflected in various texts, what we take to be family resemblances, or some other kind of "sameness" posited at various levels of abstraction. The myth of the tradition often in one way or another plays upon many of these quite unexceptional and intuitively rea-sonable claims, but it goes much further.

At its core is the reification of an analytical construct. It is the represen-tation of what is in fact a retrospectively and externally demarcated tradi-tion as an actual or self-constituted tradition. The classic texts are ex-tracted from their actual historical contexts and reconstituted as a virtual tradition with a prior synoptic meaning from which each text then takes its particular meaning. It is not simply to treat the classic texts, literally, as a "great dialogue" in which the authors consciously engaged but to as-sume that, whatever their particular circumstantial concerns, this dia-logue and their contributions to it are the most basic context for under-standing their work. It is to treat the so-called great tradition from Plato to Marx as if it were logically comparable to, although larger and more en-compassing than, for example, what many would take to be the actual tradition of Marxist thought. It is to suggest that the relationship between such individuals as Machiavelli and Locke is to one another and to politics and political ideas like the relationship of Descartes and Newton to one another and to natural science and scientific theory.

The claims about the existence and character of the great tradition are not so much a research conclusion as a rhetorical move in an argument about contemporary politics. This in no way means that such claims are in some obvious or automatic manner inappropriate, but there are problems attaching to them. First of all, they present themselves as a "historical" thesis, and although the criteria of historicity are surely far from uncon-tested ones, there is no context for evaluating the claims in these terms. Much, in fact, depends on removing the claim from any such context and placing it in the realm of revelation and prophecy. The very idea of *the* tradition is an a priori concept, and its general and unexamined accep-tance is a crucial aspect of the myth. While all this may be strategically prudent, it raises, in the scholarly context in which it is presented, the paradox of rhetorical claims in a critical academic forum. Closely related to this point is the fact that, although one might imagine circumstances in which this might be effective or supportable, such a context has not really obtained in the world of American political science and academic political philosophy where these arguments have flourished. These arguments have amounted to little more than part of a set of academic disputes and a kind of futile symbolic action that actually speaks neither to nor about politics in any significant manner.

Although one might reasonably hypothesize about the various ways that such claims might become part of political education and political change and even suggest that there is in the end no academic argument about politics that is not in some way a political argument, such a position tends to beg the question. One of the facts of American political experience is the less than easily permeable membrane that separates academic and political discourse, no matter how much one may speculate on the possibilities and actualities of interaction. Another fact, which presents an even more difficult problem, is that, although the intention or purpose of this literature may be "political," it seldom really addresses or engages the particularities of politics except in an elliptical and categorical manner. It remains a kind of abstract philosophical politics that speaks at best indirectly to and about concrete political issues and circumstances.

The myth of the tradition is a myth in nearly all relevant respects. It has become part of the academic mythology that defines and justifies the study of the history of political theory. It is only an ostensibly historical account that serves to foster a persuasive but unreflective image of our past and present. It is simply counterfactual with respect to almost any attempt that might be made to place it in a discursive or evidential context. Although these charges might seem unduly harsh given what many would take to be the laudatory motives that inspired it, there are, despite all the virtues that one might conjure up in its behalf, few competitors in terms of its contribution to the alienation of political theory.

Although what I am calling the myth of the tradition is considered here more as a syndrome than an argument that is the property of a certain thinker or thinkers and although it is deployed in various ways by different individuals and with varying degrees of reflectiveness, several common elements of the myth can be found in the work of its principal creators. My concern here is only in a secondary way with the arguments of individuals and the particular purposes of their work. Despite the many differences among the authors and the degree to which the work of someone like Strauss deserves independent treatment (see Gunnell, 1978; 1985), I wish to point out some of the concrete similarities in the literature that have converged to create the myth. Its existence and scope in the scholarly literature of political theory from textbooks to monographs and its pervasive hold on education in the field are things that I take here as givens (see Gunnell, 1979*b*).

First, there is the assertion, suggestion, or assumption that the classic texts from at least Plato to Marx are in some way the product of a distinct and conventionally autonomous activity with historically discernible continuities and transformations. These works are taken not as a canon constituted simply by academic tradition but as the principal works in an integral and independent tradition of inquiry with a career that, as a whole, can be made the subject of interpretation. What is meant by "political theory," as both product and activity, and "political theorist" is defined by this body of literature. The point is not simply that there are assumed to be various connections and relations of influence among these works and authors that might be researched and discussed but that their primary audience was each other—they were speaking to their canonical predecessors and to their anticipated successors. They are presented as engaged in what more than metaphorically could be called a continuing conversation such as one might attribute, for example, to contemporary academic political theory and the disciplines within which it resides. There is clearly an element of projection in this characterization.

Central to the contemporary versions of this myth is the notion that today Western political society is facing a crisis—a crisis usually associated in some way with modern science (and social science) and liberalism—and that the crisis is both caused by and exemplified in the decadent state or restricted circumstances of political theory. The great tradition is in decline, if not dead. But, at the same time, this crisis of politics and political theory creates the occasion, opportunity, and necessity of reflection, particularly historical reflection, that will deconstruct and reconstruct the tradition and thereby explain modern political thought and action and open the path to a restoration.

Such an explanation is offered as the starting point for a therapeutic exercise in self-knowledge that will grasp the source of the modern malaise and provide the basis for the beginning of a process of rethinking and remaking modern politics. Exactly how "we" might undertake this practical task and what in fact it would mean to the proverbial "us" are left quite vague. But, in a somewhat Hegelian fashion, political knowledge is identified as knowledge about ideational matters—theory and ideas are what is assumed to move the world, and politics is conceived as their residue. What is to be gained from this penetration of the past may differ considerably from author to author, but whether it is incremental wisdom,

substantive and instrumental truths, moral precepts, or general and transcendental imperatives relevant to understanding and solving the crisis of
modernity, these are supposed to be historically accessible and to be found
in the classic texts and the relationships among them. Most often there is
not only a point of truth that is to be discerned historically in the tradition
but one principal point of transformation that represents the beginning
of the degeneration of the tradition and the crucial source of political
devolution.

What is important in this venture is to ascertain in some way and degree the "meaning" of the tradition as a whole and its significance for the
present. This is often tied to some particular hermeneutic key, some privileged mode of access to the meaning of the texts and the symbolic crystal
of past politics that would yield methodological certainty for the interpretation and, consequently, for the wisdom exegetically extracted. But
the general meaning of the tradition is the fundamental basis for understanding the particular works and authors, for each plays a role in the
total titanic saga with its beginning, rise, fall, and hope of redemption.

Part of what makes the myth of the tradition a myth is not simply that
many of the assumptions involved may be historically indefensible but that
they are seldom if ever defended. Even though the criterion of what would
constitute an actual historical tradition may not be easily agreed upon,
there is never an attempt to demonstrate that the classic texts that have
been extracted and abstracted from various contexts do in fact represent
anything that could reasonably be construed as such a tradition. But the
propagation of the idea that what is being discussed is actually an inherited pattern of thought and action that mediates between our circumstances and the past is a crucial element of the myth. What gives power to
the myth is that it plays upon the idea of the tradition—the acceptance of
the general narrative that is presupposed and commonly accepted but
given a special and poignant meaning. Like many myths, this narrative is
designed to explain the human past. The tradition is a premise and not a
hypothesis, and it carries with it a number of basically unexamined, and in
many respects unexaminable, assumptions and assertions.

These include claims about the major participants and the roles they
have played as founders, transformers, and executioners of the tradition;
about its beginnings in ancient Greece and its modern decline; about its
determinative influence on modernity and its special relationship to some
modern crisis that has been created by the degeneration of the tradition
but that frees us for historical self-knowledge; about the problems of liberalism and social science, and many aspects of modern philosophy, as both
manifestations and causes of its decadence; about the special status of the

political realm, its contemporary demise, and the need for its reconstitution; about the emphasis on the practical implications of this "historical" investigation and the revelatory character of the discoveries achieved through a critique of the tradition; about the idea that basic grounds of practical political judgment can be gained or regained through retracing the tradition and the exegesis of the texts and that this will solve the problem of the loss of such grounds in the modern age; about the assumption that one can really speak cogently about the meaning of what Smedley Sweat called "all previous thought" (Crews, 1963); and about the role of the "historian" as prophet, preserver, and transmitter of truths in and about the tradition and in some way as a contemporary representation of those paradigmatic figures who have gone before.

Although the myth of the tradition began to take shape in the vision of the émigré scholars during the 1940s, it was not clearly manifest in the literature of political theory until the 1950s when the work of people like Strauss, Arendt, and Voegelin became influential. One of the earliest examples of this genre, and maybe the first major departure from the literature that characterized the older paradigm, was John Hallowell's *Main Currents in Modern Political Thought* (1950), which addressed a "crisis in Western civilization" caused by what he took to be the decline of political theory and the perversion of liberalism. Hallowell, during the 1940s, had pursued the theme of the decline of liberalism, which he attributed to the rise of positivism and historicism and linked to the emergence of totalitarianism. For Hallowell, the solution was to be found in a reconstruction of liberalism in terms of new philosophical and theological grounds.

Although Hallowell's arguments actually preceded the publication of the principal works of such theorists as Strauss and Voegelin, they appeared at a point at which the discourse associated with the study of political theory was undergoing a fundamental change that reflected the ideas of these individuals. A large portion of Hallowell's book was devoted to what would become a typical summary account of political thought from ancient times to the present. The story was one of the degeneration within modernity for which a decadent liberalism was in large measure responsible. Through its failure to develop a philosophical ground that could justify itself in the face of totalitarian ideologies, liberalism helped to produce "the crisis of our times" that began in the early part of the century and manifested itself in the totalitarian forces that gave rise to World War II and now threatened the West in the form of communism.

Central to this myth, then, is the idea that politics and political thought, usually in some universal and essential sense supposedly manifest in the conditions of the modern age, are in crisis. Strauss emphasizes that we are situated in the midst of crisis, "the crisis of our time, the crisis of the West" (1964a:1). For Voegelin, it is a "civilizational crisis" (1968:22), and for Arendt "a general crisis that has overtaken the modern world" (1961:140). Essential to this symbol of crisis is the idea that it is, at least when once called to our attention, in some fundamental way self-evident. Strauss suggests that the existence of such a crisis is "hardly in need of proof" (1972:217). All the particular events that we might view, for various but typical reasons, as having some attributes of crisis and "of which everyone so readily speaks" (Voegelin, 1968:22) are urged as the symptoms of a deeper and larger crisis that can be revealed by reflection and historically illuminated. The criteria for both the existence of the general crisis and its relation to actual events are, however, either unspecified or supported only by allusions. It is argument by evocation, and this is the basic genre to which the literature exemplifying the myth of the tradition belongs—political theory as evocation.

The crisis these individuals allege is both political and intellectual in character, but an essential element of the image evoked is the notion that it is most fundamentally a crisis of ideas or a "spiritual disorder" (Voegelin, 1968:22)—a dilemma of the "mind" and a break in a "tradition of thought" (Arendt, 1961:8–9). Any demonstration of an actual link between what is characterized as the debased politics of modernity and the presumptive "decline" or "decay" (Strauss, 1959:17) of political philosophy is singularly absent, but we are asked to extrapolate the events and conditions of modern politics, which are presented largely in terms of images such as "tyranny" (Strauss, 1963b:26–27), "the corrosion of Western civilization" (Voegelin, 1952:188), and "world alienation" (Arendt, 1958:6), from interpretations of classic texts holistically conceived as an organic intellectual tradition that explains the present causally and by revealing the inner meaning of modern politics.

The political dimension of the crisis is most ostensibly totalitarianism on both the right and the left, but in many respects each of these individuals is more concerned with the subtle problems that they believe are immanent in modern society and liberal democracy, which, they claim, spring from the same intellectual roots. The attitude toward liberalism is characteristically ambivalent. On the one hand, it represents, or is represented as, the loss of both spiritual and political authority in the modern age. In liberalism can be found all the symptoms of the crisis, such as the decline of the political realm and its subversion by social and private values, relativism and the weakness of political principle, and the historical regime that allowed nazism to enter the world and that now may be too weak to defend against incursions from the East. For Strauss, liberalism has become little more than "permissive egalitarianism" (1953:5–6; 1972:242), and in the end, for these thinkers in general, most of the underlying characteristics of the worst political forms and ideas that mark the decline of the West are evident in liberalism. On the other hand, liberalism is generally understood as worth saving and as the medium for political revival. It is at least a remnant of the tradition, and each views some kind of liberalism as the best practicable regime and a type deserving political defense and the effort of philosophical reinvigoration.

The problems of liberalism and its intellectual handmaiden, social science, then, not only spring from the same intellectual source as totalitarianism but may even be implicated in its appearance and certainly portend the danger of degenerating into it. The connections these individuals suggest between the events of modernity and the underlying philosophical illness of the time that they profess to reveal are largely spurious. We are asked to believe not only that there is such a crisis but that it has some fundamental world-historical meaning that is linked not only to intellectual transformations in the past but to ones that can be attributed to and located in particular authors and texts.

This literature is distinguished by the claim that the crisis has finally funneled down to the point where it is not simply a crisis of politics and a crisis of Western thought in general but a crisis of political philosophy or political theory. This is not understood to be the case simply in some generic sense. It is professional academic political philosophy, which we are asked to believe is the rump of the putative great tradition and the repository of its fate. This discipline is presented as both the problem and the answer. Here is the nucleus in which both the meaning of the crisis and at least the beginning of a solution must be sought. Strauss, for example, asks if it is not "strange" that the "crisis of modernity," which is in general a manifestation of the "crisis of modern political philosophy," should turn out to be "the crisis of one academic pursuit among many." His answer is that political philosophy is not and, until recently, had not been "essentially an academic pursuit," and its fall into that condition and its subjection to the constraints and influences of that context are part of the problem (1975:82). Voegelin's notion of the construction of a "new science of politics" and Arendt's reflections on the "life of the mind" both suggest that the crisis of modernity is ultimately not only a problem in politics but one that resides in the relationship between academic philosophy and politics and that at least in part will and must find its solution there—both in principle and practice, in philosophy and education.

Although, in each case, the autonomy of political philosophy, both historically and in the present, is stressed, political philosophy as the source of political transformation is equally emphasized. Theoretical distance yields objectivity, but the stance of the theorist is not one of unconcern. And historical exegesis is given a practical role. Strauss maintains that historical interpretation is not an exercise in "*antiquarianism*" or merely a scholarly attempt to prevent "the burial of a great tradition" but a practical demand. We are "impelled" by the Western crisis to seek the meaning of the present in the past and to begin the process of the "restoration" of political philosophy (1964b: 1, 8). Similarly, for Voegelin, the recovery of the past is a form of "therapeutic analysis" (1968:23)—quite literally a penetration of the civilizational psyche and a cartharsis through memory. It is not "an attempt to explore curiosities of a dead past, but an inquiry into the structure of order in which we live presently." It is a matter of "re-theoretization" and "restoration" that will supposedly have practical consequences (1956:xiv; 1952:1–5; 1968:15). The precise nature of this contact between academic activity and politics, however, is studiously nebulous, but it is continually discernible as the underlying motif.

A central element in the myth of the tradition is not only the romanticization of the classic canon and its authors but the transfer of those qualities to the role of the academic theorist and historian. Both the emphasis on the importance of studying the tradition and the claim to special knowledge required for, and produced by, such study were to some extent a response by these émigré scholars to the depreciation of intellectuals in the modern age in general. It was also a response to their own particular circumstances in both Europe and the United States as well as to such specific attacks on the study of the history of political theory as those leveled by behavioralism and positivist philosophy, and individuals such as Easton (1953) and T. D. Weldon (1953). Whatever the precise reasons, the myth of the tradition is closely tied to the attempt to establish the authority of political theory in its relationship to politics and social science. Yet the question of the practical character of that authority outside the realm of academic disputation is seldom confronted, and these individuals are far from sanguine about the possibilities and virtues of reaching outside the academy. Even though the purpose is ostensibly practical, the very idea of practical engagement surfaces definite reservations.

Arendt, for example, idealizes politics as that aspect of the *vita activa* she designates as action or words and deeds manifest in the public realm, and her story of the tradition is the epic intellectual and political saga of its debasement and its relegation to a "derivative, secondary position" (1958:198). From Plato on, the tendency within the *vita contemplativa* was for *theoria* to turn toward *poiesis*, with which it had "an inner affinity," and conspire "against politics and against action" in seeking a "remedy for the frailty of human affairs" through the imposition of philosophical "standards" (1958: 174, 275; 1961: 150). Philosophy, then, is a danger to politics. But so is politics a danger to philosophy.

The posture of the theorist caught between "past and future" in the modern age requires distancing from politics in order to discern where we are and where we have been. The structures of modernity, even apart from their most repressive forms, are a threat to reflection, and philosophy is in danger of becoming ideology. Marx, who Arendt claims represents the end of the tradition, effected that end in part because "a philosopher turned away from philosophy so as to 'realize' it in politics" (1961: 18). And Arendt explains, and partly apologizes for, Heidegger's flirtation with the Nazi regime on the grounds that it was an example of thought being enticed into the alien world of practice where it could not authentically reside (1978). Like Strauss, she believes that contemplation and action ultimately stand in "unequivocal opposition to each other" (1958: 275). There is no resolution of the conflict between philosophy, contemplation, and the life of the mind on the one hand and politics and the world of action on the other.

There is no doubt a genuine concern in this literature about historical and contemporary issues that involve what may be categorically termed the relationship between thought and action. And the historical background of that concern as well as the details of these thinkers' particular exploration of the contours of this issue is surely an interesting biographical matter. But part of the myth of the tradition is precisely the transformation of particular existential problems into philosophical categoricals, which are in turn reified and made the subject of history. Political issues are transformed into philosophical issues, and nowhere is this more obvious than with regard to the question of theory and practice.

There are, historically and culturally, all sorts of forms and degrees of what might be called the relationship between theory and practice. What is mythical, or at least remains mythical as long as it is simply presupposed, is the idea that these are manifestations of some transcendental structural relationship. This presupposition and the various mythhistorical philosophical schemes in which it is embedded and which give it meaning are what make this issue surface as such a crucial matter in this literature. They are also what at the same time distances it from a genuine engagement of actual problems that might be reasonably construed generically as problems of theory and practice. One of those problems is the status and role of this very literature as well as much of academic political theory. The myth of the tradition serves, in a number of ways, to obscure that role and suppress the problem. And it does so in part by subsuming this literature in the mythic archetypes that define the classic texts and the role of the theorist.

For both Strauss and Voegelin, the core of the modern crisis is the transformation of political philosophy into ideology. As for Arendt, this depreciation and degeneration of political thought must be explained historically and remedied in the present if there is to be a reconstitution of politics. A crucial aspect of what Strauss calls the "decay" of political philosophy or what Voegelin takes to be the "derailment" of the tradition is the fall of philosophy into the world of action. Political philosophy is not, Strauss would have us believe, merely a category that is simply identical with political thought but a definite calling and body of thought that was "originated by Socrates" (1963a:2) and that in the modern age is in extremis. The modern philosopher/historian is the priest and prophet of that tradition who remembers and restores the truth that it represents and thereby, in some measure at least, participates in it.

Although the decline of the tradition is a decline in the quality of thought and apprehension of truth, an essential aspect of what Strauss, for example, continually refers to as the "modern project" and its rejection of classical political philosophy is the breakdown of a clear line between political philosophy and politics. It is the project of individuals like Marx and Lenin, who believed that their millenarian dreams could be translated into practical terms. Such crossing of the line debases not only political philosophy but politics as well. Heidegger's defection symbolizes the convergence of both (Strauss, 1953:34; 1963b:218; 1972:227). Although the end of political philosophy, in an Aristotelian sense, is action and therefore practical in concern, politics cannot become philosophical and philosophy cannot become political without destroying themselves and each other. Strauss continually stresses the necessary, historically manifest, and ultimately irreducible tension between the lives of philosophy and politics. But at the same time he pursues the question of articulation and the role of the former in saving the latter.

Just as in the case of both Arendt and Strauss, Voegelin wishes to emphasize that "the history of philosophy is in largest part the history of its derailment" (1957:277). The moving force in that derailment was "Gnostic activism" (1975:298) and its attempts to emulate God, realize heaven on earth, and achieve dominion over the world through the transformation of knowledge into action. The historical evolution of gnosticism and its denial of the understanding of the differentiated orders of existence attained in Greek philosophy and Christian theology has constituted a "theoretical retrogression" (1952:79–80). This is manifest in, and the underlying meaning and "inner logic" of, all major political thought and political movements since medieval times. In its theoretic forms, the "Gnostic revolt" is evident from the historical immanentization of Christian eschatology in the ideas of Joachim of Flora, who "created the aggregate of symbols which govern the self-interpretation of modern political society to this day," through the Enlightenment to Marx, in whose "idea we find the spiritual disease" fully developed (1952:111; 1975:298). Its pragmatic or activist manifestations reach at least from the French Revolution to twentieth-century totalitarianism. In all this, there has been a continuous devolution.

If theory is to save practice, it must, according to Voegelin, be extricated from it. What historical experience and philosophy reveal is that knowledge and practice cannot be made identical and that all attempts to do so are politically apocalyptic and intellectually destructive. The failure to recognize this is what gives common meaning to all modern political and ideological movements, including liberalism, positivism, psychoanalysis, social science, nazism, communism, and their philosophical underwriters and instigators such as Comte, Hegel, Marx, Nietzsche, and Heidegger. Only now, as Western thought falls into crisis and the ideas of modernity turn inward against themselves, are we in a position to create a "new science of politics." Such a science would be the first complete, authentic, and focused effort since Aristotle and one that is free of "the ideological mortgages on the work of science" that have been characteristic of positivism and its separation of fact and value which created the intellectual paralysis of relativism in the modern age (1952:13, 26; 1956:xii; 1957:357; 1968:6).

For each of these individuals, what makes the renewal of thought possible is, somewhat ironically, the political crisis for which that thought, if not an ultimate solution, is to some degree the vehicle of restoration. Crisis is the key to renewal. The task, Strauss claims, of achieving "solid knowledge" of the "thought of the past," that is, understanding "it as exactly as possible as it was actually understood by its authors" and judging its significance for the present, has "been rendered possible by the shaking of all traditions." The modern crisis "may have the accidental advantage of enabling us to understand in an untraditional way what was hitherto only understood in a traditional or derivative way" (1963b:24; 1964a:9).

We are to believe, then, that the authority of the special vision these writers profess to possess derives in part from a crisis that shocks the reflective consciousness of the theorist dedicated to the life of thought who stands in some privileged way outside the constraints of political structures and ideology. In this respect, the attitude toward the tradition is one of ambivalence. It is to some degree a sacred object, quite literally our collective psyche and the repository of self-knowledge, but it has undergone some process of deformation or even, according to Strauss, "putrefaction" (1959:17), which requires that certain portions of it must be destroyed or at least undergo a process of purification in order to reach and sustain the healthy tissue.

The symbols of purity, contamination, fall, crisis, and redemption govern this literature. And the key to redemption is the vision of the untainted academic theorist arising in the midst of crisis with the tools and will for understanding and restoration. Cast in scholarly prose, these claims take on a kind of authority and reasonableness that quickly recede when extracted from the milieu of the paradigm. To accept the diagnosis of crisis, it is necessary to accept the idea of the tradition that Arendt maintains "had its definite beginnings in the teachings of Plato and Aristotle" and "came to a no less definite end in the theories of Karl Marx" (1961:183). What exactly the criteria would be for falsifying or justifying this kind of claim is an issue that is not confronted, but Arendt wishes to begin with the idea that this tradition has been broken and no longer serves as a bridge over "the gap between past and future" where political thinking takes place.

There is, however, as already noted, freedom in crisis. For Arendt the tradition, in an important sense, had been the enemy of politics and a source, as well as a reflection, of the decline of the public realm of human action discovered and constituted in the Greek polis. As for Voegelin and Strauss, the path of the tradition was a recession from an understanding and exercise of the highest human capacities. Although Arendt may at least ostensibly put greater stock than the others in the world of action as a mode of human realization, she still maintains the assumption of the privileged place of thought and mind, really of the academic intellectual, in the modern world where ideas have become ideology. The crisis has freed thought, at least the thought of the scholar not captured by mundane political interest, for a "critical interpretation of the past" that may save the present (1961:15).

What is unexamined, and even to some degree obscured if not unstated in this literature, is the Mannheimian thesis (and the connection is more than a conceptual similarity) that the academic intellectual, first neglected and then persecuted and cast into an alien land, is the disinterested bearer of historical memory. Wounded and estranged, but with greater sensitivity and concern for the world than those more deeply enmeshed in it, this intellectual stands above interests and perspectives and can grasp the meaning of the totality of experience in both the past and the present and point toward realistic modes of coping, if not practical root-and-branch solutions. The sotto voce claim is that practice should, and even "had better," listen to theory. The difficulty, however, is that the practical audience is only vaguely defined, and ultimately the audience contracts, except in fortuitous instances, to the world of academia and academically sensitive intellectuals.

For Arendt, then, world alienation is the problem, but it has created a reflective moment, an opportunity for stepping outside the collision of past and future and dealing with the "desperate" condition of humanity in the modern age where not only the old answers but the old questions have lost meaning. Like the psychoanalyst, Arendt tells us that our various anxieties are not only real and deeply rooted in a monumental world-historical malaise but intelligible and at least theoretically remediable. Just as Strauss impresses on us the image of a virginal perception achieved by those original philosophers in the Greek polis who saw "political things" in an untraditional way uncontaminated by the accretions of subsequent and derivative thought and "with a freshness and directness which have never been equalled" (1959:27, 74), Arendt promises to reveal truth through the destruction of the already debilitated tradition.

Strauss claims that the modern crisis allows us the opportunity to cut our way back through the distortions of modern political philosophy, to relive the quarrel between the ancients and moderns and at last come down on the right side of that debate and step over the threshold of a natural or "prephilosophic" understanding of political phenomena and political right (1975:75). As in all great myths, the present is an archetypal repetition of the past. Although Arendt may not be inspired by the same political values and notions of transcendental judgment as Strauss, she conjures up the same images of the role and possibilities of theory and in the same mythic terms. And her concern, too, is to reach that prephilosophic natural understanding of the human condition.

It is possible, she claims, because of the break in the hold of the tradition that the crisis within the tradition has afforded, "to discover the real origins of political concepts" and "to distill from them anew their original spirit," which has "evaporated" from our thought and language. Now the past will "open up to us with unexpected freshness," and we can at last "look upon the past with eyes undisturbed by a tradition, with a directness and clarity that has disappeared from Occidental reading and hearing." As for Strauss, "the beginning and the end of the tradition have this in common: that the elementary problems of politics never come as clearly to light in their immediate and simple urgency as when they are first formulated and when they receive their final challenge" (Arendt, 1961:15, 29, 94, 18). The "purpose of historical analysis," then, is to trace back modern world alienation" to its "origins" and "arrive at an understanding of the nature of society" before it was engulfed by modernity (1958:6, 7).

There is, as we shall see, a considerable continuity between this mode of argument and much of the other literature of contemporary political theory, or works that have influenced political theory, which at first, in many respects, might appear quite different. One similarity is the revelatory character of the claims—the implication that, once pointed out, the matters are quite beyond debate. And it is this characteristic that indicates what may be the most fundamental concern underlying this literature. This is the question of the bases of political judgment and the discovery of demonstrable grounds that would be authoritative. This is, as we shall see, a somewhat paradoxical undertaking in the context of academic political theory, but there can be little doubt that it is the enterprise to which these individuals are committed.

Relativism and historicism, complemented and enhanced by positivism and leading to nihilism, represent the common problem, and the panoply of "isms" moving in epic form is supposedly manifest in historical events. Part of the myth of the tradition is the reification of these concepts into historical forces that allegedly shape the present and underlie political events and beliefs. Also, it is here, most clearly, that the prejudice emerges that political problems are problems of philosophy with philosophical solutions. It is the idea that behind totalitarianism is the weakness of liberalism and that this weakness is ultimately a weakness of commitment growing out of inadequate grounds of value judgment. It is not simply that these are questionable assumptions but rather that they are *revealed mythhistorically* rather than *argued historically*.

A corollary of this emphasis on philosophy is the unsubstantiated attribution of extraordinary efficacy to the ideas of certain heroic and antiheroic individuals. Even if the often summary interpretation of the meaning and significance of classic texts were credible and even if one accepted the dubious major premise regarding the existence and constitution of the tradition, the claim that the modern crisis is the result of a "conscious rebellion" within that tradition by individuals such as Marx and Nietzsche (Arendt, 1961:21, 31) can have only rhetorical force. Not only is the beginning of the tradition located in the figure of such individuals as Socrates but, as in the case of Strauss, fundamental shifts that transformed Western civilization are identified with the conscious design of such individuals as Machiavelli and Hobbes.

One is invited, literally, to read off modernity from the texts of what is by academic convention taken to be modern political philosophy. Machiavelli's work is presented as an explanation for everything from the *Federalist Papers* to the work of Marx. Hobbes, for example, becomes the "originator of modernity" and, along with Spinoza, the "founder of liberalism" with subsequent "waves" marked by Rousseau, Nietzsche, and Heidegger (Strauss, 1959:41–51). Voegelin's philosophy of history may be somewhat more structural and less personalized, with individuals in many instances more the representations of an age than the instigators, but in all this literature the distinction between specific philosophical ideas and historical epochs and events is thoroughly conflated—and, given the nature of the argument, necessarily so. Voegelin's work, too, is replete with explanatory references to the same paradigmatic heroes and villains. If, for Strauss, Marx is Machiavellian, Voegelin claims that "at the root of the Marxian idea we find the spiritual disease of the Gnostic revolt" (1975:298).

Despite variations in the general account of the contours of the tradition and where it went awry and ran dry, and despite what may seem to be differences in the philosophical premises informing these claims, the basic story is remarkably uniform. And the variations and differences quickly recede when this work is located within the very tradition of German philosophical historicism, which it, ironically, often sees as the root of the modern problem. It is as much the crisis of that academic tradition that is being confronted here as any crisis in politics. Although it is quite fair to say that the real political concern is totalitarianism or at least that it is a real concern and a formative influence, it is, again, liberalism that is the more immediate problem. It is here that all the sins of the fathers are vested and where the problem of the intellectual and politics is most concretely confronted. Given the degree to which this literature contributed to the basic paradigm of political theory for so long, it is little wonder that in recent years the relationship between political theory and liberalism has been an unhappy one—whatever other reasons there might be for disaffection.

This literature associates a whole variety of problems with liberalism and modernity, including the depreciation of the political public realm and its corresponding virtues, the rise of mass society and technocracy, the loss of authority, and the place of social science as a fellow traveler. But modernity and liberalism are actually political metaphors for an intellectual and philosophical, if not academic, dilemma. This is relativism, historicism, and the general problem of the grounds of transcendental judgment. No matter how much this is projected on liberalism in the past or read into contemporary American politics as the underlying weakness of the regime in the face of internal and external threats, this is the core issue. Even though it does involve questions of the authority of philosophy in relation to politics, at least in the minds of these individuals, it is a metatheoretical problem and a problem that is indigenous to the very tradition to which they are bound.

Arendt may be less inclined, at least at certain times, to attribute the political crisis or the "break in our history" directly to the demise of the tradition and the intellectual confusion that followed. The break was caused by the "political" and "spiritual" chaos that allowed the advent of totalitarianism (1961:26, 34). The intellectual rebellion within the tradition by those such as Kierkegaard, Nietzsche, and Marx destroyed the tradition as a vehicle for contending with this situation. Rather than extending the tradition and creating new values appropriate to the modern age, they turned against it and inverted it by putting practice over theory and reversing the relationship within practice between the public realm and the subpolitical universe of social and economic life. Thus they brought it to an end but remained trapped within it, using "its own conceptual tools." The result was to bring us "to the threshold of a radical nihilism," which provided no way of thinking ourselves out of the modern crisis (Arendt, 1961: 18–34).

No matter how intricate the story, the basic problem—and argument—is the same. It is the historicization of value and the immanentization of meaning. With the Enlightenment, Hegel, and Marx, value is transferred to, and revealed in, the process of historical evolution. With the demise of that organic historical vision, we are left with relativism, historicism, and probably nihilism as modern philosophy in general cuts the ground out from under itself. Transcendentalism has been relegated to history and then eliminated from history. This is the essence of the modern crisis.

Although this might in some respects be a quite persuasive account of philosophy's dilemma, or understanding of its dilemma, it is hardly original with these thinkers. What is more original and definitive of this literature is the notion that this explains the crisis of modern politics and that a solution to the philosophical problem would be a solution to the political problem or in some fundamental but usually unspecified way would provide the grounds for such a solution. What is implicit in all this is the idea that the academic political theorist is, at least potentially, through education or some such device, the mediator of theory and practice. In its various versions, this story has been the story of contemporary political theory.

For Strauss, the decline of political philosophy has led to relativism, but relativism, in turn, puts an end to the traditional enterprise of political philosophy by denying the objectivity of values and asserting their relativity. Political philosophy is a matter of seeking and finding absolute truth. Voegelin argues that modernity is a "morass of relativism" that is the legacy of the last half of the nineteenth century and animates our culture both in everyday life and in the social sciences (1952:13). This "unqualified relativism" that affects the modern age is never carefully analyzed by these thinkers. It is basically an image defined in terms of dubious references to Nietzsche and attributed to the rise of historicism and positivism and leading to "nihilism" and unprincipled political acts as well as the inability, in 1933 and once again today, to find a principled basis for resisting them (Strauss, 1953:2−5).

Although Arendt does not place as much pointed emphasis on the dilemma of relativism and the need to recover absolute values as Strauss and Voegelin do, relativism is a principal aspect of her analysis of world alienation which, much as for Strauss, involves an estrangement from nature and a retreat to subjectivity. Modern philosophy and modern science are, Arendt claims, founded on "Cartesian doubt" and have contributed to "modern nihilism." Even in science, the idea of truth based on objective qualities has given way to "uncertainty" and "relativism" in the work of Heisenberg and Einstein, but this is the consequence of early modern thought exemplified in the work of individuals like Galileo, Hobbes, and Newton. The result has been the loss of the ability "to *think* in universal, absolute terms" (1958:236−38, 246). The idea of a "transcendent world disappears," and "in the place of the concept of Being we now find the concept of process." With the loss of a notion of "objective truth," human beings are freed to use thought as merely an instrument in the construction of a universe of their own making based on "the assumption that life, and not the world, is the highest good of man" (262, 266, 270).

One putative example of the intellectual effect of relativism is that political philosophy has degenerated into a historical enterprise, the history of political philosophy, and given up its search for truth (Strauss, 1959:56). For Strauss, as well as for Voegelin and Arendt, the fall into historicism must in a certain sense be accepted. There is no immediate turning back, and the task is to transform historical claims into philosophical ones or to find truth through history—to engage in historical argument so as to reach truths beyond, but once appearing in, history.

There is a strong sense in this work that the reader is invited to grasp the point that, because the modern age is intrinsically historical in spirit, philosophy, in order to speak to and about it, must itself be historical. But it is equally clear that this literature can be understood only within the tradition of German historical philosophy and hermeneutics and that the approach is not simply an instrumental choice in that it is merely one way of doing philosophy and thinking historically. The "theory of politics" must be "a theory of history" (Voegelin, 1952:1). This is transcendentalism trapped within historicism, and its only choice—no matter how much it may talk of universal standards of natural law, fundamental orders of existence and the relationship between them, or the defining structures and demands of the human condition that are accessible to reason—is to seek and reveal reason in history. It requires us to believe that it is possible to discern such things as "a civilizational cycle of world-historic proportions . . . transcending the cycles of the single civilization. The acme of the cycle would be marked by the appearance of Christ; the pre-Christian high civilizations would form its ascending branch; modern, Gnostic civilizations would form its descending branch" (Voegelin, 1952:164).

In this work, as in all great myth, truth is concretized and given the quality of historicity by locating it spatially and temporally. For Strauss, it is the thought of Plato and, especially, Aristotle; for Voegelin, the ideas of the Christian Middle Ages, and for Arendt, the mode of life of the pre-philosophic polis. Again, this location carries the quality of revelation or at least interpretative disclosure which depends on the reader accepting the general historical myth as the context of meaning. Once the deconstructive historical task has been achieved, the past will speak to us "and tell us things no one has yet had ears to hear" (Arendt, 1961:29), appear as "an intelligible succession of phases" (Voegelin, 1952:1), or make accessible "the essential character of all political situations" through the reappropriation of "*the* truth" achieved by "*the* true political philosophy" (Strauss, 1959:68–69; 1962:313; 1964a:10).

Strauss may more explicitly employ the language of natural law, but the basic claim is the same. It is the idea, revealed at some past time and now rediscovered, that there is a natural order of things that demands the obedience of the conventional world and provides knowledge for judging and acting in the world. Exactly what is to be done with this knowledge is somewhat ambiguous, and the prescription varies considerably. It is uniformly denied that it furnishes "recipes," but there is equal unanimity that in some important way it is "the indispensable starting point for an adequate analysis, to be achieved by us, of present-day society in its peculiar character, and for the wise application, to be achieved by us, of these principles to our tasks" (Strauss, 1964a:11). Strauss, significantly, does not disclose to us the content of natural law.

Once these claims are held up to scrutiny, it becomes evident that they cannot really be discussed outside the mythological matrix. Again, what makes the myth of the tradition a myth is not a single thread of argument whose accuracy might be debated on some terms and accepted in some context. It is the composite image that is advanced and the rhetorical function that it performs. And although there have been numerous under-laborers in the field of political theory who have accepted the literal burden of this paradigm, what is required is an examination of the kind of argument that is actually involved and its place in the context from which it has emerged.

It requires very little reflection to see that the works that have become part of the pantheon of classic texts have originated in a variety of quite different circumstances and can only be analytically understood as a tradition or a genre. They are not the core of what is conventionally understood as a tradition, that is, an inherited pattern of thought, that informs modern politics. To attempt to pursue an interpretation of a historical text by placing it in the context of *the* tradition is to imprison it within an alien framework and ensure a distortion of its meaning. This is not to say that there is some obvious illegitimacy attaching to such uses of the classic texts, but, on the other hand, it is to say that such uses are not insulated from critical examination because of the putative nobility of the concerns.

Central to most uses of the tradition is the blurring of any line between philosophy and history and between interpretation and commentary. This is not to say that such a line can be drawn in an a priori manner or that as a practical matter the two can or should be fundamentally separated. But the distinction is a relevant one in many instances—even when it is essentially avoided—both in terms of distinguishing what an author is doing or what kind of argument is being advanced and in terms of critically reflecting on such arguments. Those writers who contributed most fundamentally to the creation of the myth of the tradition have employed it as a vehicle of political commentary (Baumgold, 1981), and in various ways it is essential to their argument that the line be blurred.

The degree to which that employment in particular cases has been basically instrumental is not easily settled. It would seem, for example, that Voegelin takes the philosophy of history as an intelligible project. Arendt appears, sometimes quite explicitly, to use the idea of the tradition as a literary device, but at the same time her deconstruction of the tradition of Western political thought closely parallels Heidegger's analysis of the historical fate of philosophy. In the case of Strauss, the propagation of the belief in the literal truth of the tradition would seem to be essential to the rhetorical force of his claims. But my concern here is less with the motives of these individual authors than with their contribution to the myth of the tradition and entailed notions about political theory, the political theorist, and the relationship between political theory and politics.

The precise manner in which the idea of the tradition has been utilized, the strength of literal belief in the construct, and similar issues are of considerable importance for understanding contemporary academic political theory. Whether the idea of the tradition has been accepted as historical reality, employed rhetorically and instrumentally, or both, it is a myth that is no longer supportable and one that has contributed significantly to the various dimensions of the alienation of political theory. But, in view of the persistent domination of this myth in the study of the history of political theory, and even the identification of this enterprise with this myth, it is important to emphasize that its rejection does not in any way entail a wholesale rejection of a case for the importance of studying the classic texts (Kateb, 1968; Sabia, 1984), and it does not automatically involve the acceptance of some other specific approach to these works.

We might want to say that in an important sense this work is not really historical (e.g., Skinner, 1969), but this need not imply some uncontentious notion of history and historicity or a concern with relegating the classic texts to historical objects and confining them to their historical context. Even if one were reluctant to accept the idea that a treatment of the texts as historical objects and autonomous bearers of meaning is a necessary prelude to considering their significance for the present (on the assumption that, if we do not know what they mean on their own terms, it is difficult to find them meaningful in ours), it is necessary at least to free them from the Procrustean confines of the myth that has dominated the field for so long. This myth, even apart from literal attachments to the work of the individuals discussed above, continues to inform notions about the classic texts and the study of political theory, and it is necessary to resist this restrictive and bankrupt image of the history of political theory. In fact, it is only through a rejection of this myth that the texts can be freed for a fresh understanding in their own right and as vehicles for creative political thinking and education. But it was not simply the classic texts that suffered from this approach to the study of political theory and this definition of political theorizing.

The myth of the tradition, no less than the behavioral image of science, estranged academic political theory from any substantive exploration of the nature of political phenomena, and, despite the ostensibly practical concerns of the purveyors of this myth, it estranged the discourse of political theory from actual political issues and the particularities of politics. Above all, it has distanced political theory from an authentic understanding and consideration of its relationship to politics—and philosophy. No matter what the practical and political concerns that originally gave rise to the myth, it more and more became part of a debate within academic political theory about the value of studying the classics and the extent to which behavioralism was merely part of the modern debasement of political thought. If it was political commentary, it was only in a categorical and abstract sense. Political issues were transformed into pseudophilosophical issues and solved accordingly. Real political events, and even crises, became devalued because they were only symptoms of the big underlying crisis. Even though the formative experiences of these individuals may have been real and important political events, such events were to a large degree moved out of focus as the emphasis was placed on the world-historical forces that allegedly produced the great crisis in the great tradition.

With varying degrees of sophistication, two generations of scholars have dedicated themselves to sustaining and elaborating this saga. To reject the myth is not, for example, to reject the idea that the past is relevant to the present or that a particular text might have explanatory significance for modern politics. The myth of the tradition is precisely the acceptance of the complex of elements that constitute the arguments of individuals like Voegelin and Strauss. Together these elements compose an image that only appears to be open to internal criticism and discussion. There are no criteria that would allow this construct to be placed in the realm of corrigibility, and its power, like all myths, depends precisely upon that privileged position. Like epistemological claims, there is no context in which meaningful discussion can occur. The force is rhetorical, but, once extracted from the context of substantive claims about particular political phenomena and from contexts of real political argument, it is an alienated enterprise that only seems to be about the past and the present in much the same way that epistemology only seems to be about knowing the world.

The myth of the tradition is an example of political theory that has fallen into inauthenticity. The point is not to question the depth of commitment of the authors of this myth or even the uses to which they wanted to put it. It is, however, important to question the manner in which it came to constitute, for the discourse of academic political theory, the limits of thought and served to produce an intellectual estrangement from politics in terms of both theoretical and practical matters. To some degree the myth was a denial of the necessary or circumstantial distancing inherent in a mode of academic political theory that aspired to be more but could not be more and yet remain secure within the academy. It attempted to solve the existential dilemmas of theory and practice philosophically and by reference to abstract claims about education and scholarship as a political act that were either truisms or unexamined hypotheses. But in this search for transcendental grounds of political judgment that would carry political authority, an image was generated that held two generations of scholars—and their students—captive.

Although there is a basic sense in which the myth of the tradition Europeanized political theory in the United States, the usual domestication of foreign ideas also obtained. Whatever difficulties attach to the myth of the tradition when viewed discursively, it is clear that it was to a large extent, particularly in the work of Strauss and Arendt, a kind of philosophical politics as much as it was political philosophy. The problem of the status of such discourse was a significant one, and it was a problem that would remain at the heart of the alienation of political theory during the 1970s. In its search for political meaning and contact, political theory ran headlong into the chains of academic philosophy. But equally important was the fact that the myth became increasingly literalized. The basic notions of political theory and theorizing generated by the myth provided the defining characteristics and self-image of political theory as not only a distinct academic discipline but a profession.

The image of political theory created within the myth of the tradition was not one that could easily be reconciled with the academic enterprise. There was an exodus of political theory from political science in the 1970s, or at least there was an inversion of the original relationship. Those elements of political theory in political science that were not congenial to the behavioral definition of the study of politics increasingly became reflections of the wider institutionalized field of professional political theory. Behavioral, or what was now mainstream, political science was condemned as either irrelevant and apolitical, if not antipolitical, or perniciously biased. The idea was that "traditional" political theory would not only provide a counterpoint to behavioralism but spring loose from political science and establish an authentic and autonomous theoretical enterprise. But the notion of theory that emerged was largely a projection of the myth of the tradition rather than a realistic assessment of the state and possibilities of academic political theory and its relationship to politics.

Although the myth of the tradition was in large part forged within the context of controversies in American political science, the basic concerns, and certainly the principal intellectual structures, that the myth originally contained were somewhat alien to that discipline. Although Strauss, for example, was indeed a severe critic of behavioralism or the "new political science" (1962), his engagement was a highly mediated one. In the work of Sheldon Wolin, we can see more clearly the adaptation of the myth of the tradition to problems more concretely rooted in the context of political science and politics and the projection of that myth into a new vision of political theory as an autonomous enterprise. Furthermore, in Wolin's work, both the literalization of the myth and the problem of the relationship between academic political science and politics are more clearly, consciously, and concretely manifest.

Wolin's work deserves careful and systematic attention for several reasons—not the least of which is the fact that it brings the problem of the myth of the tradition most clearly into focus. But only in Wolin's work, despite its difficulties, is the question of academic political theory and its relationship to politics joined in a manner that allows it to be critically and realistically discussed. Probably no one else in the field has attempted to think through so carefully what the theoretical enterprise entails, what it has involved historically, and what it might involve today. His vision is, I would suggest, ultimately a tragic one that is in many ways reflected in his analysis of Max Weber.

Although the myth of the tradition was, by the 1960s, not only the basic paradigm governing education and scholarship in the history of political theory but even the basis on which behavioralism understood the activity and subject matter of historians of political theory, the concept of the tradition was not clearly articulated. It was a vague but powerful piece of academic folklore centering around the notion of the classic texts as a "great dialogue" and "ongoing conversation" that constituted a distinct and autonomous body of thought, which had both influenced and represented the politics of the past and which explained and held promise for the politics of the present. This was the explicit message of most texts and commentaries, but an examination of any of these works yields very little in the way of evidence and criteria. In a certain sense, it was important to the work of such individuals as Strauss that the notion of the tradition remain "flexible" and somewhat ambiguous in order to perform its rhetorical functions. The particular arguments of people like Voegelin and Arendt were sufficiently disparate that the concept of the tradition was somewhat hard to pin down with regard to specifics, and it seldom became an object of reflection among those who embraced it. It was the unexamined premise of teaching and research.

Wolin's concerns were, generically and probably to some degree historically, similar to the concerns of the émigrés that created the myth of the tradition. It may be fair to say that Wolin stood, intellectually and temporally, halfway between the idea of the tradition as it had emerged in American political science in the work of individuals such as Sabine, and the critical perspective that informed postwar work in the history of political theory exemplified in the work of individuals such as Arendt. Wolin's arguments are closely allied to those of Arendt, to whom he gives a special place in the field of political theory. He claims that her work "came as a deliverance" which changed the "recent history of political theory in the United States" from its status as "a special branch of the history of ideas" that was "neither political nor theoretical" into an enterprise that spoke to the great issues of the age: war, totalitarianism, and racial oppression. Her concern with "authentic politics" raised the idea of the political and the status of the classic texts to a new "dignity" (1977:93). It is interesting that Wolin's assessment of earlier scholarship in the history of political theory is similar to Easton's; at least he finds in Arendt's work an answer to the critics of the field. But there is no doubt that Wolin adopted the concerns that marked the work of the émigrés.

What is worth noting is the extent to which positions that might conventionally be construed as politically antithetical, such as those of Strauss and Marcuse (1964) (who in many ways shared a similar world-historical vision and rationalist perspective), were in fact remarkably similar in their diagnoses of the ills of the modern age. Concrete political differences were overshadowed by common concerns about liberalism; materialism; the rise of social conformity in an age of mass society; the complicity of social science and positivism, if not natural science itself, in contemporary problems; relativism; the loss of political authority and the primacy of political association; and similar issues. They were also at one in their attempt to integrate all this in a synoptic historical explanation of the rise and fall of modernity, and Wolin participated in this project.

Wolin, probably more than anyone else, attempted to look at the idea of the tradition analytically and give it substantive meaning. This was at once necessary and impossible. It was necessary to articulate a vision of politics and political inquiry, and their relationship, comparable and contrary to that of behavioralism (which was clearly a principal goal of Wolin's work). At best, Strauss's symbolism of a struggle between the ancients and moderns or the old and new political science and Voegelin's idea of a new science of politics offered only philosophical intimations of such an enterprise. Furthermore, the idea of theory, what it had been, and what it might be, in contrast to the notion of theory in political science, was far from fully explicated in this work. The task assumed by Wolin was ultimately an impossible one, because it was impossible to transform the philosophical myth of theory into reality and give it historical existence. Once extracted from the general philosophical arguments in which it was embedded, it was too vulnerable.

*Politics and Vision* (Wolin, 1960) cannot, despite some thematic, substantive, and formal similarities, easily be lumped together with the work of Strauss and Voegelin—or even Arendt. Although it is in many ways close to the latter in terms of overall concerns and claims, it is still a different project in a different context. For one thing, it is tied to the discourse and tradition of American political science and politics in a way that these other works were not—despite their impact on academic political science. With regard to internal characteristics, the treatment of individual theorists and texts is considerably more historically—and even textually—sensitive. They do not appear merely as actors in an epic drama or as literary devices. Also, even though Wolin is clearly a political moralist, there is no easily identifiable transcendental historical and philosophical argument that informs, or is reflected in, his interpretative essays and his more segmented and less organic treatment of the history of political theory. The work is clearly not exactly of the genre of Sabine, and it is not exactly of the genre characteristic of the émigrés. Yet it shares features of both, and the linchpin in the connection is the idea of the tradition.

Ten years after the publication of *Politics and Vision*, which more than any other work of the period attempted to give substance to the idea of theory and tradition, Wolin noted that "the notion of tradition presents difficult problems for the study of political theory" and that the task of clarifying it remained unfinished (1970*a*: 592). He might have added that the relationship between academic political theory and politics remained equally problematical. Wolin's project and its problems are evident in his discussion of "Political Theory" in the *International Encyclopedia of the Social Sciences* (1968*b*).

This entry reflects the institutionalization of the idea of political theory as a distinct field of study and subject matter, and Wolin attempts to give real content to this idea as he did the next year in "Political Theory as a Vocation" (1969). In this piece Wolin is attempting to establish that the classic texts, and in turn the contemporary study of those texts, represent a definite tradition of political inquiry that is of major significance for the present. He is also suggesting that positivistic social science in general as well as behavioralism in political science, and their notions of scientific theory are, in many ways, an unfortunate and barren branch in the evolution of that tradition, which possesses characteristics that could lead to the "sterilization of political theory" (Wolin, 1968*b*: 328). Wolin might disagree with Strauss about the specific meaning of the texts and the intentions of thinkers like Hobbes and Locke (e.g., Wolin, 1960: 306–7, 478–79), the significance to be elicited from the tradition as a whole, and the precise reasons for studying it, and he might believe that Strauss's "moral fervor" and "intellectual certainty" were nearly as abhorrent as scientism (Schaar and Wolin, 1963: 150). But he sought to validate the general image of the tradition and even such general and common claims as that

Hobbes was responsible for the shift toward an emphasis on science which eventually "came to ursurp the place of philosophy" in the "classical synthesis" (Wolin, 1968*b*: 319).

Applying the Kuhnian framework, more explicitly employed in a similar argument about scientific and traditional theory (1968*a*), Wolin presents and evokes a picture of the history of political theory as the evolution of a field governed by "certain fairly well-developed conventions relating to methods of inquiry, the constitution of the subject matter, and the purposes of inquiry." Despite crises, challenges, and changes, Wolin argues that a half-dozen elements, ranging from a search for the best polity to systematic comparative analysis, defined the enterprise and framed the endeavors of the classic authors who, consequently, worked within a definite tradition of discourse. There is a distinct sense conveyed that these characteristics are not retrospective, analytically imposed attributes but aspects of a discernible self-constituted activity. Wolin claims that even if the tradition, or a tributary of it, went astray, the basic form is still present and rooted in that intellectual synthesis that "took shape in fifth century Athens." The "point of departure" was the idea of political theory as formulated by Plato and Aristotle, and this "truly classical paradigm" is the starting place for understanding "later alternatives" (Wolin, 1968*b*: 319).

One sound generalization about myths is that, at the point at which they become self-consciously articulated and defended as realistic claims, they are no longer viable. And this is the case with the myth of the tradition. The myth had been instrumental, and the propagation of the idea of the tradition had not been an end in itself. Although the claim about the tradition is still instrumental in Wolin's argument and part of a practical concern about political education and political commentary, much greater weight is given to substantiating that claim independent of other ideas such as the authority of a particular text or set of values. Wolin is much less bothered, for example, by the issue of relativism and is content to see the tradition as the source of incremental wisdom and general enlightenment. Heroes and villains do not stand out sharply, and it is more the very "intellectual enterprise" (1960:v) of theory that he wishes to endow with value and preserve. But that enterprise was more an idea than an actual activity. In Wolin's work, a very large step was taken in the invention of political theory—both in endowing it with a past and in preparing its foundations as an academic activity in its own right.

Like Arendt, Wolin's specific focus is on the decline, or loss of identity, of the political realm in the modern age or "the sublimation of the political into forms of association which earlier thought had believed to be nonpolitical" (1960:429). As much as anyone, Wolin has contributed to transforming "political" into a noun and infusing it with a sense of essentiality. It is as much the myth of politics as the myth of the tradition that emerges. Even though he insists that "the field of politics is and has been, in a significant and radical sense, a created one" rather than something "written into the nature of things," he argues that "the adjective 'political' has had a more or less stable meaning" since the time of Aristotle (5, 61). That stability is now in danger as we face the loss of the integrity and identity of politics and a concomitant loss of a distinct kind of thought about it. In Wolin's work, more than that of any of the others, political theory itself, and its survival as a form, is the primary focus.

Wolin has, to be sure, his own distinctive reconstruction of the general path of political decline over the past twenty-five hundred years and his particular sense of the meaning and significance of the tradition as a whole (see Gunnell, 1979*b*: 53–55), but, again, his treatment of particular texts and authors is considerably less encumbered by the task of justifying that reconstruction. There is, however, no mistaking the genetic connection of *Politics and Vision* to the myth of the tradition, and many of the same kinds of claims that characterize the work of Arendt, Strauss, and others are evident. Yet, on the whole, the myth that Wolin attempts to sustain is in some ways less the myth of the tradition per se than the myth of politics and political theory—and the relationship between them. He is in some ways less concerned with what the tradition demonstrates than with demonstrating its existence and the need to continue it.

Wolin seeks to *describe* the history of political theory as an actual historical tradition and not merely to play upon the presentational symbolism. It is, he claims, "a special tradition of discourse" that is a "species of philosophy." The texts are not simply a series of works with family resemblances or analytically imposed criteria of sameness. They are the product of an "activity whose characteristics are most clearly revealed over time" and that has "acknowledged masters" and a "continuity of occupations" centering around knowledge of public things (1960: 1–3). The relationship between political history and the tradition of political theory, as the chronology of classic texts, is, however, obscured in two basic but somewhat contradictory respects in Wolin's work.

First, the classic authors are given, without demonstration, a significant and even causal role in practical politics. The modern understanding, and even constitution, of politics is presented as a "legacy accruing from the historical activity of political philosophers" and their continuing dialogue on the dialectic of politics and order (Wolin, 1960: 5). Second, at the same time, despite the claim that the concerns of the political philosophers or theorists were in an important sense practical and a response to political crises, they are presented, in a still more important sense, as detached from political action and ideology. It is this detachment that is the source of their theoretical insight.

Although it is reasonable to suggest that the classic authors were, in general, responding to practical issues and that they were, for various reasons, estranged from political action, what is mythical is the notion that these texts were the product of a conventional historical enterprise that fundamentally shaped the particular works and that this vocation had an integral formative relationship to the Western political tradition or traditions. Although the authors may have been constrained by the circumstances of an epoch to which their imaginative reconstructive visions were a response, Wolin claims that, "of all the restraints upon the political philosopher's freedom to speculate, none has been so powerful as the tradition of political philosophy itself." Here we are at the core of the myth.

Wolin argues that "most formal political speculation has operated simultaneously at two different levels"—one that reflects a concern with "a vital problem" of the day and one where the work has "been meant as a contribution to the continuing dialogue of Western political philosophy." He makes it clear that this second level is the most important and that the authors have self-consciously wished "to participate in the perennial dialogue" and "contribute to the tradition of Western political speculation." He argues that "the theorist enters into a debate the terms of which have largely been set beforehand" and that the theorist is bound by the "inherited body of knowledge" and "cultural legacy" of the great tradition (1960:22–26).

This is a dubious claim, which Wolin does not concretely defend but which is crucial both to the idea of the tradition he develops and to the notion of political theory that informs his work. How *any* text in the classic canon could be so constrained by the context of a tradition that had not been invented is not easily answered. Even the most generous interpretation of the argument leaves it unconvincing. Although in varying degrees the authors may have been addressing or may have mentioned earlier writers and thinkers who are now within the classic canon and taken account of possible successors, it would be difficult to demonstrate in any case that this was more than a strategic element in their argument or a secondary concern. But, whatever the situation might have been in a particular instance, it is a mistake to raise these two levels of distinction to the status of a general interpretative premise.

The story of the "invention of political philosophy," and politics, in Greece to the eventual decline of both in the contemporary world is for Wolin, just as for individuals such as Strauss, a didactic admonitory tale that seeks to remind us of what we have "discarded" and the entailed dangers and to point toward its reconstitution. Such a history is necessary for explaining "our present predicaments," providing a language for thinking about them, and gaining substantive wisdom for understanding politics and making political choices. It is thus, he suggests, like the others, "not so much a venture into antiquarianism as a form of political education" (1960:v,27) and is in itself a kind of practical or political argument. The notion of political education is crucial because, again like Strauss, the image evoked is one of a pitched titanic battle between political theory and positivistic political science for the minds of citizens and the authority of knowledge.

The question that remains begged in all this is that of the real relationship between academic political theory and politics. To the extent that it is answered, it tends to be answered in terms of images from the myth of the tradition regarding the position of the theorist vis-à-vis politics. But, for Wolin particularly, the purpose of talking about the past is to establish the idea of the "vocation" of political theory as both the precursor of modern political science and the remnant of political philosophy "in its traditional form," which this new political science has "marked hostility towards, and even contempt for" (1960:v). In the discussion of this vocation, the dilemma of academic political theory and the problem of its relationship to both politics and political science appear more clearly than anywhere else in the contemporary literature of the field.

For Wolin, modern social science "depletes the world by depriving it of history, value, and common experience" (1973:356). It reflects and contributes to a situation in which politics in the classic sense of a sphere of meaningful human action has given way to "giant, routinized structures" that are "impervious to theory." Yet, Wolin suggests, that world, dominated as it is by organizational and constitutional forms that suppress democratic action and aided and abetted by the "methodism" of social science and its hidden ideology, is in crisis. It "shows increasing signs of coming apart" and threatens to become "anomalous." Much like Strauss's image of political science fiddling while Rome burns, Wolin argues that "amidst this chaos political science exudes a complacency which beggars description" (1969:1081). However, the concepts of theory, politics, crisis, and chaos that emerge here are images from the myth of the tradition. And the idea of a vocation of political theory and its practical mission, that prophetic and noble but maybe, in Wolin's view, ultimately futile endeavor, is a projection of that same myth. In this argument, we come face to face with the modern alienation of political theory.

Wolin's attempt to reconstruct his claims in terms of Kuhn's theory of scientific revolutions was not much more effective than behavioral political science's attempt to underwrite its version of its history through the application of this metatheoretical framework (Wolin, 1968a). Apart from the question of the adequacy of the framework on its own terms, the idea that the classic authors were to politics as Newton and Galileo were to science—creators and destroyers of paradigms—is not a convincing analogy. It assumes the very premises that are problematical in the myth of the tradition, including that of the relationship between those authors and politics. Any such analogy presumes what is most at issue—the idea that there is some historical sameness to the classic texts that extends beyond retrospectively imposed or noted similarities. The idea that *anyone*—even Marx—stood in relationship to politics as revolutionary scientists did to science is not a claim that is intuitively convincing and that can be accepted without detailed historical evidence. If there is any reasonable analogy at all that can be drawn in this area, it might be in terms of philosophers of science, revolutionary scientists, and science on the one side and political philosophers, great political actors, and politics on the other.

In another context, Wolin suggests, in a way that would seem to contradict the image of the theorist as a revolutionary scientist, that there has been "from Plato to modern times an epic tradition in political theory" that has been distinguished by "heroic" motives and the "hope of achieving a great and memorable deed through the medium of thought" and by "an attempt to compel admiration and awe for the magnitude of [that] achievement" (1970b: 2, 4–5, 10). This would seem to be a much more historically credible argument as far as the characterization of the motives of the classic authors is concerned, and clearly the notion of tradition *here* is one that has been analytically and externally constituted. Such an argument offers little in the way of corroborating the claim about political theory as a distinct historical and conventional form of inquiry and the suggestion that "testimony that such a vocation has existed is to be found in the ancient notion of the *bios theoretikos* as well as in the actual achievements of the long line of writers extending from Plato to Marx" (Wolin, 1969: 1078). The latter claim is the essence of the myth of the tradition.

For Wolin, there are really two vocations of political theory, but his argument seeks to link them historically—if not to suggest a certain dimension of identity. The first, the vocation supposedly exemplified in the classic canon, is mythical. The second, the vocation of those "who preserve our understanding of past theories" and are engaged in "teaching about past theories," is academic political theory which, although not mythical, is endowed with mythical attributes as it is contrasted with the "methodism" of political science. Wolin sometimes seems to imply that the conditions of modernity may have even rendered the first vocation, the "vocation by which political theories are created," extinct—an implication that is also apparent in the work of Strauss and others. But this makes the task of remembrance and education all the more important and allots to the historian of political theory a nearly sacred mission.

The thrust of much of Wolin's argument is in the direction of demonstrating that the study of the history of political theory is, despite the charges of individuals such as Easton, far from normatively and empirically irrelevant to science and politics. It is, on the contrary, the "history-less" attitude of political science that renders it sterile and threatens to sterilize theory. It has rejected the "political wisdom" and "tacit knowledge" that is "so vital to making judgments, not only about the adequacy and value of theories and methods, but about the nature and perplexities of politics as well." It is the historians of political theory who are now the heroic figures "who sharpen our sense of the subtle, complex interplay between political experience and thought," "who preserve our memory of the agonizing efforts of intellect to restate the possibilities and threats posed by political dilemmas of the past," who are "engaged in the task of political initiation" and of "developing the capacity for discriminating judgments" and the "sense of significance" necessary both in "scientific inquiry" and in "exploring the ways in which new theoretical vistas are opened" (1969:1070–71, 1077).

What Wolin is attempting to establish is the autonomy and authority of academic political theory by creating an image of it as a distinguished and heroic patrimony of which the modern age is in danger of being divested. The context of the argument is clear. It is the debate about political theory in political science. And maybe the rhetorical force of the claim was pragmatically justified. What is unfortunate is that it is a claim that cannot withstand critical scrutiny outside the terms of the confrontation between traditional and scientific theory. It contributed to a self-image that academic political theory can neither live up to nor, in good faith, ascribe to itself any more than behavioral political science could sustain the extravagant image of theory it had advanced. The myth of the tradition could no more validate the enterprise of the history of political theory than the fictions about theory derived from the philosophy of science could legitimate the behavioral program. And in both cases these chimeras, both individually and through their conflict with one another—a conflict that served as much to exaggerate as to critically illuminate the respective images—impoverished and alienated political theory.

Wolin's notion of political theory as education, however, begins to reach the core of the dilemma of academic political theory. This is by no means merely education in the narrow sense of the classroom. What Wolin means by "theory" is largely a certain kind of activity more than, for example, a particular product. It is an activity that stands in many respects aloof from politics and takes a posture of critical realism. It is conceived as a combination of hermeneutical mediation between the past and present and a sort of Enlightenment rationalism. The problem in this formulation, as in much of political theory, involves the question of the authority of these external claims in general, as well as that of the particular values they embody regarding both the primacy of the political realm and the particular attributes ascribed to it. They clearly are not conceived as entering politics on the same level as ordinary or conventional political participants. Furthermore, there is the question of exactly how such claims could in fact enter politics beyond the extent to which academic discourse is part of the totality of society.

The ironic truth is that the figures Wolin selects from the classic canon as paradigms could not as a whole be construed either as pragmatically successful or, in any uncontentious sense, as the purveyors of universal wisdom—no matter what particular meaning and significance one might find in their work. But neither is it accurate to project on them the image of academic political theory. Although, at a certain level of abstraction, there may be resemblances, such as the frustration born of having a claim to political knowledge that is not politically acknowledged, most were more intimately involved politically than contemporary, institutionally separated, professional, academic political theorists. References to the classics are of little help in confronting the problem of theory and practice as manifest in the political theory of the academy. Wolin's arguments, however, are of particular interest in this respect because, unlike most, he has explicitly attempted to both think and act through the issue. The results are instructive in many respects, not least for understanding the problem. The principal difficulty in Wolin's reflection on this matter is that he remains bound in his discussion of theory not only by the less than always apposite model of the classic canon but by attributes of that model spawned by the myth of the tradition.

Wolin, in some instances, attempts to bridge the gap between theory and practice by denying that there is in fact any such significant distinction. In this explicit claim, he reflects an assumption that is implicit in most contemporary political theory. Wolin argues, first, that political "theory" and political "commentary" are two different forms, modes, or species of political interpretation. They are "political" in two senses: they are "concerned with the interpretation of politics," and they "engage in interpretation in a political way." The conclusion he reaches from these premises involves a significant leap: "they *are* politics expressed through the act of interpretation" (1980:190; emphasis added). The difficulty with this kind of argument is obvious. These are analytical distinctions and categorical claims. In some circumstances with certain referents they might apply, but in many cases they may not. If Wolin wishes to suggest, which would seem to be the case, that contemporary academic political theory is in fact, in this time and place, a form of politics, the claim not only is dubious but obscures the real issues involved. This, however, is not exactly the overt line of argument.

Wolin argues that most of the classic texts, that is, the tradition from Plato to Marx (his paradigm of theory as a product and activity), involved both specific and general elements of political commentary. Some of these same authors, however, as well as many others such as Locke, Mill, and Weber, engaged in a separate, more direct and practical, "more uninhibitedly political" activity and mode of commentary, which amounted to a different and less constrained "symbolic form" and which was directed toward a wider audience. Such commentary, he claims, is an extension or "intimation" of the theory and is designed to implement it and affect politics by affecting political actors and their perceptions (1980:191–92). Wolin concludes that in the contemporary world where political understanding is largely "secondhand" or where political perceptions are filtered through various interpretations of the media, politics is functionally identical with interpretation. The implication would seem to be that academic political theorists can, then, in principle at least, act politically by doing what they do—for example, interpretative and conceptual analysis. Politics can at last in the modern age become a fully ideational matter open to the authority and manipulation of the intellect. This has become a pervasive assumption in the academy of political theory and one that is hardly eschewed by those who see all or part of their heritage in Marx.

The difficulty in modern society, Wolin suggests, is "that the most familiar forms of political commentary are untheoretical" and the rationalizing instruments of institutionalized interests in society such as those in government and the corporate economy. It fails to perform a critical function and instead keeps the citizenry "gently oscillating between resignation and hope" (1980:194–96). It is also untheoretical in the sense that it accepts the theory inherent in the "text" of society. There is no critical or theoretical distance such as in the case of Plato or Weber that makes the text of society a "problem" rather than a contextual given and allows the limitations inherent in its system of explicit and tacit principles to be held up to examination in a manner that would surface contradictions and expose hidden agendas.

Here, on the cusp of appearance and reality, the role of the theorist exists, not only to expose and criticize but to provide "a glimpse of reality, of a better social order, of a more authentic life." Because of this complementary positive vision, the extension of political theory into political commentary is not only natural but "a necessity," both for testing the vision and for "political education" in terms of it. Wolin suggests that to do less would be inauthentic and leave theorizing unjustified (1980:203).

It would be shortsighted not to note that this argument was offered just prior to the publication in 1981 of the journal *Democracy*, "A Journal of Political Renewal and Radical Change," edited by Wolin (and published by the Common Good Foundation). The argument about political theory and political commentary could reasonably be construed as both the justification of that project and an expression of the vision that informed it.

What is required is a sensitive critical assessment of the theory and practice of political theory in this case. Although it might be tempting for some to suggest that the disappearance of *Democracy* after a relatively short time can be explained by the inadequacy of the idea of political theory that informed it, the exclusiveness of its ideological position, or the intractability of the social and political regime and the rationalizing commentary (e.g., *Public Interest*) that it sought to combat, the crucial problems were probably much more mundane. Nevertheless, some observations can be offered.

The notion of political theory that Wolin advances conforms in many ways to historically discernible characteristics of classic texts and the circumstances of their production (see, e.g., Gunnell, 1979b: chap. 5). But, once extracted from the context of the myth of the tradition, this parallel has little relevance for understanding institutionalized academic political theory today and prescribing its activity. This notion of theory was surely one held by many of the individuals in question, but it was not an account of their actual relationship to politics. To think that the megalomaniacal vision of someone such as Hobbes regarding the intellectual's ability to transform politics and political education provides a model for political theory today is an illusion. And they were far from the inhabitants of the modern academy. For example, many struggled, like Plato and Machiavelli, to enter politics directly, whereas modern academic political theorists would seldom forsake the university for the uncertain world of actual politics or even engage directly in the structurally significant politics of the polity in which they most immediately reside—the university. Political theory is seldom guilty of practicing what it preaches. But *Democracy* can be understood as an attempt to do so.

For the most part, *Democracy* did not, like so much of academic political theory and the journals associated with it, merely transform political issues into philosophical ones or treat them in terms of abstract hypothetical examples. In this sense, it made a real move in overcoming the alienation of political theory from politics. But, despite its address of concrete and practical problems, there was, on the whole, an inability to engage those issues in a manner that transcended the confines of academic discourse. It may not be impossible for academic political theory to find an Aaron either as another mode of itself in the form of political commentary or in some ancillary type of practical discourse. It surely cannot do so, however, as long as it persists in the academic and philosophical prejudice that assumes that, because politics is ultimately in some respect a matter of perception and ideas, academic theory and theoretically informed commentary *about* politics are simply tantamount to politics.

The real institutional distinctions and relationships between the academy and conventional politics in late-twentieth-century America, and their historical evolution, were elided. *Democracy*'s particular prejudice was the assumption that the particularities and ambiguities of political interests, movements, and structures could be bypassed in favor of an appeal to an undefined disembodied Hegelian public consciousness and that democracy could be pursued as an idea without an institutional and behavioral dimension. It was the belief, the academic prejudice, that, if political action can no longer be a transformational force in the contemporary age of rationalized structures, then political change can emerge through the force of ideas and education. As for individuals as diverse as Strauss and Habermas, the notion is that somehow academic political theory can change the world and even that the university is the locus of that change. But there is yet a deeper problem connected with the relationship between theory and practice which pervades the world of political theory and which is especially and ironically evident in Wolin's arguments.

There is no way in which one can consistently defend the compatibility of democracy and revelation. But contemporary political theory, as much as the behavioral policy scientist's claim to instrumental and substantive rationality on various grounds, proclaims the authority of privileged knowledge. If it is not knowledge of natural right, the direction of social evolution, or other immanent and transcendental foundations of judgment, it is knowledge of the principles and contradictions that govern social and political forms. The point is not that such claims to knowledge are meaningless but that they carry no automatic authority and that they are not validated without argument by references to the special position of the theorist and the objectivity that position allegedly entails. Political theory is not the theoretical dimension of politics any more than the philosophy of science is the theoretical dimension of science. If such metatheoretical or metapolitical claims wish to enter politics, particularly in the service of democracy, they must enter it on equal terms with other participants—not simply on the basis that they can see what others cannot.

Wolin speaks perceptively of Max Weber's theoretical alienation (1981), but it is difficult not to sense in this analysis a wider significance regarding the tension between political passion and academic confinement. The picture Wolin paints is one of theory without a field of practical action, which is an image easily evoked by the examples of such classic authors as Plato and Machiavelli. In the case of Weber, Wolin suggests, the intractable structures of society finally drove him to engage in a "politics of mind" and a philosophical or "ontological politics" in which his real political urges were sublimated. In this situation, theory is transformed into "prophecy," which "is closet-theory in the age of science," and into "methodology." The latter, "as conceived by Weber, was a type of political theory transferred to the only plane of action available to the theorist at a time when science, bureaucracy, and capitalism had clamped the world with the tightening grid of rationality" (Wolin, 1981: 406). What Wolin argues is that, politically frustrated, Weber's "political-theoretical impulse was turned inward upon social science" where, instead of founding a political order, he attempted to defeat rivals (politics), revolutionize social science, and lay down (constitution) principles of "theoretical inquiry" as a normal science. "Methodology is mind engaged in the legitimation of its own political activity," and social science becomes "the postmodern form of political theory" (406, 408, 416).

This is, to say the least, an intriguing image. Whether Weber's ventures into methodology were in fact sublimated politics and political theory or, as he himself claimed, a "pestilence" and aberration forced on him by the philosophization of inquiry in his time is a matter that deserves detailed historical investigation. Weber's own strictures against metatheory and methodology would seem, in fact, to be very much on the order of those of Wolin. One might make a better case for his substantive social science as displaced politics. It seems more revealing to read this as Wolin's assessment of the dilemma of contemporary political theory, and it is tempting to turn the analysis back as a framework for understanding Wolin's attempt to found political theory as a mode of inquiry, give it a history, and do battle with its modern rivals.

Wolin's analysis of the modern condition of political theory at least coincides closely with what I have called here the alienation of political theory. Political theory to a great extent is prophecy and methodology and a kind of politics of the mind in which substantive theory has been transformed into a series of philosophical issues and estranged from politics and political phenomena as objects of inquiry. This is less, however, because of the "iron cage" of modernity conceived as intellectually depressing and disempowering rationalized structures than because of the iron cage of academic discourse and the institutionalization of political theory. As Wolin himself notes, "the fate of the meta-theorist is not, perhaps, a great loss. He has turned out to be a theorist *manqué*, his methodology a displaced form of political theory confined within the walls of the academy but serving a legitimation function once removed" (1981:420)—or, one could add, a critical function equally removed.

Wolin's treatment of individual thinkers tends to reflect his general account of the history of political theory as the displacement of politics by organization. Just as Wolin sees Weber's political impulses transformed into the symbolic action of social science, he finds in Marx's work a turn from a commitment to revolutionary action to a metapolitical theory of structural determinism. This interpretation of Marx deserves some detailed attention, because whether or not it explains Marx, it reveals a great deal about Wolin's position and his understanding of the relationship between academic political theory and politics.

The change in Marx's argument, Wolin claims, was the result of his inability to hold together a structure of intentions that included a scientific "commitment to the search for truth," a belief in theorizing as action or "a political mode of activity," and a notion of "action as an extension of thought" (1983*b*: 80–81). At the core of Marx's problem was a "theoretic failure" to sustain an idea of theory and action as "complementary modes of activity" and to make "philosophy political while making action philosophical." The cause of this failure was the fact that "theoretical inquiry" produced results that undermined "the aims or project of action" and led to a conflict "between Marx's theoretical findings and his political commitments." Wolin pointedly suggests that "commitment to truth always carried that possibility and with it the possibility that theory and action might be compelled along divergent paths" (80, 82–83).

The specific conflict that Wolin finds in Marx's work was between his eventual theoretical conclusion that capitalism would not be overthrown and his "political intentions" regarding the revolutionary activity of the proletariat. The outcome was that the role that had been assigned to the proletariat was replaced by deterministic predictions that turned out to be theoretically "false" but symbolically "true to action" (84). Marx came to the painful conclusion that the evolution of society had produced "an uncontrollable order of things," and, consequently, his hopes for a "power-laden theory" diminished (87, 89). Gradually his concepts of revolution and proletariat and the idea of "action of heroic proportions" tied to such "traditional themes" as "political education and political virtue" gave way to his economic analysis of "capitalism as a system of power" (96–97). The idea of the proletariat as a historical actor was transformed into an abstract "impersonal unity of forces to overcome the totality of forces represented by the bourgeois organization of productive forces" (99). Similarly, the idea of revolution gave way to the idea of the "metapolitics of an industrial cosmogony" and the theory of the crisis of capitalism—"an institutional revolution" that was only a "solace, a memorial to an older faith in the power of human action" (107). But the problem was psychological as well as theoretical.

Wolin argues that Marx fell into "despair at the cumulated massiveness of the modern world, which disposes men to cling to the past even while they are engaged in changing the present," and that he, as well as the world, was overwhelmed by the "malady" of "tradition" (92). Wolin presents an image of Marx as engaged in a dialectical theoretical struggle through the past "in imitation of the history of social formations" until, like society itself, his theory reached "a crisis of overproduction" which contributed both to the "defeat of heroic intentions" and to the "theoretic failure" of "incompleteness." In all this, Marx was constrained by his "remarkable concern for existing intellectual traditions," for treating truly great thinkers with utmost seriousness, and for taking "careful account both of the reigning ideas and their antecedents" (93).

This is an ingenious interpretation of Marx, but despite the textual and historical sensitivity with which it is executed, it is the integrity of Wolin's structure of intentions that is most clearly at issue. It is principally Wolin rather than Marx who sees modernity at odds with humanism and the classical political ideal and who sees the imminence of theoretic and practical failure. Whatever Marx's philosophical and existential dilemmas regarding the relationship between theory and action may have been, the nature of Wolin's uneasiness is relatively clear.

What is heard in this essay is a story about the inability to articulate theory and practice. Although Wolin attempts to present theory as a form of political action, it is largely symbolic and doomed to remain so. What he claims are the contradictions in Marx's work and life are also manifestations of his own attempt to reconcile commitments to theory and practice, and deal with the involvement of academic political theory in the "malady" of tradition and the crisis of scholarly "overproduction." It is less Marx than contemporary academic theory that is bound to the task of historical interpretation as "a succession of forced entries into occupied domains" (93). It is Wolin who sees the ineluctable conflict between the imperious structures of modernity and hopes for democratic change; it is he who believes that the concept of a "'democratic state' is a contradiction in terms" (1983a: 10). But there is also the more subtle paradox that theory ultimately debilitates the will to action.

At the end of his encomium to Arendt, Wolin demurs somewhat mildly regarding her explanation of the decline of "authentic politics" or "the political" and its displacement by labor within the *vita activa*. Although it is ostensibly the modern state and capitalism that threaten politics and democracy, Wolin suggests that, at a deeper level, the trouble with modernity must be attributed to the ascendency of "Absolute Mind" which, with its "abstractions," now "reigns supreme, everywhere incarnate and universal" (1977: 104). This claim is in fact, on its face, not at all at odds with Arendt, and we can only assume that Wolin is hinting at something more than a different distribution of emphasis, and that in the end the problem is as much the impotence of action in a world of theory as it is the impotence of theory in the world of action.

As long as contemporary political theory is understood as a remnant of the great tradition struggling for survival in a politically and intellectually alien world, as long as it fails to understand itself as the academic enterprise that it is, it will live in bad faith and inauthenticity. If it aspires to more it must first face up to what it is, and to be more it may have to come to grips with the need to transform itself rather than attempting to figure out how it can remain a quintessential academic activity and construe itself in some tortured way as a form of political action. In its present state, it tends not even to speak *about* politics, let alone act within it.

As in the case of behavioralism, the myth of the tradition left political inquiry with no theories. It produced no theory of politics and no explicit theoretical controversy. What it produced were *ideas* about theory and the theoretical enterprise and metatheoretical images of politics, largely in service of justifying the professional academic enterprises from which these claims emanated. This is not to suggest that no "politics," ideology, or theoretical assumptions were involved, but they were submerged and sublimated in debates about the idea of theory. Whether it is called critical theory, interpretative theory, or theoretical politics, it has produced not so much substantive theory as metatheoretical claims about the nature of theory and the foundations of its knowledge. And a critique of political theory must engage this problem.

# 4
## Theory and Metatheory

Philosophy reduced to "theory of knowledge," in fact no more than a
timid epochism and doctrine of abstinence—a philosophy that never gets
beyond the threshold and takes pains to *deny* itself the right to enter—
that is philosophy in its last throes, an end, an agony, something inspiring
pity. How could such a philosophy—*dominate*!

NIETZSCHE

REFLECTION ABOUT political theory has virtually ceased
to exist in mainstream political science except as a form of legitimating
various research strategies. This might be understood as a healthy development and a sign that the discipline had in fact evolved to a stage in
which theory is fully integrated with empirical investigation. It is not
surprising, given this state of affairs, that political scientists (e.g., Keohane,
1983) would seek a self-image in such philosophical constructions as Imre
Lakatos's notion of a "scientific research programme" (1970). This concept attempted to preserve some of the basic structural or formal characteristics of the orthodox reconstruction of scientific theory and the history
of science and yet account for contextual arguments such as that of Kuhn.
The concern, in the face of what was (mistakenly) taken as the challenge to
the objectivity of science, was to preserve the idea of epistemic continuity
between changes in theory and to retain the principle of factual givenness
as the criterion of theory evaluation. Such "evolutionary" approaches
to the problem of theoretical commensurability became common (e.g.,
Goodman, 1978; Hesse, 1980; Laudan, 1977; Shapere, 1984; Toulmin,
1972). Although they might serve as a basis for continuing to justify political science to itself, the perennial difficulties remain.

The old questions of the relationship between philosophical reconstructions and the practice of political science continue to be begged, and the discredited philosophical assumptions about theory (such as instrumentalism) are embedded in the practice of the discipline and continue to guarantee the poverty of theory. Although one might disagree with some of the claims offered under the rubric of "biopolitics," they do at least touch substantive theoretical issues about political phenomena. Theory in political science remains, however, almost without exception, as a heuristic for better understanding and (now with the policy turn) manipulating the world as given in everyday understanding. Political theorists outside the realm of normal political science (although maybe professionally residing within it) largely ignore the problems of political science. They are willing to leave these to the discipline, just as the discipline is willing to grant to them the autonomy of their concerns. To a large extent, pluralism and complementarity are the order of the day. Leading journals studiously avoid controversy, and each enclave is given its due as esoteric articles on classic texts are juxtaposed to applications of social choice theory without a hint of paradox.

Reflection on political theory as an activity and product has been largely confined to interdisciplinary political theory, but here the mood is also largely pluralistic. Separation from political science was viewed as a condition that would produce "great vitality." Releasing political theory and political science from interdependence suggested that they both might "prosper" (Kateb, 1977). Autonomy has been taken as a signal that political theory is no longer "on the verge of extinction" (Richter, 1980:6), and the standard interpretation is that political science and its brand of theory can live beside, and complement, other kinds of political theory and philosophy. Everywhere the signs are that political theory has risen from the ashes of the early 1960s and that the work of individuals such as Rawls and Nozick and the "very strong resurgence of Marxist thought" as well as other trends "truly represent the rebirth of political theory" and an "upsurge in creative political theory" (Freeman and Robertson, 1980:6, 11, 21).

There are at least two things wrong with this picture. First, this image of a virile, prolific political theory is little more than a reflection of its professional academic autonomy and its productivity. What it signifies in a substantive sense is extremely vague. Second, the image of political theory's rebirth is predicated upon the vestiges of the myth of the tradition and the persistence of the same philosophical notions of science that had legitimated it in earlier years.

For many, as for the editor of *Political Theory*, the apparent health of the field continues to be a consequence of its escape from political science or at least its independent status within the discipline. "Political philosophy continues to flourish within the discipline of political science—for which, however, the discipline remains curiously ungrateful." The judgment is that "political science had lost its bearings" and a "sense of purpose following the demise of the positivist project," but political theory and philosophy evidenced direction and purpose (Barber, 1982:491). But an attempt to examine the "prospects and topics" of political theory in the coming decade yielded only an invitaton to "a number of thoughtful senior colleagues . . . to get on with what they were thinking about," on the assumption that this was "representative of both the scope of the field and the pushing forward of its concerns" (Barber, 1981:291).

What can be said with confidence, it seems, is that "political theory is what political theorists do." Because this varies "enormously in style, concern, technique, and ideological viewpoint," it is reasonable to suggest that the present "upsurge" in "political theory today is more pluralist in all these respects than it ever has been" (Freeman and Robertson, 1980: pref. 1, 11). Although there have been some attempts to take a more critical look at what political theory is and might be (e.g., Nelson, 1983), the basic mood is self-congratulatory. The characteristic judgment is that there was, by the mid-1970s, an "outburst" of political theory and that it has "re-emerged as a distinct intellectual activity" evolving largely out of academic traditions in political science and philosophy and constituting a "mixed mode of thought" composed of deductive, empirical, and normative elements. These have a "practical, action guiding character" and an ability to engage politics by moving between "social conditions and political concepts" (Miller and Siedentop, 1983:1–3).

Such claims, as a matter of fact, have been typical since the first blush of postpositivism in the mid-1960s when it was declared that political theory was alive again. This had been a somewhat tentative recognition of life signs, and there was little willingness to go much further than suggesting that there was some recession of the influence of (positivist) "linguistic philosophy and behavioral science," that "prescriptive discussion of political issues was not meaningless, and that deductive argument and empirical evidence can be brought to bear on it." Laslett was quick to point out the excesses of past political theory with its "*a priori* sociology," "disguised prescriptivism," and "grandiose" ideas, but now, chastened and reborn, it could move forward "at once more careful about its claims and more securely grounded in the established results of economics, psychology, and political science" (Laslett and Runciman, 1967:3–4).

The image of political theory that evolved during the succeeding years was basically one that attempted to give substance and parity to the metatheoretical categories that were the legacy of positivism (logical, empirical, and normative) and the variations (historical, critical, and interpretative) that were required to take account of new metatheoretical trends. It was in these terms that the past of political theory was understood and the program for its future was planned. Political science and political philosophy were identified, and the relationship between them understood, in these terms. Questions about the real relationships between political science and political theory and the actual relationship of both to political "facts" were neglected. Metatheoretical answers to metatheoretical issues became the prevalent mode, and the persistent myth of the tradition became the fictional past of the analytically contrived present.

In all this talk of renaissance and resuscitation that has become characteristic of the discourse of academic political theory, what, precisely, is being revived is seldom explicitly confronted, but the implication is clear. It is the great tradition. There is even, in some cases, a willingness to admit that the behavioral and positivist attack on political theory was in some respects warranted, because writing "histories of political ideas is not in itself the writing of political theory" (Freeman and Robertson, 1980:2). In fact, it is suggested, "very little original creative construction of theories about political reality and morality was done between, say, the death of Mill and the (publishing) birth of Rawls." Now, however, there is "a return to political theory in the grand manner" and "attempts to do what the great men of the tradition did, to write constitutions, devise institutional designs, on the basis of presuppositions about man's basic nature" (Freeman and Robertson, 1980:2−4, 11, 21). There might be few who would subscribe to *quite* such a fatuous account of the situation, but such claims reflect the general mood and image of political theory that began to develop by the late 1960s and tend to govern the conception of the field today.

It is difficult to factor out the attributes that are imposed on the classic texts, by viewing them as the precursors of academic political theory, from the characteristics imputed to academic political theory by suggesting that it is the revival of the great tradition. But perceptions of both, and their relationship to politics, are fundamentally distorted in the process. The dispersed, pluralistic—if not substantively detheoretized—character of political theory makes it impossible to focus on arguments that define the field. If political theory is to be understood as what political theorists do, there is little in this respect to indicate an identity. There is certainly no theoretical identity. But there are characteristics and trends that dominate the field and that run deeper than a description of the various enclaves and their particular pursuits would indicate. The unity and identity of political theory, apart from its institutional or professional coherence, which is now rather sharply delineated, inhere principally in the features that constitute the various dimensions of its alienation and philosophization.

Political theory understands itself and its activities in terms of metatheoretical categories and modes of analysis; it sets for itself metatheoretically defined problems for which it offers metatheoretical solutions; and it approaches and deals with the existential issue of the contingent relationship between political theory and politics in terms of variations on the metatheoretical theme of theory and practice. Professional autonomy has allowed the field to settle into complacency, but it has little about which to be complacent. Its metatheoretical propensities have deprived it of intellectual autonomy, entrapped it in a range of issues that even in their own terms, let alone as ways of "doing" political theory, are of dubious validity, and estranged it from what it most prided itself on achieving, particularly in contradistinction to behavioral science: a theoretical and practical engagement of politics. The arguments of political theory have, for the most part, become forms, or reflections, of epistemology, methodology, philosophical transcendentalism, and foundationalism.

Wolin was correct when he noted that one of the things that made the application of Kuhnian categories inappropriate in behavioralism's account of itself and its history was that it possessed no "initiating theory" (1968a; 1969: 1063–65). Apart from the extent to which theories, and values, were unreflectively embedded in the "facts" and conceptual frameworks of behavioralism, it was theoretically empty. But the critique of behavioralism gave rise to little in the way of what might be reasonably understood as such a theory, a theory functionally analogous to a theory in natural science or any autonomous practice of knowledge. There has not even appeared much that could be construed as discussion of substantive theoretical issues. The syndrome of "methodism" that characterized behavioral science is not unlike that which now characterizes political theory. The most dominant works in political theory today do not advance or include theories in the sense of claims that potentially constitute domains of facticity as much as they retail *ideas* about what theory and theorizing are, and might be, that have been wholesaled by philosophy. If some of the main traditions in academic philosophy associated with epistemology and foundationalism are in trouble, then so are the main traditions in political theory. A crisis in one becomes, lockstep, a crisis in the other.

The problem of the relationship between political theory and epistemology (and other metatheoretical claims) is not simply a matter of these arguments in the philosophy of science and philosophy of social science influencing political theory. Nor is it merely the fact that political theorists repeat those arguments and assume, much like behavioralism, that in some way they constitute theories and approaches to inquiry. Here we can see the problems that political theory has unwittingly and unreflectively appropriated in its search for identity and that have alienated it from substantive theory, but the problem of the philosophization of political theory has a more fundamental dimension. This involves a distinct parallel between the fate of modern philosophy with its foundationalist tendencies and its relationship to the practices about which it professes to speak on the one hand and political theory and politics on the other. Both philosophy and political theory have in large measure become alienated activities. And they are alienated not simply in the sense that the philosophy of science, for example, is not science. They are alienated in that they have not achieved an authentic understanding of their relationship to their subject matter. Before we return specifically to the condition of political theory, it is necessary to look at the situation in philosophy.

The contemporary critique of the foundationalist epistemologies that have dominated modern philosophy, since at least the time of Kant, has been a telling one. This is true not only in the philosophy of science with the work of individuals like Kuhn, Feyerabend, Toulmin, and Sellars but in the broader perspectives developed by Stanley Cavell (1979) and Richard Rorty (1979).

Cavell suggests that the traditional "epistemological quest" has involved generic questions about knowledge of generic objects outside of practical contexts where there are or could be substantive criteria of knowing. Epistemology has attempted to provide transcontextual, foundational, but, at the same time, practically authoritative answers about the empirical and rational possibilities and grounds of knowledge. The quest is inauthentic. It is only an abstraction from, and projection of, actual, "ordinary," or "natural" situations and the language of doubting and knowing appropriate to those situations. Competing epistemologies are competing projections whereby philosophers seek to say something, not so much about particular claims of their own as about the validity of the claims of others in everyday life or some specialized practice of knowledge. What is sought is a kind of selfless, translinguistic, supradiscursive, philosophically specifiable given that is independent of our responsibility for, and criteria of, claims in particular contexts but that can, at least in principle, undermine or underwrite such claims.

One difficulty with Cavell's position is that, despite his concern about the "professionalization" of philosophy (e.g., 1984:31), his argument remains bound to the life and times of academic philosophy. He indicates little appreciation of the significance of these issues outside philosophy or of the consequences of the extensions of epistemology in areas such as social science. There is an important sense in which the "transcendental illusion" (219) is insignificant as long as it remains in philosophy. Another problem, also evident even in Rorty's more historical approach to the problem of modern epistemology, is that the difficulty is presented as a somewhat inexplicable pathology of philosophy, which is to be cured in an equally vague way by better or less foundationally oriented philosophy. Nevertheless, Cavell cuts to the heart of the issue, and even its origins, when he suggests that such philosophical claims are "protestations of knowledge, entreaties that I be credible. Not one of them, in their rootlessness, would remove a doubt [or create one, it might be added]; they are signs to ward off doubt" (217).

The "world" about which the epistemologist has doubt, anxiety, and certainty, with regard to both its existence and its character, is only a mythical world. Even that, however, may be granting too much, because this world is not even hypothetically specified. Conjectures and refutations regarding it are only the abstracted grammatical forms of substantive knowing and criticizing. The result of these kinds of claims is ultimately to block discussion, retreat to authority, and, by stepping outside the context of saying anything particular, effectively seal philosophy off from life and make it irrelevant. In this situation, skepticism and foundationalism, relativism and absolutism, are really mutually required, and each provides the necessary problem for the other as natural doubt and certainty are projected on a transcendental screen. This, as Wittgenstein noted, is language and thought on a "holiday"—"an engine idling."

The open question of "How do you *really* know?" and the claim "*really*" to know, both extracted from all practical conditions of knowing, are meaningless. There are no criteria of "really" knowing as opposed to the criteria operative in particular conventional contexts. Epistemology lives in a vacuum somewhere between psychology and scientific theory. General skepticism is as mystical as general certainty. Both lack a context. But, with regard to both empirical and normative issues, both science and morality, the philosophical quest has been for this necessarily elusive and illusive grail. The search for foundations of knowledge with respect to science is no different than the search for the foundations of moral judgment—from Kant to the present. The idea that every particular claim to knowledge raises implicitly the question of how knowledge in general is possible and also tacitly answers it is simply the heritage of the dubious metaphor of knowlege as something possessing foundations and the assumption that knowledge and justification are the same. "Knowledge," "truth," "certainty," and the like are categorical modal terms that have criteria of application in human practices and nowhere else.

Human practices are not species or tokens of a greater transcendental practice, nor are there immanent universal criteria of validity that are more than abstractions from or family resemblances between actual practices. There always seems to be a nagging doubt that by giving up foundationalism we are giving up the ability to judge and adopting a Nietzschean posture that relegates science and morality to matters of individual decision and will. But the fact is that, as in the case of rejecting the positivist interpretation of theory, all that is given up is the particular philosophical foundationalist reconstruction, and all that is adopted is a distorted interpretation of Nietzsche. To reject foundationalism is no more to reject the validity of science than, for example, to reject the "new criticism" is to reject the idea of poetry as meaningful. All that is involved is an incredible philosophical scam to which certain special disciplines have succumbed in the hope of gaining identity and authority but on whom the philosopher's stone lies as an oppressive burden. It is one thing to understand how philosophy came to take up the epistemological quest, but it is another thing to explain why political theory endorsed it and participated in it.

In attempting to demonstrate how philosophy, in its search for identity and authority, has become irrelevant, Rorty has suggested that it has been "as a whole shrugged off by those who wanted an ideology or self-image" (1979:5). Although this may be the case with natural science, it is hardly the case with social science and political theory. Epistemology seemed to offer precisely what these disciplines wished: a way in which to establish *their* identity and authority with regard to politics in much the same way that philosophy wanted to understand itself in relationship to science and escape from history and particular contexts to a universal suprascientific foundation of either method or value. Such a foundation would in turn give it autonomy and significance in a world (at the end of the nineteenth century) where it was being diminished by particular specialized disciplines and even by internal threats to its Kantian dominion. Before examining the problem of philosophy's relationship to other fields, it is necessary to look more closely at its own integrity.

Like Cavell, and even like Popper (despite his apparent contradictions), Rorty is adamant about demonstrating that all knowledge is propositional and that justification is a relationship between propositions rather than "privileged relations to the objects those propositions are about" (1979: 159). We might say, with Althusser and Bachelard as with Kuhn, that the objects of science are constituted by theoretical practice. Influenced by the critiques of empiricism mounted by individuals like Sellars and W. V. O. Quine, Rorty sets out systematically to undermine the epistemological tradition and the theories of mind on which the notion of privileged representations rested. In doing so, he calls into question much of the contemporary practice of academic philosophy and its search for grounds of rationality that would underwrite knowledge in general and solve the skeptic's problem of how to pierce the "veil of ideas" and bring subject and object together. For Rorty, epistemological problems, as philosophical problems, are pseudoproblems, often grounded in philosophy's ill-fated search for a privileged status and role as the guarantor of science. "There is no wholesale, epistemological way to direct, or criticize, or underwrite, the course of inquiry" (1982:162).

It is necessary to think carefully about the implications of these arguments for political theory, but it is also necessary to be wary of these arguments and conscious of the danger that they may simply be appropriated as another philosophical claim to be incorporated into the image of political theory and political theorizing. In addition, despite their critique of philosophy, it is necessary to remember that they remain very much a part of an internal critique. The growing concern about language, communication, community, conversation, hermeneutics, edification, and the like, which Rorty and Cavell find exemplified in the work of Wittgenstein, Heidegger, and Dewey as opposed to the futile philosophical attempt to assuage Cartesian doubt, in many respects merely echoes the concerns that produced that attempt. It is another philosophical recommendation about the possibility and growth of knowledge which is not unlike that advanced by J. S. Mill, Dewey, Peirce, Popper, and others.

What philosophy—even as represented in this deconstructionist trend—cannot bring itself to do is to extricate itself from philosophical solutions to philosophical problems. In destroying the roots of certain myths in philosophy, it aids in destroying the "volunteers" and "suckers" that choke intellectual growth in other fields, but, for the most part, philosophy refuses to make those fields, or other practices of life, in their particularity, the object of analysis, to engage in what might be called empirical epistemology. And it is in this respect also that political theory mirrors philosophy—in its refusal to engage politics authentically as either a theoretical object or a practical concern.

The implication of the arguments of Cavell and Rorty that deserves emphasis is that judgment is not only a contextual matter but a matter of what might be called substantive theories in those contexts. The search for the foundation of all foundations was, I will argue, originally a move in the justification of a theory, before philosophy took up the search as a task independent of any particular theory and before social science brought those philosophical reconstructions back in the service of its identity and mission. Whether it is what Kuhn calls paradigms and exemplars or what I am calling substantive theory, it is that class of claims that establishes a domain of facticity—what exists and the manner in which it exists—and provides the criteria of explanation, description, evaluation, and prescription. But the poverty of theory in political theory is a function of its subservience to philosophy in both style and content.

The explanation of this problem is not simply a matter of the recent history of political science and its relationship to philosophy—or of the recent history of philosophy. Before turning to a brief excursus concerning this historical issue, which is largely neglected by Rorty and Cavell, I want to return to the related problem of the extent to which their work escapes the dilemma they ascribe to contemporary philosophy. Their arguments posit only a vague idea of an alternative kind of philosophy, which they see exemplified in Dewey and Wittgenstein. Rorty believes that this "edifying" trend is characterized by Wittgenstein, Heidegger, Foucault, Gadamer, and the whole hermeneutical tradition stressing conversation rather than closure. This position has much to recommend it, but there are at least two fundamental problems, both of which are instructive for thinking about political theory.

The first is that, although Rorty may *find* edification in the work of these individuals and derive significance from them, they are not all easily lumped together and described in this manner. They may all have challenged the traditional epistemological quest, but to suggest that Heidegger, for example, is not attempting to offer apodictic claims about the history of thought and structures of human existence that are just as authoritative as those of Kant and as philosophically chauvinistic is, I believe, to make a basic mistake and abstract historically and philosophically from the context of his project. Much the same could be said of Gadamer, and certainly to take Foucault as a model of liberal conversation is a quick if not facile move. Heidegger and Foucault, despite what one may find stimulating in their work, are prophetic and world-historical philosophers. Even if there are substantive aspects of their work that suggest the principles Rorty embraces, the mode of philosophizing is not so fundamentally different. Even in Rorty's case, the notion of edifying philosophy seems to be largely another, even if seemingly softer, way to justify an authoritative role for philosophy that will save it from being dragged down by the edifice that, in effect, has already collapsed. To "edify" may only archaically mean to build and establish, but it still carries more the force of didactic instruction and improvement than a conversation among equals.

T. D. Weldon may have been wrong when he suggested that, as a matter of logic, moral and political principles were "stop signs" to discussion (1956), and Cavell may be right in suggesting that we should "think" of morality and, by extension, politics as an essentially contested universe that is open to reasoning and argument. The fact is that, descriptively, Weldon is closer to the truth, and although it may serve some purpose to recommend a model of democratic academic discourse as a way of thinking about science and politics, it helps little as a way of explaining either. Traditionally, epistemology was meant to be a conversation stopper, but although Rorty may grasp this point, he fails to see the degree to which this is also true of his models. Any careful attention to Dewey's political thought would indicate that he was an edifier in the old sense as well as a deconstructor. Epistemology is by its very nature, whatever its particular message, authoritarian and revelatory, and this is why it has appealed to political theory. But, simply because some strands of contemporary philosophy challenge the old rationalism, we should not jump to the conclusion that they do not carry the same aura of presumptive authority and closure and underwrite definite ideological and theoretical positions that are more evoked than defended.

The second problem in Rorty's argument is that the actual relationship of philosophy to the practices of knowledge and life is not directly confronted. It may be salutary to offer a vision of philosophy as a critical enterprise that is pragmatic in its orientation, enters substantive conversations at the same level as other participants, and carries no a priori principles of truth, but the question of the real relationship of philosophy to other activities is rather systematically begged. It seems quite apparent that the implication is that, although something else should be learned from philosophy than what was learned before, the game is still therapeutic, and therapy, no matter how liberally conducted, is still therapy and implies the authority of the therapist. The explicit message may be "philosophy without foundations," but the implicit message is still that philosophy is the teacher. This may be a suspect message, one that neglects the extent to which practices such as science, and politics, are grounded in theory and the immanent criteria of judgment that theories provide. But even if in principle one could satisfactorily sustain the idea of the therapeutic role of philosophy, the existential practical problem of its relationship to other conventional practices remains.

Although Rorty is cautious about the idea of philosophy claiming authority over forms of everyday life and specialized disciplines, he believes it might play the role of clarifying, liberalizing, and, much like lawyers, giving weight to various positions as it adopts an adversary role in the world of substantive discourse. Clearly, Rorty does not supply much ammunition for those who want to find strong critical purchase for political theory in philosophy, and one might suspect that he is relatively complacent about liberalism. He is to philosophy as Charles Lindblom is to social science. Pragmatism, tolerance, pluralism, and usable knowledge are the watchwords. But in both cases the vestiges of the idea of academic authority are unmistakable, and the problems of the relationship of theory to practice are not confronted.

The historical roots of the problem of epistemology remain unclarified, and until they are illuminated the kinds of problems discussed above cannot be adequately addressed. Cavell presents the problem of epistemology as if it were just "there." Although Rorty has a number of truly tantalizing comments about the historical situation and gives considerable attention to the seventeenth century and the origins of the Cartesian problem and Lockean epistemology, he is overwhelmed by the philosopher's prejudice of projecting contemporary academic philosophy backward. Plato becomes the paradigm of Platonism, Descartes becomes the struggling but ultimately mistaken professional analyst, and Locke the precursor of logical empiricism.

The ultimately unexplicated claims go in the direction of suggesting the extent to which epistemology is apology (Gunnell, 1982; 1983*a*) and was originally rooted in apology. Rorty says, for example, that "investigations of the foundations of knowledge or morality or language may be simply apologetics, attempts to externalize a certain contemporary language-game, social practice, or self-image" (1979: 10). It seems quite clear that this is the use, even though sometimes unreflective, to which social science and political theory have put their epistemological borrowings from philosophy. But this apologetic role in philosophy and science must also be explored. Similarly, he argues that the critics of Kuhn "were right in seeing that Kuhn's criticism of the tradition went deep, and that the ideology which had protected the rise of modern science was in danger. They were wrong in thinking that the institutions still needed the ideology" (333). It might be, as Rorty also often suggests, that philosophy was trying to protect itself and its autonomy as much as it was trying to protect science.

Something about the origins of epistemology are indicated here, yet Rorty does not tell us enough about why philosophy wanted to escape from history via metaphysics and epistemology. He indicates that epistemology in the modern sense did not really appear until the eighteenth century and maybe did not become fully established in a way that gave rise to some of our present problems until the late 1800s. Yet he treats earlier thinkers as if they were dealing with the same issues and not merely functionally similar ones. The following argument can only be offered in summary and promissory form, but it is crucial to the critique of political theory undertaken here.

Just as there is a sense in which academic political theory is still tied to its political origins, philosophy, and particularly the philosophy of science, cannot get over its practical or scientific beginnings. This is not to say that political theory and philosophy should reject practical concerns, but, as academic fields, they must come to grips with the problem of their relationship to the practices they now take as their object. They cannot simply choose to be identified with these practices when it is convenient and be above them when it is persuasive to do so. At present, in many instances, they move within a fourth dimension, a shadow world, where they play out a kind of academized surrogate form of political and scientific practice. Epistemology and political theory not only have been tied together as political theory has sought authority in epistemology but have a similar evolutionary structure, which explains, at least in part, their common alienated status.

It is important to distinguish, immediately, between what might be called functional, or practical, epistemology on the one hand and professional, or disciplinary, epistemology on the other hand. It is in part the failure to make this distinction that clouds the projects of Cavell and Rorty as well as other antifoundationalist literature. By functional epistemology, I mean the justification and legitimation of certain substantive knowledge claims. Such epistemology is characteristically either embedded in some practice such as science or closely tied to such practice. Professional epistemology, by contrast, is a relatively autonomous, circumscribed body of literature confined largely to academic philosophy and concerned with the foundations of knowledge and rationality per se. The historical connections between the two are important, because the latter largely evolved out of the former and exists as an alienated mode of the former.

One of the difficulties with Rorty's argument is that he quite consistently conflates the two. For example, he persistently treats Plato as if Plato were a prototypical, if not archetypal, foundationalist in the professional sense. We might never have a satisfactory answer to what Plato was doing in works such as the *Republic*, but to approach the dramatic ironic discussion of knowledge in that context in the literal unhistorical manner that characterizes Rorty's analysis is of dubious benefit. In the case of Descartes, despite the typical treatment of Descartes's work as a series of abstract philosophical perplexities, there is considerable evidence to suggest that he should be understood less as a professional epistemologist and methodologist than as a scientist attempting to defend and secure his substantive claims against religious sanction and rival authorities. The case of Locke and what is philosophical, political, and rhetorical is equally complex. But there is little to suggest that in these instances epistemological issues can be any more than functionally or analytically distinguished. As Rorty himself often indicates, professional epistemology is a quite recent enterprise that arose as a way of legitimating philosophy in an age of science—legitimating its claim to a special and autonomous status and legitimating it by performing the role of underwriting the rationality of science.

What, in retrospect, we might understand, functionally, as epistemology and methodology, that is, claims about the criteria and foundations of adequate knowledge and how to acquire it, played a rhetorical/apologetic/critical role integrally tied to various social and political practices. Although it might be difficult to disentangle this mode of discourse from others in, for example, ancient myth, the point at which claims to knowledge are self-ascribed is clearly a juncture at which epistemology is functionally distinguishable. Whether it is Homer's invocation of the Muses, Hesiod's affirmation that it is he they love and to whom they speak the truth, Thucydides' empirical challenge to the deficiencies of former accounts of the past and modes of knowledge acquisition, or Plato's intimations regarding noetic access to the grounds of *episteme* and his rejection of the methods of his rivals that produce only *pistis* and *doxa*, the question of the difference between appearance and reality is at issue and epistemology comes into play.

As noted earlier, what distinguishes epistemological amd methodological claims is not so much that in themselves they are really a matter to be debated as that they are claims to authority regarding substantive matters that are at issue in some field or realm of discourse. All such claims about the foundations of knowledge are basically incontestable and incommensurable—and designed to be so. There may be contentious historical questions regarding the instances in which epistemological controversies became distinct and autonomous or when and how the transformation from functional epistemology to professional epistemology might be understood as generally having taken place, but certain things seem relatively clear.

The origins of the genre of claims that we associate with contemporary professional philosophical epistemology can be found in the literature of early modern science. Whether in the form of separate or somewhat separate treatises, such as the work of Descartes and Bacon on method, or embedded in substantive discourse, as tends to be the case with Galileo or Newton, such claims were primarily justifications of the putative inductive or deductive procedures from which their theories were gained and of the empirical grounds on which they rested. For Galileo and Descartes, the problem of religious authority and political sanction required a delicate statement of the basis of scientific rationality. The process of the transition from practical to philosophical epistemology, first of all, had much to do with the attempt of that portion of philosophy that had not been transformed into differentiated practices of knowledge such as natural science to give itself identity and legitimacy. Second, the increased legitimacy, autonomy, and internal differentiation of natural philosophy meant that less and less metatheoretical legitimation was required to defend it both epistemologically and ideologically. One might suggest that Kant was attempting, still, to justify science and provide it with a metatheoretical foundation, but he was surely also attempting to justify philosophy by demonstrating that it could, or even did, validate science. Science needed philosophy less than philosophy needed science.

Epistemology and methodology, then, as they emerged in the context of modern science, served the function of metatheoretical legitimation. Such claims were basically ex post facto, often ad hoc, apologies for particular theories and even scientific practice itself. This is not so much to make the common, and not very historically meaningful, point that science had not yet cast off its "philosophical" origins as it is to say that certain elements of philosophy have their historical roots in scientific practice. It is not the case, as Habermas, for example, claims, that first there was epistemology and then it degenerated into the philosophy of science. It is more accurate to say that first there was the philosophy of science, which expanded into philosophical epistemology. Newton, for example, did not address methodological and epistemological issues in any detail until he was forced to do so in defense of his "theory" of optics, which had been challenged as a "hypothesis" by rivals like Hooker and the Jesuit Pardies and neglected by others. Newton wished to substantiate his position by demonstrating that he arrived at his claims by "reason" and "experiment" and that he did not make hypotheses.

Whether by design or mistake, by the nineteenth century philosophers had begun to produce a fundamentally inverted image of the actual relationship between epistemology and scientific practice. They characterized the functional epistemology embedded in science as statements of the procedures that had made substantive scientific knowledge possible and the bases (usually psychological) on which it rested. Thus was born the idea of the scientific method and the idea of the foundations of scientific knowledge as well as the notion that there could be a philosophical distillation of this method that could be employed not only as an explanation of the logic and epistemology of science but as a critical and methodological framework for practicing it. In the work of John Stuart Mill, who apparently knew very little about the actual substance and practice of natural science, we have the paradigm case of this syndrome as well as one of the first clear examples of the suggestion that, because natural science is a paradigm of rationality, this mythical method could be extended to the field of social studies in order to emulate the success of the natural sciences.

As the philosophy of science emerged as a distinct discipline in the late nineteenth century and professional epistemology began to take form, they were largely still parasitic on developments in science. These developments were responsible for the basic intellectual shifts in the philosophy of science regarding matters of induction, the relationship between theories and facts, and the like. Epistemological issues were basically determined, in turn, by issues in the philosophy of science. Even the roots of logical positivism are to be found not simply in an attempt to make philosophy scientific but in an attempt to account for basic transformations in physical theory. But what is significant is the fact that while this movement was in one sense still trying to validate science philosophically it was also attempting to interpret science in a manner consonant with prior philosophical doctrines about scientific knowledge. As time went on, the philosophy of science and epistemology acquired a life of their own—but an alienated life—largely detached from the substantive practice of science and other forms of life. They generated their own philosophical issues, which they solved accordingly. Part of this new and separate life involved their relationship to social science. Alienated philosophy became the source of emerging social science's self-image and even the guide to its practice.

What has characterized claims about science and natural science in the social sciences, from Mill to the present, is that they have not simply been mediated through works in the philosophy of science and tertiary summaries of such works in both philosophy and social science but have largely been constructed entirely from such sources. This is not, however, a recent phenomenon. In this respect, the social sciences were alienated enterprises from the beginning in that they sought a philosophical identity and increasingly became a kind of philosophical practice. Early social science in seeking a scientific self-image, for both internal reasons and reasons of political and social authority, drew upon the philosophy of science and epistemology. What started out, however, as a form of legitimation was increasingly transformed into a methodological mandate that was progressively detached from both substantive social scientific matters and the political context. What occurred was an inversion of epistemology and inquiry or metatheory and theory—an inversion that in large measure explains and defines the contemporary alienation of political theory. There was once a good deal more self-consciousness about this matter. This is evident in the work of Weber and Lenin.

The *Methodenstreiten* of the late nineteenth and early twentieth centuries were grounded in ideological or political disputes, questions of the relationship between theory and practice or the vocations of science and politics, and matters of science and the authority of its knowledge. These were all integrally related issues, as is so apparent in the case of Weber, but however one might read Weber's methodological essays and whatever he was in fact doing by what he said, it is clear that he recognized the problem of metatheoretical alienation. Although the controversy regarding the nature of social science explanation and its degree of symmetry with the logic of explanation in natural science, exemplified in such disputes as that between Karl Menger and Gustav Schmoller, was one that in its basic form would be repeated many times in social science and political theory, it involved, and reflected, a real competition between concrete practices of inquiry and the problems of legitimating them. And it was related to some concrete political issues. What distinguishes that debate from modern versions in the philosophy of science and political theory is that in large measure the discussion is about *ideas* of inquiry only vaguely related to real practices, and the political concerns have become equally distanced and philosophized.

Reluctantly, and paradoxically, Weber entered the realm of the *Wissenschaftslehre*. His methodological essays were not the reflective redaction of the procedures he employed in sociological inquiry and the practical guide to research that subsequent generations have characteristically taken them to be. They were instead primarily a rather unsystematic set of arguments that were the product of an attempt, first, to legitimate a form of historical inquiry in the face of attacks from scientism and the taint of intuitionism. But, second, and maybe even more importantly, he wanted to resolve and clear away a number of metatheoretical intrusions that threatened to diffuse substantive social scientific and political issues and inhibit theoretical work and concrete research. To a very great extent he engaged in metatheoretical argument to demonstrate its dangers, and he was not unaware that his venture might contribute, as it did, to the very problem about which he was concerned (see Burger, 1976; Oakes, 1977). It is ironic that, whether one was for or against methodism, Weber became the paradigm.

For Weber, social scientific involvement in metatheory was a form of "dilettantism" that had, in part, caused the *Methodenstreit*, served to prolong it, and enticed social scientists into a realm of discourse not of their own making, and with which they were not really prepared or equipped to deal. The "embellishment" of social science with "epistemological investigations" had created a "methodological pestilence" that drew attention away from "*substantive* problems." Weber's argument, so historically sensitive and logically acute, was that "methodology" could "only be self-reflection on the means which have *proven* to be valuable in actual research. Explicit self-reflection of this sort is no more a condition for fruitful research than is knowledge of anatomy a condition for the ability to walk 'correctly.'" And just as a person who did so would be "in danger of stumbling," so would "the scholar who attempts to base the aims of his research on a foundation of extrinsic methodological consideration" (Weber, 1975:14–15). Weber's prophetic remarks presaged the alienation of political theory.

Another voice that pointed to the danger of metatheory in the early years of the social sciences was that of Lenin, who not only indicated the general problem of philosophical intrusion but focused on the distorted idea of theory that would come to dominate positivistic social science. Lenin's problem and the connections among social science, philosophy, and politics were clear. He was attempting to do for Marxism, in a practical way, what Althusser and numerous other contemporary philosophers, with varying degrees of practical concern, would attempt to do in a more academic but consequently intrinsically contradictory manner— validate the scientific status of Marx's theories.

Lenin viciously attacked the trends in the philosophy of science that had begun to emerge around the turn of the century in the work of Ernst Mach, Karl Pearson, J. H. Poincaré, P. I. Duhem, and others. He saw, first of all, that the instrumentalist interpretation of scientific theory in this work, an interpretation that would dominate the tradition of logical positivism/empiricism and eventually the image and even practice of social science, was, in its attempt to secure objective foundations for science, ultimately, and maybe ironically, based on philosophical idealism. It was idealist both in the Kantian sense that it saw theories in a formalistic manner as constructs of the mind for organizing experience, "theory as only a systematization of experience, a system of empirio-symbols" (Lenin, 1950:287) and in that it reduced the facts and foundational language of science to sensations in its attempt to produce an idea of grounded knowledge. What Lenin wanted explicitly to defend was what he called "naive realism," which he believed was the foundation of a "materialist theory of knowledge," against both Kantian idealism and empiricist (e.g., Humean) skepticism about the possibilities of knowing the world. It is also clear that Lenin sensed in a more general way the danger of this philosophy to substantive theory, the notion of theory as a realistic claim about the domain of facticity, and the problem of philosophical reconstructions as guides to science—particularly as they related to the study of society.

Lenin, like Weber, noted that the philosophy of science was "conditional" on the practice of science and not vice versa (1950:138), and he warned of the danger of scientists being "led astray by professional philosophy" (44). Of course, for Lenin these "official professors of official philosophy" (40) were wittingly or unwittingly involved in legitimating more than science, a message that need not be forgotten. He also noted that epistemology is, and always was, a "*partisan* science" (356). Today it is still a partisan science, but one confined to the world of academic philosophical politics. Apart from his specific concerns, there is general wisdom in his claim that "if natural science in its theories depicts not objective reality but *only* metaphors, symbols, forms of human experience, etc., it is beyond dispute that humanity is entitled to create for itself in another sphere a *no less 'real'* concept" (361). Philosophical empiricism does less to ensure the objectivity of science than it does to destroy the critical force of theoretical claims.

It is against this background of the historical connections between epistemology and social science that we must understand several dimensions of the alienation of political theory that are connected with the epistemological quest and the attempt to substitute metatheory for theory. But there is also a structural parallel between the fate of philosophy and that of political theory and its relationship to politics. If there is a way to rehabilitate philosophical epistemology, there may be a way to rehabilitate political theory. Just as it was necessary to distinguish functional and professional epistemologies, it is useful to distinguish between what might be understood as political theory *in* politics and political theory *about* politics or functional and academic (professional) political theory. To conflate the two, slip into the habit of suggesting that the latter is the historical extension of the former, or assume that they are equivalents has become characteristic of the literature. It is precisely such moves that avert the problem of the relationship of political theory to politics in both its current and historical dimensions.

The social sciences in the United States to a large extent began, during the last half of the nineteenth century, as reform movements directed toward the abolition of slavery and, eventually, the curtailment of modern industrial capitalism and political corruption. Even though originally somewhat amateurish intellectual societies, they were organized for purposes of political action and reflected political passion or at least displaced religious and secularized moral fervor. Not a small factor in their eventual entry into the world of academic professionalism and their disciplinary differentiation was a search for social authority and the belief that professionalization would give force to their political ends. The academic institutionalization and professionalization of the social sciences were, however, major factors in their deradicalization (see Poschman, 1982; Seidelman, 1985).

By the time political science appeared as a distinct discipline and profession, it was already a relatively conservative field that identified its relationship to politics in terms of political education, bringing increased efficiency to public administration and effecting social control through the machinery of the state. The practical mission remained, and, at least through the years of the progressive movement, a distinct critical/reformist perspective retained considerable influence. Although the idea of political science as a policy science has gone through cycles of varying popularity, it has been the most dominant image in the field. Nevertheless, the evolution of professionalism in political science increasingly served to distance the field from the particularities of politics—in both a practical and a theoretical sense. This tension has been especially manifest in political theory, which, although it has reflected the general contours in the development of academic political science, has felt a special mission, much like the philosophy of science, to criticize and/or underwrite the activity from which it sprung.

Once closely identified with concrete political ends, academic political theory about politics evolved a life of its own quite apart from the practical problems that gave rise to it and the ideas and theories in politics with which it had been closely tied. Although maybe never entirely unresponsive to actual political issues and political change, political theory came increasingly to reflect problems generated in its disciplinary context and, for some of the reasons already discussed, problems defined by the philosophical contexts into which, for various reasons, it was drawn. Much like epistemology, once abstracted from its practical context, political theory lost touch with actual political issues and theory in politics, yet sought to make authoritative claims about the foundations of empirical and normative political knowledge. It still saw its role in part as that of legitimating and exposing political claims, but paradoxically it increasingly operated in a world of philosophical politics where its arguments had neither a real political context nor a political object (or objective). It was a world as divorced from politics and theories in politics as epistemology and the philosophy of science were divorced from science and theories in science.

In all the claims about the "decline" of political theory, the notion of decline is, at least subtly, tied up with the academization of political theory, but in each case there is a failure to confront directly the issue of how political theory can perform in a preacademic manner and remain academic. In each of these cases there is also a genealogical mistake that has a great deal to do with political theory's inability to come to grips with its true identity.

The point is not that contemporary political theory is totally unrelated, either historically or in terms of the kinds of concerns that identify it, to the classic texts in political theory but rather that the canon is not its most direct and immediate ancestoral background. It persists in a mythical image of the tradition that it identifies as its family tree. Just as both current defenses and critiques of epistemology seek their past in the work of individuals such as Plato and Descartes, or academic images of these individuals, rather than in the apologetic discourse embedded in early modern science, political theory looks for images of itself in the classics rather than in its social scientific parentage and the relationship of social science to politics. Similarly, the question of whether there is an authentic future for academic political theory is not only linked in a practical way to the future of philosophical epistemology to which it has been so beholden. There is a distinct conceptual parallel regarding the problem of the relationship of theory to practice that makes the question of the redemption of epistemology relevant for thinking about the state of political theory.

What characterizes political theory today is an inversion of the proper relationship between theory and metatheory, if not the displacement of the former by the latter. This situation can be explained, at least in its broad outlines, by looking at the academic invention of the very idea of political theory—particularly, as we have seen, beginning in the 1950s with the rise of the behavioral image of science and the philosophical rationalization and critique of this image; the transformation of the idea of the great tradition into the myth of the tradition; and the issues springing from the conflict between the two. The latter in a fundamental way informed the differentiation and constitution of contemporary political theory as an autonomous interdisciplinary academic field with its various enclaves governed by respective philosophical images of theory as a product and activity.

Whatever the details of the historical development of this problem may be, in terms of both the discipline of political science and the wider background of philosophy and social science, the basic point is that political theory by the mid-1980s was as a whole distinguished by its absorption with metatheory—with methodology, epistemology, transcendentalism, and various forms of philosophical foundationalism. The issue at hand is the possibility of cutting through this syndrome and rethinking what theory is and can be in political theory, what the relationship of political theory to philosophy should involve, and coming to grips with the question of the relationship of academic political theory to politics. To accomplish this requires thinking through some more immediate manifestations of the metatheoretical inversion.

One of the basic lessons that should be learned from the history of epistemology is that there are no metatheoretical answers to theoretical problems. The search for an indubitable realm of fact and a method for apprehending it was, as a philosophical project, a futile quest. It was based on both a category mistake, because "fact" is really a term that refers to a class of propositions (maybe those in which we have substantive criteria for belief), and the mistaken notion that metatheory could do the job of theory in a particular practice of knowledge —create a domain of facticity and the criteria of empirical knowledge. Political theorists in mainstream political science leaped into the metatheoretical dilemma for at least two reasons. They believed in the positivist image of science as a form of knowledge at once about and grounded in *the* facts and the idea of *the* scientific method, and they sought an authoritative basis for their enterprise and its claims. But the search for transcendental methods and facts that would ensure scientific rationality was only one aspect of the alienation of political theory.

No less than the positivist social scientist, the antipositivist political theorist and political philosopher sought grounds and methods of transcendental judgment, which in many respects became more important than any particular substantive judgment about politics. There was a sense in which the difficulties were exacerbated in this case. Although there may have been normative implications and biases in the frameworks and "facts" of behavioral political science as well as a certain claim to authority in matters of public policy, the political philosopher more directly sought, at least in the abstract, to substitute philosophical judgment for political judgment and discover the incontrovertible grounds of such judgments. Here also there was a failure to recognize that theory must precede metatheory, that ultimately an evaluative claim must be grounded in a theory of what kind of thing it purports to evaluate. And there was a failure to come to grips with the general practical issue of the relationship between political theory and politics, an issue that could not be solved philosophically or categorically by general claims about theory and practice.

Whether the position was positivist or postpositivist, the self-image of political theory, by the 1970s, was based on a metatheoretical framework grounded in positivist philosophy. Even while attempting to extricate themselves from it, political theorists remained bound by it. The language attaching to the so-called fact/value problem structured the discourse of political theory. The mistake was to assume that such issues as distinguishing descriptions from evaluations, dealing with bias in empirical research, determining how normative concerns and even general cultural perspectives influence problem selection and the interpretation of data, and deciding how empirical claims relate to normative judgments were particular manifestations of a more general problem about values that admitted of a general solution, one that could be extended to particular cases. Political theory increasingly became involved in an attempt to work its way out of a metatheoretical problem in metatheoretical terms.

Some remained content, as in the case of behavioralism and its political science offspring, with the philosopher's claim that "the basic judgments of human beings may be divided into three fundamentally different categories: (1) logical judgments, (2) factual judgments, and (3) value judgments" (Kemeny, 1960:292). Political scientists, maybe at first for rhetorical reasons but eventually because it became their view of the world, accepted the idea that, although in practice these types are likely to be mixed, the factual aspect of a proposition refers to a part of "reality" and "can be tested by reference to the facts" whereas the evaluative "aspect of a proposition . . . expresses only the emotional response of an individual to a state of real or presumed facts" (Easton, 1953:221, 224). Parenthetically, one might wonder, if values are basically irrational preferences and commitments, as Easton suggests, what he might have meant by his recommendation that political scientists construct value theory, but this metatheoretical image of the framework of judgment was almost liturgically accepted by political scientists.

It would be a mistake not to recognize that the separation of fact and value, both in positivism and in social science, was not merely a function of scientism and a depreciation of evaluative concerns. It was, like the idea of value relativism, part of liberal ideology. The autonomy, and equality, of value judgments, from Weber's arguments onward, was as much, although less noted, an implication of the fact/value dichotomy as the autonomy of science. And it is no accident that the rejection of that dichotomy and the rejection of relativism were almost always tied to the critique of liberalism. For liberalism, particularly in the American context, transcendental political values were safely embedded in its "facts." Relativism was, at least for a time, a luxury it could afford and still defend the idea of freedom inherent in the autonomy of values and morality. Science might be free from values, but values were free from science.

Whatever the contextual reasons that made the fact/value dichotomy appealing or a matter of concern, it was a philosophical problem within a philosophical framework bequeathed to political theory by philosophers and their interpreters. Like relativism, which was little more than a version of philosophical skepticism and which required its twin, absolutism, to be intelligible, it provided identities for various positions, both positivist and antipositivist, and a basis for the division of labor in social science and political theory. Many might have been dissatisfied with it and the assumptions that inspired it, but such philosophers and political theorists largely accepted the definition of the dilemma. They saw the problem in terms of providing grounds for values; demonstrating that, in the end, evaluative and empirical statements could not be disentangled; and giving form and content to what positivists had in effect designated as a non-activity—normative theory or political philosophy.

It is worthwhile looking at Weber's analysis of fact and value both because, conceptually, later analysts were never able to go far beyond his account of the matter and because, historically, his arguments had a significant effect on the manner in which later social scientists viewed the problem.

Weber insisted on an irreducible "logical distinction between 'existential knowledge,' i.e., knowledge of what 'is,' and 'normative knowledge,' i.e., knowledge of what 'should be,'" which makes propositions regarding these matters "absolutely heterogeneous" (1948:51). This was hardly a matter of abstract logic for Weber. His concern was in part the intrusion of certain ideological positions into the activity of the academy, and his purpose was to argue that the acceptance of the logical distinction and the need to make value judgments "explicit" was "an imperative requirement of intellectual honesty" (2, 10). Given his practical and rhetorical motives and concerns, it is not surprising that Weber lumped together, under one basic logical category, a number of very different things, including evaluative judgments, ideals, interests, and moral and cultural perspectives. Beliefs and choices belonging to this realm, as opposed to scientific statements about "empirically observed facts" where "validity" is a matter of universal "empirical truth," are grounded, he suggested, in will, feeling, and conscience, and "the *validity* of such judgments is a matter of *faith*" (53–60).

Weber's second, and equally important, practical concern was to establish the autonomy of values and human action, including politics. Evaluative judgments and perspectives might be matters of choice and compromise and not scientifically demonstrable, but when Weber claimed that "there is no (rational or empirical) scientific procedure of any kind whatsoever which can provide us with a decision here," he was seeking to secure the autonomy of normative claims as much as the autonomy of science (1948:19). Values might not be scientific, but they could not be replaced by scientific rationality. There was also at least one other practical concern that informed Weber's analysis. Part of his purpose in separating these two realms of discourse, and the activities that he suggested corresponded to each, was to demonstrate that there were important relations between them, a point that could not be forcefully made until the distinction was clear.

After establishing the heterogeneity of values and facts, Weber argued that there was, after all, "no absolutely 'objective' scientific analysis of . . . social phenomena," because all knowledge is "always knowledge from *particular points of view*" which inform problem and data selection as well as interpretation and analysis. Even the belief in scientific truth is a "subjective" belief. Yet he maintained, much in the way that later philosophers distinguished between the contexts of justification and discovery, that even though there is "presuppositional" empirical science, there is objective logical and epistemological validity to causal and descriptive scientific claims, independent of the investigator's "conceptual framework," that makes "scientific truth . . . *valid* for all who *seek* the truth" (1948: 72–84). But this claim was important to Weber not merely to preserve the autonomy of science but to demonstrate that it was relevant to normative and practical issues. Science may not be able to ground values, but it can, among other things, specify means to ends, describe and explore values and the relationships between them, estimate which means and ends are practically viable, provide reasons for choice, and predict the consequences, both intended and unintended, of holding certain values.

The fate of Weber's discussion of fact and value is instructive. Within the tradition of social science, this was probably the classic and definitive rendering, and it provides a clear example of the path of the alienation of political theory. Weber's analysis of the problem consisted, as in the case of his other metatheoretical claims, basically of a set of strategic and rhetorical arguments located in a definite theoretical *and* political context. They were subsequently abstracted from that practical context and treated as if they either defined the conditions of social scientific inquiry or undermined the possibility of political philosophy. Extracted from their context, even the context of his own argument, they became free-floating metatheoretical propositions that could be, and characteristically were, reconstituted and contradictorily interpreted both as the paradigm case of subjectivism and value domination in social science and as the archetype of the belief in objectivism and value freedom in these disciplines (e.g., Rudner, 1966; Strauss, 1953). This is not to suggest that metatheoretical arguments lost all their rhetorical function and force. They have been characteristically employed on both sides of the modern *Methodenstreit* for validation and criticism. But increasingly, as in the case of the "value/ fact fetish" (Austin, 1962:150), they were reified and treated as autonomous substantive problems that defined the practice of social science and political theory. To the extent that the fact/value framework derived from positivism, it was rooted in a theory of linguistic meaning, but that theory itself receded from view as debates between seemingly disparate positions were carried on within that framework.

Nagel represented the characteristic philosophical view accepted by social scientists. Starting from the assumption of the unity of science, he suggested that it may be difficult but hardly impossible for social science to achieve "objectivity" and "the 'value-neutrality' that seems so pervasive in the natural sciences," because "there is a relatively clear distinction between factual and value judgments." It is always, at least "in principle," possible to decide "whether a given statement has a purely factual content" (1961:485, 488, 502). On the other hand, Strauss took the position that there can be no "strictly factual" accounts of social phenomena, because "it is impossible to study social phenomena . . . without making value-judgments"—especially when, as in the case of a description of a concentration camp, for example, the account cries out for the application of evaluative terms such as "cruel" (1959:21, 22, 52). The point is not that Nagel and Strauss hold the same basic philosophical assumptions— although they may be a good deal more similar than they appear. Both, for example, are in the end transcendentalists looking for the foundations of knowledge. What is most important is the fact that their claims— whether wittingly for rhetorical purposes or unreflectively—have been shaped and constrained by a theoretically unanchored metatheoretical issue and language.

Arguments such as those of Strauss did not become the main response to the positivist/behavioralist account of the relationship between facts and values, but the framework continued to dominate in all areas of political theory. The framework was parasitic, as in the case of Weber, on a practical context and, in the case of positivism, on a metatheory already at least once removed from any theoretical substance and practical concern. Increasingly, the move was back to a position that closely reflected a formal rendition of Weber's analysis—autonomy and complementarity. Within this now abstract alienated conceptual structure were unlimited possibilities for categorizing and inventing aspects of political theory and finding metatheoretical solutions to metatheoretical problems. Political theorists and philosophers of social science alike accepted versions of the idea that the fact/value dichotomy represented two forms of language, which in turn were reflected in two kinds of activities. Nearly everyone was willing to talk about the relevance of one to the other, but hardly anyone wanted to be associated with "condoning attempts to sabotage the distinction between facts and values" (Braybrooke, 1958:989). There was something in this distinction for everyone.

The problem for political theory or political philosophy became basically one of giving content to the side of the equation that positivism had called into question and providing some sense of a significant relationship between empirical political science and normative claims. Lurking in the background were both the myth of the tradition and the philosophical myth about scientific theory, which were quite generally accepted by all parties as the content of the activities representing the binary division of the language and practice of political inquiry. The questions were ones of status and relationship, which were asked and answered within the commonly accepted metatheoretical framework. Political scientists stressed what they took to be the newfound autonomy of empirical science grounded in empirical theory and empirical language, and political theorists searched for a way to resurrect the significance of normative claims.

Robert Dahl's statement was a classic representation of the position of behavioralism. Dahl did not question the idea that values influence empirical research in many ways. Claims to the contrary could only be associated with the "extreme (and now somewhat old-fashioned views) of the early Logical Positivists." But he maintained that it is nevertheless "possible to isolate and test the empirical aspects of our beliefs about politics . . . entirely independent of our values" (1963:103, 106). Not only, it seemed, did language have factual and normative elements, but our beliefs could be factored out in a similar way. Exactly what kind of theory of mind and language would support such notions is difficult to say, but it is clear enough what the metatheoretical assumption was that was reflected here— even if in a distorted way. For Dahl, this logically entailed two different kinds of inquiry and theory, and his assumptions were in no significant manner distinguishable from the characteristic positivist analysis. Dahl argued that empirical and normative inquiry, political science and political philosophy, reflected the "logically" distinct character of "decisions about what '*is*' and decisions about what '*ought*' to be." Propositions embodying the former are judged by the extent to which they correspond to "the real world," whereas the latter rest on "preference" (8, 103).

Hardly anything could be more consistent than the manner in which this position was stated by political scientists for over a generation and reinforced by the mediational literature in philosophy and social science.

Easton's arguments over the years provide a good example of this consistency. He argued that "facts and values are logically heterogeneous" and that ethical evaluation and empirical explanation involve two different kinds of propositions" that constitute the difference between "causal and value (moral) theory." The validity of the former is "determined by the correspondence of a statement with reality," which is in turn "verified through the known procedures of good reasoning and observation," whereas the latter "can ultimately be reduced to emotional responses" (1953:221, 226; 1965a:7). But what is most interesting, at least in retrospect, about this claim is not its pervasiveness and persistence.

The same basic argument had been part of the core of political science's understanding of itself from its beginnings. And even though those who were now at war with one another saw the relationship between the two endeavors as more problematical than their ancestors did, the tendency to identify themselves in this manner is not surprising. If there was any significant difference in content in the argument of those who sought a scientific identity, it was only a matter of some increase in sophistication as a result of more direct contact with philosophy where the argument was systematically elaborated. Neither was its rhetorical use in the context of the behavioral era surprising or difficult to understand. What *is* interesting, however, is the inversion of justification and practice, that is, the way in which the metatheoretical framework increasingly became one to which political scientists attempted to give content in accordance with philosophical ideas about the demands of empirical theory and which political theorists sought to fill in by finding grounds for restoring the classic vocation. It is here that we must seek the cause of the alienation of political theory.

In many respects, that alienation was more severe in the case of what came generally to be understood as normative political theory. No matter how theoretically deficient mainstream political science might have been; how much estrangement there was between what it did and what it professed, or hoped, to do; how deeply enmeshed it was in the myth of the given and the political as well as scientific values it entailed, it was at least a practice. There was "empirical theory" and research—and not just a philosophical image of political science and what it might be even if one totally discounted its worth and ultimately judged it worse than nothing. Normative political theory, on the other hand, remained largely an *idea* of a practice and a disembodied rationale for it, a search for substance that would give it parity and weight in the fact/value balance. By 1970 it was estimated that one-third of the people identified in political science as political theorists "practice Normative Political theory" (Eulau, 1969:13), but one would have been hard put to say what constituted that practice. There were severe questions of whether normative political theory could practice within the confines of political science where the fact/value distinction was basically invidious and whether in fact it was practicable at all. After 1970 political theory, conceptually and professionally, embarked on a quixotic quest in search of its Self—a self that had largely been defined by others.

The definition of the task to which the next generation of political theorists dedicated themselves was incoherent. The notion of creating an identity for normative political theory, or re-creating the activity of political theory, had little to do with thinking through what kind of a practice academic political theory was, had been, or could be, how it related to politics, and how it related to political science and philosophy. It was not a real issue at all but rather a dilemma defined in terms of a metatheoretical category and a series of metatheoretical problems dealing with theory and practice and the grounds of political knowledge and value judgment.

The question of the possibility of political philosophy was reduced to the philosophical issue of whether there was procedural and substantive rationality in ethical reasoning. The difficulty was not simply the collapse of the issues surrounding political theory into this monolithic philosophical problem but also the dubious character of the philosophical problem itself as well as the answers to it. Political theory, which already had a propensity to think in metatheoretical terms and to seek authoritative answers from philosophy, appropriated the standard version of the dilemma of postpositivist ethical theory.

Like philosophers of science who, when faced with a crisis in their account of science, asked whether objective scientific judgment is possible, philosophers faced with the traditional positivist account of rationality and its relegation of metaphysics and ethics to meaningless or only emotively significant claims asked whether moral reasoning is possible. In neither case were any real questions about either science or morals being posed. The assumption that such issues were at stake was a function of the philosopher's belief, or pretension, that philosophy underwrites life or that philosophy has or should have some authority over the practices of life that are its object. Such assumptions were adopted by political theory in part because they belonged to the philosophical ambience into which the field was drawn as well as because the increasingly interdisciplinary character of the field brought it into closer identity with philosophical discourse. But there was more to it. Given the historically characteristic conflation of political theory *in* and *about* politics and the self-interest attaching to that blurred distinction, it was only natural that political theory would equate its dilemmas and solutions with those of politics.

Although few political theorists actually took much ostensible notice of Arnold Brecht's claim about the "tragedy of 20th century political science" (1959:8), the problem he diagnosed was structurally the same as that which would dominate the field of political theory for the next generation. Whether it was termed relativism, which was the Continental favorite, or defined as a situation that "called into question the logical status of all ethical statements" (Laslett, 1956:ix), this was the issue that animated the discourse of political theory. As in the case of Brecht, this had been the problem at the core of the concerns of the émigrés. Although those more tied to the Anglo-American tradition of political theory were more wary of the historicism and natural law claims of individuals such as Strauss, the problem was basically the same. And so was the cause —positivism.

What was remarkable about this literature was the absence of any clear reference to a political problem. The standard but somewhat vague argument persisted that totalitarianism had bloomed in a climate of positivism and relativism and might do so again. But apart from occasional allusions, and the symbol of the "crisis of the West" held up by the myth of the tradition, there was little attempt even to suggest that in fact existential politics and morals were being swept away in a tide of relativism or lack of standards of judgment. The motivation in certain cases was a concern about ideology in politics, and though some suggested that it was in fact at an end, which meant that consensus could take the place of conflicting political judgment, others wanted to find a way to rise above it, or get below it, to more solid ground. Political concerns were not totally absent from this literature, but they were at best vaguely articulated. What *was* clearly at stake here, however, was the role of academic political theory both in the academy and in relation to politics. It identified itself with its ability to make authoritative normative claims about politics.

The whole dilemma cannot withstand scrutiny. For Brecht, the argument was that value justification had been endangered by scientific rationality, but he simply identified science with philosophical positivism and logical empiricism in the philosophy of science. He concluded that, despite the value of scientific reason, its "logical" implication—and its "seamy side"— was relativism and the inability to get from an "is" to an "ought" (1959:6–9, 118). The "tragedy" of political theory was, supposedly, the loss of rational foundations. Similarly, Laslett argued that positivism had "set up rigorous criteria of intelligibility" that "threatened to reduce traditional ethical systems to assemblages of nonsense," and "since political philosophy is, or was, an extension of ethics, the question has been raised whether political philosophy is possible at all" (1956:ix).

These arguments amounted to little more than philosophical truisms. They were not really about anything. Someone like Weldon might argue that references to political principles were logically outside the realm of rational discussion and that choices of principle were nothing more than decisions of commitment, and someone like Laslett might wonder whether or how ethical and political judgment was possible. But this was no different from the debates between skeptics and foundationalists in epistemology and the philosophy of science. Neither political nor scientific judgments were at stake—only the authority of philosophy and/or political theory to make them or underwrite them. They, of course, could do neither, but they persisted as if this were within their power and purpose. And this ensured the alienation of political theory.

Brecht's and Laslett's arguments are good examples of the cultural lag between political theory and philosophy. By the time they had articulated the dilemma of political theory in terms of the positivist theory of linguistic meaning, some of the most influential work in postpositivist ethical theory (e.g., Hare, 1952; Toulmin, 1950) had already appeared. This work, much of it inspired by Wittgenstein, contributed to exploding the positivist myth of the rationally deficient character of normative argument and judgment. And, just as similar work in the philosophy of science attempted to look more carefully at the internal structure of scientific reason in the context of scientific practice, it sought to reconstruct the autonomous character of moral reasoning. There were, however, at least two significant and related problems with this literature as it began to have its predictable impact on political theory. One involved the relationship between political theory and philosophy, and the other involved the character of this literature itself.

Just as it was a mistake to think that philosophical positivism signified that normative political theory was impossible, it was a mistake to think that the rejection of positivism made it possible—as if such an activity, if there actually were such an activity, depended on philosophical endorsement. The claim could be, and in some cases was, more modest. It was not that the great tradition was being resurrected but that it was possible for academic political theorists to think about critical and prescriptive analyses of politics as a reasonable kind of activity and that they need not feel inferior to empirical social science and theory. This was surely, in principle, a defensible notion, but if political theory and/or political philosophy were such a fragile enterprise that it required this kind of reinforcement one might well have wondered about its staying power.

There was, in fact, very little clear idea of what such an activity would concretely involve apart from the usual allusions to the great tradition. The idea that one can perform certain linguistic acts without speaking nonsense does not create a practice and define its relationship to politics, but the reassessment of the situation offered by Laslett and others (Laslett and Runciman, 1962), that the belief about the break in the tradition of political philosophy was premature, amounted to little more than this. Isaiah Berlin claimed that value judgments could not be reduced to empirical or merely logical assertions in a "pluralist society" where "ends collide," and therefore political philosophy was possible and could never "wholly perish from the earth" (1962: 6, 8–9, 33).

The well-known trilogy of statements about the fall and redemption of political philosophy, in succeeding volumes of *Philosophy, Politics, and Society*, ending with the observation that it was "alive again" (Laslett and Runciman, 1967), represented a general climate in the literature that saw "revival" in various forms, whether it was, as Laslett noted, the "prescriptive discussion of social and political issues" along with attention to "the methods and results of the social sciences" (Laslett and Runciman, 1962) or whether it was the work of individuals such as Strauss, Voegelin, and Arendt (e.g., Germino, 1967). But, again, apart from the untenable claim or assumption regarding the reconstitution of the great tradition, little was signified here except the growing differentiation and autonomy of academic political theory, which largely identified itself and its context in terms of the very positivist metatheoretical structure that created the artificial dilemma that shaped its understanding of its situation. It was an attempt to demonstrate that the category of normative theory or political philosophy did have content and to work out its relationship to social science.

Laslett argued that the rebirth of political theory was tied to the "impact of linguistic philosophy and behavioral science on social and political theory," and he took pains to disassociate the revival from the "*a priori* sociology," "disguised prescriptivism," and "grandiose" notions that had characterized the work of "traditional theorists" (Laslett and Runciman, 1967: 3–4). It was to be a chastened and more humble theoretical phoenix that would arise from the ashes of the tradition. There was much work to be done before it was possible to "undermine the orthodox fact-value distinction," make an impact on behavioral political science, and achieve a philosophical imprimatur that would "credit judgments of value with status of facts." But it seemed safe to say that "prescriptive discussion of political issues is not meaningless, and that both deductive argument and empirical evidence can be brought to bear on it" (3–4). This must have come as a great relief to political actors! Maybe what is most apparent here is the beginning of the institutionalization of political theory as it settled down to stake out its place in the new academic trivium.

By the mid-1960s this kind of argument had been extensively elaborated in some of the literature of the philosophy of social science. W. G. Runciman suggested that, despite "the positivistic excesses of some of its practitioners," the "autonomy of [empirical] political studies has been a useful development" (1963). Although the "logical relation between a (more or less empirical) proposition in political sociology and a (more or less prescriptive) proposition in political philosophy is a complicated and intractable problem," the former should not be understood as displacing "the sorts of utterances made by traditional political theorists" except in those cases where they "lacked evidence" or were simply trying to "justify" certain states of affairs rather than make empirical claims. Thus "political theory remains a separate, philosophical discipline which neither the positivism of political science nor of linguistic analysis has outmoded, though they both may have been very good for it," because "there has always been a necessary link between empirical conclusions about politics and political theories" (42).

What is clear in such claims is that there is no real confrontation of the issues involving the relationship between political science and political theory and there is no significant analysis of either enterprise and its relationship to politics. It is a discussion that remains bound to the "value/fact fetish" and is little more than an extrapolation of it. Reflected in such arguments were the claims characteristic of the new work in metaethics, such as the idea that rationality in morals is a matter of good reasons that are often factual in character. As Runciman suggested, "whatever philosophy of politics a person puts forward, we may ask him his reasons for believing it" (1963 : 168). Probably no one outside academic political theory ever thought otherwise. These "discoveries" and "solutions," cast at the level of the idea that the factual assumptions in moral judgments make them amenable to empirical test and that factual claims presuppose positions that make absolute value freedom impossible, had no real significance for the life and death of political theory. Nevertheless, Runciman concluded, from this logic, that "neither the philosophers nor the social scientists . . . are likely to get on very well without each other" and that "the empirical and philosophical study of politics may have more to gain from a maximum contact with each other" than had been previously assumed. Much like medieval faith and reason, political philosophy and political science cannot displace one another and in fact complement one another (86, 108, 134). It was, of course, quite true that they could not get

on without one another, any more, for example, than relativism and absolutism or many other metatheoretical dichotomies.

More was involved, however, than simply a matter of form, the per-
petuation of the positivist framework, and begged questions about the
relationship between political theory and politics. Not only was the framework the same, but in this attempt to interpret the situation as the functional, if not the historical, reconstitution of the great tradition in terms of
the complementarity of normative and empirical discourse or political
philosophy and social science, many of the other old myths about ephemeral values and given facts and their respective languages were carried forward. In the search for the autonomy of normative theory, the positivist
image of science and the myth of the given was largely accepted and the
old Weberian structure was unreflectively reappropriated. The characteristic picture that emerged was something like the concept of separate but
functionally entwined powers in the United States constitution—two logically distinct spheres, but with elements of each mixed with the other to
ensure checks and balances as well as complementarity and ultimately
common purpose. Charles Taylor's argument (1967) was another paradigm case. It is here that Wolin's critique of Weber might be appropriately
applied.

Taylor argued that in social science "the adoption of a framework of
explanation carries with it the adoption of the 'value-slope' implicit in it,"
with its "gamut of possible politics and policies" and "conception of human needs, wants and purposes." Thus it "secretes a notion of good and
a set of valuations" and "cannot stop developing normative theory"
(1967:42, 55−57). But, Taylor claimed, not only do values inform empirical social science in this way (a claim, by the way, that even the most
hardhearted positivist never disputed), but "the business of normative theory, making recommendations and evaluating different courses of action,"
must be tempered by the "facts." The "findings of political science" are
relevant for "establishing particular sets of values and undermining others."
If we would but think about it, this is what the "greats" of the tradition
teach us—that "one form of inquiry is virtually inseparable from the
other" and that we must "recognize a convergence between science and
normative theory in the field of politics" (26−27, 32).

This kind of argument, which by the 1970s became a dominant mode
of rationalizing the situation in academic political theory, was not coherent. The analysis was still bound by the vestiges of the logical structure
and theory of linguistic meaning characteristic of positivism. The idea was
still that there are two basic types of meaning and that such activities as
political science and political philosophy (which was a quite vague entity

apart from constant references to the great tradition) could be understood as coterminous with the respective types. There was a systematic conflation of types of propositions and the relationship between them, on the one hand, and activities and their universes of discourse, on the other. And the idea remained that "facts" are somehow in the end incorrigibly "given," while values can be supported or undermined by reference to them. The whole scheme did not actually describe anything and solved no real problems of any practice in either social science or politics. Political theory was once again trying to understand itself and find a role in terms of philosophical images. And, like the philosophy of science to which political scientists turned for sustenance, the metatheoretical arguments that inspired these solutions were not without their problems.

# 5
## *The End of Political Theory*

"Liberation" is a historical and not a mental act.
MARX

POSTPOSITIVIST work in metaethics had an impact on political theory for a number of reasons. In part, it was simply the usual
deference to philosophical authority, the utility of the scheme for solving (philosophically) the problem of normative judgment as it had been
framed in the positivist tradition, and its provision, at least conceptually, for reintegrating conflicting elements of academic political theory
in a period of professional consolidation. But above all the literature
seemed to offer a new way to escape from relativism and achieve some
form of judgment that transcended political contexts and ideology.

If this literature had been content with simply establishing the autonomy of moral reasoning and investigating the logic and types of reasons
characteristic of moral argument, in much the way that Kuhn and
others had approached the philosophy of science, the situation might
have been considerably different. Although this type of work was not
absent from the literature, the most influential treatises adopted a much
more rationalistic approach. The aim, much like that of the traditional
philosophy of science, was to find *the* nature of moral reasoning and
*the* ground on which it was based. Most of the work aimed at something more than demonstrating the descriptive inaccuracy of the
emotivist theory of ethics and the deficiency of its notion of validity as
effectiveness (e.g., Stevenson, 1945). The traditional epistemological
quest was evident in this literature, which sought procedural and substantive grounds of moral judgment.

Very early on, Toulmin set out to demonstrate, in the face of positivism, how reasoning in ethics was possible and how there could be, and were, "factual reasons" for "ethical conclusions" (1950). His arguments, however, were still caught, at least initially (cf. 1958) in the binary framework of fact/value, description/evaluation, consequentialist/deontological, and science/morals. He was still bound by the idea that there must be *a* fundamental way in which "is" relates to "ought," *a* particular structure of moral reasoning, and *a* basic purpose or function for these spheres of language and activity that constitute their ultimate justification. In the case of ethics, the purpose was to "harmonize people's actions" (1950:145). This was clearly a substantive claim disguised as a logical and descriptive feature of moral reasoning. It is easy to see how political philosophers could come away from Toulmin's work with the notion that they had discovered the how and why of doing normative theory and solving related problems, even though this clearly was not his basic concern. Other work, that of Hare, for example, was clearly more didactic.

The spell of the fact/value scheme was indeed strong in Hare's work (1952). Although his aim was to defend the autonomy and rationality of prescriptive discourse, he was equally intent on demonstrating that moral claims could be supported by "descriptive" statements. This he attempted to do by showing that value claims have a certain descriptive meaning that allows descriptions to be logically relevant to, and good reasons for, prescriptive claims. It is, parenthetically, not too difficult to see the basis of the kind of rapprochement between empirical and normative theory advanced by Runciman and Taylor. The problem for Hare, then, became one of figuring out how one *logically* could bridge the gap between these linguistic forms if, as he insisted, they are fundamentally heterogeneous. His answer was formal deductive logic. Because there was, in his view, no getting logically (deductively) from an "is" to an "ought," the major premise in a moral argument (syllogism) was a universal moral principle which, in turn, was ultimately a matter of decision and commitment.

Hare's notion of reasoning as justification was as limited and constraining as that of the deductivists in the philosophy of science. In addition, he, as well as Toulmin, and like the philosophers of science, did not focus on particular moral issues and problems at all. Moral argument was simply equated with a certain logical form of language (prescriptive) identified in terms of its presumptive function (reaching consensus), and the examples were hypothetical paradigm cases. The liberal ideology reflected in these supposedly "logical" claims about reasoning is apparent. All along, however, the problem was not simply how to get from an "is" to an "ought," or from basic assumptions to particular judgments, but the ultimate basis of justification. As in the philosophy of science, the problem was how to justify the theoretical principles, and Hare's answer was not much different from that of the logical empiricists.

In *Freedom and Reason* (1963), Hare turned explicitly to the question of the apparent conflict between the decisionist basis of morals and reasoned judgment. Still embracing deductivism, but now of the Popperian variety, he argued that it was a matter not only of deducing particular moral judgments from general principles but of testing hypothetically universal principles in terms of the acceptability of their logically deduced (actual or hypothetical) consequences, that is, the particular prescriptions that they yielded. The question, of course, was the criterion of acceptability. Hare argued that what could be depended on here were individual "inclinations," which would be equivalent to observations of fact in science, serve as the foundations of moral knowledge, and give meaningful content to moral principles. His assumption was that "people's inclinations about most of the most important matters in life tend to be the same" (1963:97), because (except in the case of fanatics and others who are outside morality anyway) everyone is governed by "self-interest." When our principles are hypothetically universalized, and finally to the point where we would see them applying to ourselves, we would all tend to reach the same conclusion about their acceptability, just as dedicated scientists would tend to agree on the same observable facts.

The arguments of Hare are significant as an example of the direction being taken in metaethics and related work in political philosophy. First of all, the arguments were not really about the language of morals at all in the sense of the claims and reasoning embedded in moral practice. The subject was supposedly "moral" concepts (e.g., good) and formal logic, but neither the concepts nor the logic were peculiar to morality. It was certainly not about what Peter Winch has called the particularities of morals, any more than logical empiricist philosophy of science was about the particularities of science. Although Hare argued that his analysis was relevant for the description, explanation, criticism, and improvement of moral reasoning, the discussion was in fact in terms of deductive logic in a context of hypothetical and highly structured artificial examples and somewhat limited definitions of the purpose and scope of moral reasoning. Second, as in all such cases, the highly abstract model of rationality reflected somewhat concealed, but definite, substantive notions of morality. In Hare's peculiar Kantian/Hobbesian structure, the "logical" thesis is clearly in effect a defense of liberal utilitarian values and of the ultimate identity of instrumental rationality and morality. All of these characteristics would become the attributes of alienated political theory.

Attention to the structure of moral reasoning was in many respects a great advance over the positivist dismissal of the subject, but it still reflected philosophy's desire to underwrite the rationality of the practice toward which it turned its attention and to suggest that philosophy had discovered the basis for criticism and improvement. And almost always it affirmed, at least indirectly, some set of substantive values associated with that practice. It was a search for the philosophical grounds of moral certainty. There is no doubt that conceptual analysis and the analysis of moral reasoning, inspired by Wittgenstein and linguistic philosophy, opened up new ways of doing political theory, exemplified by work such as that featured in the continuing series of *Philosophy, Politics, and Society* and other literature in this analytical tradition. But, for the most part, this work was only categorically about politics and political problems. And exactly what it understood itself to be doing by doing what it did was not entirely clear in all cases.

Much of it, however, was an attempt to reach methodological and substantive grounds of authoritative political judgment—to answer the question of "how rational political theory is possible" (e.g., Kettler, 1967), just as philosophical ethics attempted to answer the question of how moral judgment is possible or philosophers of science attempted to demonstrate how scientific objectivity and certainty were possible. Often these notions of rationalism and critical rationalism were employed as ways of providing an epistemological justification of liberal democracy or some other real or hypothetical state of affairs. James Ward Smith, for example (and T. L. Thorson, 1962), suggested that the fact of human "fallibilism" demanded that in science, morals, and politics the basic categorical of rationality must be "Never block the road to inquiry," and thus "the justification of democracy is methodological" (1957:109). Increasingly complex variations on this theme would distinguish much of the literature of political theory during the next two decades.

The idea was that there was a dilemma in politics, sometimes perennial and sometimes part of a modern crisis, resulting from an inability to provide reasoned justification for values. The difficulties with this position had at least three important dimensions. First, the assumption that this was a real political problem and anything more than a projection of a philosophical problem springing from positivism was seldom, if ever, convincingly supported. The idea of a general crisis of moral judgment was a philosophical myth to justify a philosophical solution. Second, although there may have been reason to suggest that one of the defining characteristics of moral, and political, discourse is the essentially contested character of many concepts and judgments, what was at least implicit in most of this literature was a concern about the basis of substantive closure or a way of arriving at it. In effect, much of this analysis regarding the language of morals and moral reasoning was a form of revived rationalism, transcendentalism, and methodism that aimed at reducing morality and politics to a moral code and a particular structure of justice. The purpose was to attain moral agreement and justify it. It was not just a matter of pointing out that there was a rational structure, and good reasons, in morals. It was a matter of demonstrating what in general that structure was, or must be, and what kinds of reasons really were good ones. Third, the question of the relationship of metaethics and metapolitical theory to morals and politics was not carefully considered, although the assumptions were relatively prominent.

Postpositivism in ethical philosophy appealed to political theorists because it offered a way to deconstruct the false philosophical dilemmas regarding normative reasoning and opened up the idea of the investigation of politics and of political discourse as an autonomous object of investigation. This, however, was only in part the case, and it was not the basic cue to which political theorists responded. The analyses of political concepts that began to appear, and which culminated in Rawls's study of justice, were in many ways illuminating and useful, but they had little more to do with actual political life and language than most metaethics had to do with actual moral issues. Although they usually were in some attenuated way parasitic on some set of substantive values and abstractly reflected a certain kind of practice, they largely represented a way of doing political philosophy without really engaging politics except in a somewhat categorical sense. An underlying purpose was to find authoritative philosophical criteria that transcended mere *political* rationality.

Richard Flathman, for example, following the lead of Toulmin and Hare, notes that "the purpose of moral reasoning is to guide conduct" (1966: 186). This may in some general sense be factually correct, but the idea that there is something that can be called *the* purpose of moral reasoning (or science, politics, etc.) is dubious. And it is even more dubious that it can be taken as definitionally correct and constitute the major premise in moral reasoning. But what is still more contentious is the claim that "the point of metaethics is to facilitate moral decisions" (xiv). It is, however, on the basis of this assumption that Flathman's analysis, for example, of the concept of "public interest" and public-interest reasoning as a species of moral reasoning proceeds. He argues that it is the responsibility of public officials to use their authority to serve the public interest, and "they must ["ought" to] utilize the decision criteria required by the logic of 'public interest' in reaching and defending public policy decisions" (189). This logic, he claims, is philosophically "specifiable" and "defensible." It is inherent in our language, which is part of our public life, and it provides criteria for the description, explanation, evaluation, and procedural facilitation of public decision making that are particularly needed in a time when "the destiny of mankind is in the hands of the state" (191–94).

The question of the relationship between academic political theory and politics is a complex one, both descriptively and prescriptively, and it is not one that can be settled in any general noncontextual manner. But this issue has been either neglected or assumed to be settled on the basis of the idea that academic political theory speaks to politics with rational authority. This notion is, of course, most characteristic of the work of individuals such as Strauss, but it is hardly absent from political theory practiced as conceptual analysis. Here political theory still speaks at least, as Hanna Pitkin claims, with therapeutic force. Pitkin's analysis of Wittgenstein suggests many ways in which linguistic analysis might facilitate criticism and understanding in political analysis and the analysis of political concepts, but the concern runs deeper—the issue in the end is "political theory and the modern predicament" (1972: 316).

What Pitkin means by the modern predicament is not unlike the other notions of modernity that surface in political theory. It is the idea of the paralysis of judgment in the face of imperious and impervious social structures and the collapse of traditional intellectual authority. "All significant modern thought," she claims, is "a response to this predicament and an attempt to escape it" (1972: 317). What is clear in her description of this predicament, however, is that both the problem and the solution are philosophical images. It is not really the dilemmas of politics that are under investigation in considerations of matters such as "total doubt and the sense of unreality" but the dilemmas of philosophy. It may be quite true, as Cavell, Rorty, and, often, Pitkin suggest, that what Wittgenstein, as well as certain other modern philosophers, offers, or what we can gain from this work, is a way of breaking the pictures that hold us captive in both philosophy and everyday life. But something more is at stake in Pitkin's idea of a "Wittgensteinian way of theorizing about the political" (325).

Unlike such theorists as Plato and Marx who, Pitkin suggests, distorted their own subject matter in their attempt to deal with its problems, Wittgenstein might offer a more concrete and practicable way "to liberate us from the paralyzing weight of our alienation" (Pitkin, 1967:328). What is it, however, that is really at the core of the modern predicament and our alienation that Wittgenstein can aid us with? It is, as for Arendt, the lack of "some foundation in stable truth" (329). Pitkin does not suggest that Wittgenstein offers political theory a new version of the failed foundationalisms of the past and their quest for certainty, but she does suggest that he offers something to take their place that sounds very much like what Rorty would later speak of as edification. When we realize that foundations belong to our human conventions, our language games and forms of life, we can face our problems more realistically and, like the better aspects of the implications of the work of Nietzsche, Marx, Freud, and Einstein, learn to face up to the pluralism and relativism that are simply the human condition. It is not a doctrine of resignation but one of critical self-reflection that restores to us the power for creative change.

In this argument, there is a subtle move from the unexceptionable to the questionable. What Wittgenstein offers, it might be agreed, is a basis for solving the old philosophical dilemmas and rejecting the quest for transcendental certainty. But what this means for the practice of political theory is not clear, because, Pitkin suggests, there cannot really be a Wittgensteinian political theory. The question is how, exactly, Wittgenstein relates to political theory, and how political theory relates to politics. Pitkin suggests that Wittgenstein was "truly not a political theorist but a philosopher, giving us a clear vision of the current state of affairs. Nor, evidently, is his teaching of a form readily accessible to large numbers of people" (1967:339).

In Pitkin's case, it seems, the argument is still that philosophy is the teacher of political theory, and political theory still has the ability and authority to teach politics. How it can accomplish this, as a practical matter, is never really confronted except to suggest that university education is the key to the dilemmas of our public life. But the idea is that political theory, at least in principle, has this authority because it sees clearly what the average person cannot see. Following Wittgenstein and other philosophers, it can distinguish between appearance and reality, and thus, even though it may not have *the* truth, it still represents truth vis-à-vis politics. The idea of epistemic and moral privilege is not dead even though in Pitkin's case it remains more in form than in substance. Here truth, as with Flathman, is to be drawn out less by looking at actual political discourse and forms of politics than by an examination of our public language and political concepts (e.g., Pitkin, 1967), which supposedly bridge the gap between theory and practice or philosophy and everyday life.

Political theory has become so absorbed with justifying itself as a practice, seeking an identity, and securing some ground of rationality that would validate its claims to authority that it has increasingly failed to speak to or about politics as either events or a kind of phenomenon. The search for identity has sealed it within the domain of philosophy from which it sought a self-image. It should not be surprising that John Rawls's *Theory of Justice* (1971) became the most important political theory event of the era.

Since the publication of that work, a considerable portion of the literature of political theory has been devoted to explicating, defending, and criticizing it. This in itself tells us a great deal about political theory which has essentially made academic texts and other literary artifacts its principal object of analysis. Rawls's book might be, and has been, understood in various ways, ranging from the claim that it is a validation that the great tradition has finally been resurrected in both body and soul and that it has directly descended from Kant and Mill to the suggestion that it is an abstract but systematic apology for liberal ideology. What it is above all, however, is a quintessential example of contemporary academic philosophy. This is not necessarily to denigrate it, but it is to call into question the idea that political theory can find in it what it seeks.

Rawls's work is not about any human practice; it is not about any state of affairs. It is about concepts and logic. But even then it is about the force of concepts such as promising, freedom, equality, and justice and not about the use and criteria of their application in any determinate practice. It is about justice in the same way that logical empiricism is about scientific explanation. The issues are philosophical issues located in the context of philosophical discourse and only categorically about political matters. And this is the case with much of the literature that has grasped the imagination of political theory in recent years, such as the work of Nozick (1974), Dworkin (1977), and Ackerman (1980). They are works that attempt to answer questions about the grounds of political obligation and the bases of rights in the same way that epistemology sought to answer questions about the foundations of knowledge and rationality. To the extent that they do relate to politics, they constitute a kind of displaced or philosophized ideology. "Justice" in these works usually amounts to little more than a philosophical version or "extension of our considered judgments" (Rawls, 1971:195), which constitutes both premises and conclusions. By attaching themselves to this realm of discourse, political theorists have become alienated from theoretical issues regarding politics—issues they have rejected in order to play the role of master political moralist.

It should not be surprising that much of this work seeks a basis in

Kant—the paradigm epistemologist and metaethical philosopher. But Kant is employed, as in the case of Hare and others who have revitalized the universalizability thesis, to reconstitute an image of liberalism. The model is abstract, in the sense that it seeks to rise above all contingency, but the argument, despite its obvious but rarefied ideological content, is also so severed, with regard to both its analysis and its prescriptions, from any concrete political context that it is meaningful only as an academic conversation. It is an attempt to get a kind of Kantian universalism in step with a neoliberal model of instrumental economic rationality.

There was a time, in the 1940s and 1950s, when the debate about liberalism, which in many ways gave rise to the structure of contemporary political theory, had real political content. But both the image and numerous critiques of that image (e.g., Wolff, 1969) have been drawn away into a realm of estranged philosophical discourse that is meaningful only to the participants. Liberalism is characteristically discussed as if it were a historical and political phenomenon with its roots in Locke, when, as the subject of the contemporary literature, it is only a philosophical construct opposed by other philosophical constructs. The debate about liberalism, its end, its revival, its idea of justice, and so on, is not really a debate about any political practice or belief. Like many discussions of democracy (e.g., Barber, 1984), these works are discussions of philosophical concepts and academic hypotheticals. What keeps the discussion going, in addition to professional survival, is the search for the philosophical grounds of authoritative political judgment.

Michael Walzer has claimed that the "prestige" of this work on neoliberalism is today very high and has had significant influence on those who shape public policy. And he believes that this influence is grounded precisely on the fact that philosophers are once again doing work that "raises again, after a long hiatus, the possibility of finding objective truths" (1983:75). Walzer neither substantiates this common claim about influence nor gives any evidence to support what he takes to be its basis. Even if such influence exists and even if the cause is correctly stated, there is no obvious reason to be sanguine about this relationship. Walzer may applaud what he believes to be the practical influence of Rawls and Dworkin on practical jurisprudence, but would, or does, he approve equally of the influence of right-wing natural law? Or need one be pleased, for example, with the "prestige" of logical empiricism and the impact of its search for objective knowledge on the practice of social science? Walzer recognizes that in a democratic society there is at least implicitly a particularly sharp conflict between the authority of the philosopher and the political authority of the community, and he concludes that "democracy has no claims in the philosophical realm, and philosophers have no special rights in the political community" (98–99). But the issue is not simply one of complementarity and mutual tolerance.

Walzer performs the typical move of casting the academic political philosopher in the image of the heroes of the great tradition and philosophers such as Descartes, but this is a shaky parallel that serves to mystify rather than clarify the relationship. He claims, much like Strauss and Arendt, that "the political philosopher must separate himself from the political community, cut himself loose from the affective ties and conventional ideas," in order to ask and answer the deep and general questions about political life (1983:93). But the alienation of Plato and most other classic figures, their relationship to politics, and their alternative visions were of a very different sort than those characteristic of academic political philosophy (see Gunnell, 1979b, chap.5). Walzer's basic criterion for differentiating between political theory and politics manifests rather clearly one of the root assumptions behind the contemporary alienation of political theory. He argues that although the function of the democratic political community is that of "authorization," it remains the case that "the most general truths of politics and morality can only be validated in the philosophical realm; and that realm has its place outside, beyond, separate from every political community" (1983:98).

The idea that political theory, in imperious isolation from the real institutions, interests, and political processes, can proceed to formulate and answer questions about political right and its criteria of validity dooms it to alienation. The relationship of political theory to politics in the sense of issues regarding such matters as what has been, is, can, and should be the influence and posture of the former is a very complex problem and one for which there are probably few general answers. But it is one with which political theory must grapple situationally rather than adopt the self-satisfied stance that its task is one of "validation." Validation also belongs to the realm of politics. Political theory might contest it just as it also might, if it really were the successor to the classics, contest authorization. It is precisely the pretension that validation is something distinct from practice and reserved to philosophy that has brought much of contemporary philosophy to its present condition and set it on a futile course in search of the foundations of knowledge and moral obligation. As long as political theory charts the same course, it will drift farther and farther away from the continent of politics it professes to seek.

One way, the common way, to think about what is happening in contemporary political theory is to conceive of the situation in terms of such matters as a controversy between rights based liberalism and more communitarian, Hegelian, and neo-Marxist positions. But this misses the more important elements that each shares. These include a basic alienation from the particularities of political phenomena as well as from questions regarding the substantive nature of such phenomena and the pursuit of transcendentalism. Again, the concern about relativism is in the end a concern about the grounds of judgment in academic political theory in relationship to politics. This is the only dilemma of modernity that is really at issue. Alasdair MacIntyre's arguments are typical (1982).

MacIntyre suggests that our ability to make judgments has been disabled by the failure of the Enlightenment's individualistic theory of rationality and the relativist implications of the claims of Weber, Nietzsche, and positivist or emotivist ethical theory. But, once again, he mistakes an academic perplexity for a political one and at the same time assumes that the former is the cause of the latter and the site of a solution. So, MacIntyre suggests, what is required is a return to Aristotle and to a notion of moral objectivity based on a teleological view of human nature and embedded in communitarian social structures that would allow us (whoever exactly "we" are) to treat moral and evaluative statements as true or false or as factual statements.

Such an argument, maybe even in the work of someone like Strauss, might be construed as having a certain rhetorical force and possibility. But like most such arguments in academic political theory, it is really about nothing political and addressed to no one outside the academy. What it does represent is the transcendental urge, but that urge, displayed in the world of academic political theory, is, much like what Montesquieu describes in the case of the eunuchs of Tonquin, the manifestation of a situation in which "the enterprises of despair become a kind of enjoyment." Yet it is not even that, for even the political passion is often only an intellectual affectation.

Although the relationship of political theory to politics is, in general, not a matter that can, or should, be settled categorically, certain aspects of that relationship are essentially given as long as the respective activities remain conventionally differentiated and constituted in the general forms that now exist. One such aspect involves the fact that politics is the object of knowledge in political theory. The degree to which philosophy and political theory, or any second-order enterprise, accept this is a measure of their authenticity. What has characterized much of contemporary philosophy, however—both the philosophy of science and metaethics, and consequently political theory—is precisely the fact that it has turned toward a philosophical analysis of philosophically constituted objects. No matter what attitude—descriptive, prescriptive, evaluative, explanatory—political theory may take toward politics, it must confront implicitly or explicitly, claims about the nature of political phenomena.

The acceptance of the metatheoretical structure represented in the "value/fact fetish" propelled political theory, even in its rejection of positivism, on a quest for the foundations of normative judgment, which trapped it within the discourse of postpositivist metaethics. Similarly, its unhappiness with the positivist image of empirical inquiry inspired it to reconstitute the other side of the equation, and this led in the direction of an attachment to postpositivist metatheoretical work in the philosophy of social science regarding the nature of social scientific explanation. Just as political theory substituted claims about normative rationality for normative claims, it substituted claims about the theoretical bases of social scientific understanding for substantive theoretical claims about social (and political) phenomena.

There is no need to be generally unsympathetic to the literature that has characteristically been considered a landmark in the postpositivist philosophy of social science (e.g., Schutz, 1967; Winch, 1958, 1972). Without the presence of this literature, as well as the work of individuals such as Kuhn, the deficiencies of the positivist perspective and the very idea of alternative notions of social scientific explanation and its autonomy might have been a long time surfacing. In retrospect, there is, however, much that one might say in criticism of this literature. For example, it was in general completely mesmerized by the positivist image of science, which it, as much as its opponents, identified with the practice of natural science. This assumption significantly shaped the arguments, which were almost as much arguments designed to justify the distinction between social science and natural science as they were arguments about the nature of social scientific understanding itself. This acceptance of positivism as an adequate account of natural science caused no end of trouble for those in political theory who were influenced by this literature.

This literature was no more clear about what it was doing than was positivistic philosophy of social science—that is, whether it was saying something about the character of actual social scientific practice, offering an approach to that practice, or providing a philosophical account of what the logic and epistemology of such practice must in effect be, given the nature of social phenomena. It simply did not do the first. It often implicitly, but erroneously, seemed to suggest that it was, or could be, doing the second. But it could only reasonably be construed as doing the third. Although this literature, which came from different philosophical traditions, had quite different concerns in many respects, it seemed, at a certain level of abstraction, to be making basically the same argument about social scientific explanation. There were a number of closely allied themes and arguments in Anglo-American linguistic analysis and Continental phenomenology (which to some degree had a common philosophical ancestry; note Wittgenstein). But, whatever might be said in criticism and defense of this literature, the basic problem was less with the work itself than with how it was received by political theory and the uses to which it was put.

Although this literature did address the question of the character of social phenomena and justified its account of the logic and epistemology of social scientific explanation on this basis, it did not develop extended and substantive claims about the nature of social reality. Similarly, its critique of the practice of the social sciences was mediated through abstract images of positivism. There was already an inversion here of theory and epistemology. Theoretical claims were employed in a rather ad hoc manner in defense of an epistemological argument about the nature of explanation and human understanding. It was basically an argument about *understanding* rather than an argument about *what was to be understood.*

Political theorists engaged in the critique of positivism in social science had sometimes made the same basic mistake as behavioralists by assuming that alternative notions in the philosophy of science offered an approach or framework for inquiry. The same fundamental mistake was represented in turning to the new work in metaethics as a way of doing political theory. The same problem was also now evident in the manner in which political theorists construed postpositivist philosophy of social science as an alternative method and a theory of political inquiry. It was not that this work was actually utilized in the practice of inquiry in any clear sense. It became, instead, the basis on which an *idea* of theory and theoretical practice was advanced—an idea that found part of its justification in an attempt to reconstitute the empirical side of empirical/normative division.

Even more so than in the case of normative theory and metaethics, secondary and tertiary accounts of this literature were retailed by philosophers and political theorists as paradigms of empirical inquiry. Such accounts were offered either as a replacement for positivistic social science (which was usually simply represented in terms of the positivist reconstruction rather than as an analysis of the actual practice of social science) or as an "interpretative" alternative to the "naturalist" approach (e.g., Bluhm, 1982; Moon, 1975) that would take account of both the "humanistic" or intentionalist and the more "scientific" and nomological dimensions of social behavior and action. Part of what is apparent in such formulations is still the hold of the fact/value dichotomy and the idea of the need to give meaning to each category and find complementarity between them. What also persists is the notion of theory as an instrument—as a perspective or way of looking at kinds of phenomena that are in some way constituted independent of theory. The problem, however, is not one of reconciling and deploying complementary philosophical accounts of inquiry. It is one of engaging, in depth, the issue of what constitutes social phenomena.

To say, for example, that natural scientific explanation is, or should be, of a certain sort is the kind of claim of which one might well be wary today. If recent work in the philosophy of science has any significance for social science, it is the message that any talk about science as a whole is a dangerous abstraction. The positivist assumption was that there is a philosophically specifiable paradigm of rationality that was most clearly approximated in the various natural sciences, and thus one might speak of the logic of scientific explanation, which by necessity underlaid all successful science. To talk about scientific explanation, however, is at best to talk about an abstraction based on certain family resemblances between scientific practices. The criteria of scientific explanation in any particular case are a function of a disciplinary matrix, which has at its core certain theoretical claims that constitute the domain or domains of facticity. In this sense, any philosophical account of scientific explanation presupposes certain substantive theories. This is why there has been a conscious convergence in recent years of the history and philosophy of science. Any such convergence has been fundamentally absent from the social sciences.

Most of the arguments in the philosophy of social science are pursued outside any theoretical context. They are the philosophical legacy of the continuing *Methodenstreit* spawned at the turn of the century, and they suffer from essentially the same difficulty as their positivist counterpart in their attempt to state, almost in the form of a Kantian deduction, the nature of social scientific explanation. For the most part, these arguments are simply an extrapolation of some philosophical account of human understanding. The basic claims are hardly new. On the Continental side, they reach back to the mid-eighteenth century and the German hermeneutical tradition, and, on the English side, they are rooted in the work of people like Collingwood. Recent work in phenomenology and linguistic analysis reinvigorated the respective positions and provided a convenient rhetorical critical counterpart to the positivist legitimation of modern social science. The difficulty, as in the case of positivism, was that philosophical claims about explanation were confused with theory and modes of theoretical practice.

It might be the case (e.g., Gunnell, 1968;1973) that, at a rather high level of abstraction, the arguments of individuals such as Winch and

Schutz did provide, as had Weber, a reasonable overview of the nature of social scientific explanation—to the extent that social science is, and should be, concerned with illuminating forms of social action and its artifacts. For the social scientist unhappy with positivism, this work provided, as had Kuhn, critical purchase and an indication of a direction of fruitful theorizing. But that was not its principal fate. Its fate was to be repeated and reprinted ad nauseam as part of a continuing affirmation that social inquiry was not like natural science. It was trivialized and distorted by positivist philosophers (e.g., Rudner, 1966) attempting to defend their flagging enterprise. It became one pole in an attempt to provide a synthetic philosophical account of social scientific explanation that would take account of both positivist and humanistic positions, or what commonly came to be understood as the difference and relationship between "explanation and understanding" (e.g., Von Wright, 1971). And it became one of the foci in a debate about whether social science could posit transcendental grounds of rationality (e.g., Wilson, 1970). Theory and metatheory were effectively inverted.

The alienated character of this "idea" of a social science, which became the concern of political theory by the early 1970s, is well illustrated in the arguments of Charles Taylor, which present nearly a paradigm case of the difficulties. Taylor had earlier attempted to develop a philosophical reconstruction of the explanation of human action that challenged the behaviorist and positivist assumptions of much of psychology and focused on its purposive or teleological character (1964;1970*a*;1970*b*). Drawing inspiration from the increased concern with hermeneutics in the work of individuals like Gadamer, Ricoeur, and Habermas, as well as the general thrust of the postpositivist philosophy of social science, he suggests that the concept of "sciences of man" can best be explicated in terms of an analogue with interpretation (1977). At least three features of Taylor's argument demand critical examination.

First, he does not offer, even at a general level, any coherent theory of human action that would make sense out of the mentalistic vocabulary (beliefs, attitudes, etc.) he employs or the idea of a "subject," which he claims is the bearer and receiver of meaning. Second, he assumes that the positivist/empiricist model is an adequate account of explanation in natural science and provides an adequate contrast model for understanding the demands of social scientific explanation. And, third, it is reasonably clear, although not explicit, that his real concern is less with the details of what an interpretative social science might involve than with seeking some form of quasi-transcendental judgment as the basis of authority for political philosophy.

It may be the case that interpretation is the proper category in terms of which to think about social scientific inquiry, but Taylor offers no detailed account of either the concept of interpretation or of what would be necessary to give substance to such a concept, namely, a theory of what is to be interpreted. Instead he presents the typical general image of human practices, including politics, as a world grounded in intersubjectively shared meanings belonging to linguistically constituted modes of "social reality" that form "the background of social action" (rep. 1977: 119, 121). From this he rapidly extrapolates an image of the requirements of at least a large portion of social scientific explanation that must rely like any interpretation on "insight" and "intuitions" and remain bound to the limitations of the "hermeneutical circle" (126–27). He never really rejects either the philosophy or the practice of positivist social science but only suggests that it is too narrow and partial an approach.

The problem is not that Taylor's claims are wrong but rather that they do not say very much, or at least anything new. There is nothing here that goes beyond the arguments, for example, of Winch, A. R. Louch (1966), or numerous secondary accounts of such claims. Ricoeur, for example (1971), elaborated the text-analogue argument much more fully. But this judgment must be juxtaposed to the intention of Taylor's argument, which involves, first of all, an attempt to differentiate natural science and social science.

Taylor wants to distinguish "the criteria of judgment in a hermeneutical science" from what "logical empiricists" represent as the demands of science in general, that is, "verification" in terms of "brute data" or those facts "whose validity cannot be questioned by offering another interpretation or reading," but he suggests that "the progress of natural science has lent great credibility to this epistemology" (rep. 1977: 104–5). It is difficult to see how, after Kuhn and company and the widespread discussion, in both philosophy and social science (e.g., Gunnell, 1969; Wolin, 1968a;1969) of the problem of the disjunction between this image of science and the actual practice of science, one could simply equate the two. But such an equation is consistently made by Taylor. His whole discussion of social science turns on the contrast with natural science as a mode of investigation characterized by "certainty" rooted in "brute data," universal predictive laws, and the like.

Although Taylor notes that the philosophy of science must be viewed critically, particularly with respect to the empiricist tradition in which "epistemology dictates ontology" by assuming the existence of "brute data" (1980: 89), he is quite willing to extend this model as a description and prescription for much of social science. The reason for this willingness is, first, that his basic concern is to demonstrate the uniqueness and autonomy of social science as interpretation—to create a distinct image of interpretative as opposed to natural scientific theory. But, second, he has a considerable stake in the idea of certainty, the overcoming of Cartesian doubt, and the concept of a knowing subject. To undermine it in natural science would surely be to undermine it in social science.

In response to the relativism that he fears is propagated in the work of individuals such as Foucault, Taylor claims that "the advance of our civilization of a scientific understanding of the natural world" is something "we have every reason to believe represents a significant gain of truth" (1984:179). Taylor does not specify what those extrascientific reasons are, but they have to do with science's instrumental success and the way its rationality has dispelled social myths of the past. In Taylor's argument can be seen the same transcendental urge that has characteristically animated academic political theory. It is not so much any practice of interpretative social science that he is concerned with or the real differences and similarities between it and natural science. It is, despite the bow toward subjectivity, a concern with reconstructed grounds of moral judgment. The notion of meaning and intuition that had plagued earlier forms of the idea of an interpretative social science as *Verstehen* could be reconstituted, as had already been demonstrated by Winch and others, along the lines of a more objective notion of public language that made access to other minds a more cogent notion. But, in various but sometimes vague ways, it also seemed to promise grounds for something quite different—the authoritative judgments of an interpreter who not only could discover what people believed and, consequently, why they acted in the way that they did but could determine what they should believe and how they should act.

For Taylor, meaning is to be grounded in something he vaguely refers to as a "subject," because, he assumes, without such "appeal to a subject," social meanings are "arbitrary" (rep. 1977:102). It does not seem that this notion of a transcendental subject, which Taylor admitted is not "unproblematical," is necessary to a notion of social meaning, but this is one of the theoretical issues that is elided in such discussions. It may, however, be necessary to Taylor's purpose. Man, he suggests, is a self-interpreting animal, but "inauthenticity, bad faith, self-delusion," and the like are possible. "Our aim is to replace this confused, incomplete, partly erroneous self-interpretation by a correct one" and achieve self-knowledge (111). There is thus always a tension between the explaining interpretation when it "attains greater clarity" and "the lived interpretation" (111–12). The question is, in exploring a universe in which claims are based on "insight" rather than "brute data," how do we arrive at even a measure of closure? Taylor does not say explicitly, but the answer is not too remote.

"Sensibility and understanding" are required; this is "not a study in which anyone can engage, regardless of their level of insight." It requires reaching a position of "superiority" whereby "one can understand one's own stand and that of one's opponent, but not the other way around." Such a "gap in intuitions" is in effect more than that; it is a conflict between "different fundamental options in life," and so theory touches practice and fact becomes value and description becomes prescription. This means we can speak of "error" and even "illusion" with regard to beliefs and the practices of life in which they are embedded (rep. 1977:127). For Taylor such "illusions" are apparent in the ideological extremes of liberal "bargaining society" and utopian revolutionaries whose visions make "a valid science of man impossible"—a science that requires "a freedom from illusions, in the sense of error which is rooted and expressed in one's way of life" (128, 130).

What is really involved in Taylor's somewhat Mannheimian argument is what is involved in the myth of the tradition, behavioralism, and most of alienated academic political theory and the philosophical foundationalism that it has found so congenial. It is a search for the authority of academic political theory vis-à-vis politics. It is one thing to call for a critical theory or an interpretative/critical theory that would make claims about the difference between "appearance and reality" (e.g., Connolly, 1981), but it is another thing simply to vouchsafe those claims positionally. It is easy to give up the idea of verification via brute data as authority when one can substitute for it the authority of "position." What bothers Taylor about Foucault, for example, is what Taylor understands, whether correctly or incorrectly, to be his destruction of *the* subject, the author of meaning and "conscious action" that would make interpretation possible; "his Nietzschean refusal of the notion of truth as having any meaning outside a given order of power"; and his failure to see the march of liberality as the meaning of Western culture (1984:160). Of course Taylor, no more than most, who use Nietzsche as a symbol of relativism—Strauss, for example—gives any careful account of Nietzsche's arguments in this regard.

It is very difficult to quarrel with the general idea of social theory as understanding and self-reflection that have, it is hoped, practical significance. Taylor's problem, and the problem of a wide range of similar arguments, is the assumption (or surreptitious claim) that academic political theory, because it might be defined categorically as concerned with understanding and reflection, is therefore validated as the authoritatively reflective dimension of social life—the thinking part of the body politic that challenges its mindless behavior (1983). It is not difficult to think of the classic texts from Plato to Marx as holding society up to examination and exposing its ideological constraints while at the same time offering alternative visions, but what those individuals were extremely sensitive to were the gap and contingent relationship between reflection and action and their lack of authority. Taylor tends to treat this gap between these modes of action and discourse as if it were just the logical relationship between thinking and doing and as if theory "transforms its own object" just as thought in an individual transforms behavior (74).

With regard to the question of "validation" or what it is for a theory to be right, Taylor suggests that it is a matter of the extent to which it clarifies and changes things. He notes that in political theory, unlike scientific theories with their "brute" facts, this is a very "controversial" matter and involves much more in the way of persuasion. There are, he suggests, no final answers to theory choice in any field, but he has faith that people do at times cure themselves of self-delusion both as individuals and as a society when "valid theory" appears (1983:85). This may very well be the case, but the question of how and why professional political theory can perform the role of creating and propagating such theory, which is the only real issue in contention, remains begged. The tenor of the discussion indicates the familiar assumption, so characteristic of criticisms of Kuhn, that if political theory cannot discover transcendental grounds for distinguishing between truth and illusion the basis of judgment in the practices of life, whether science or politics, collapses. All that collapses, in fact, is the ability of political theory to claim a noncontingent privileged position.

It is very difficult for political philosophy and political theory to conceive a self-image outside the context of a search for the authority of knowledge and the specter of relativism and nihilism, and thus it has condemned itself to seeking an answer to that problem. It is not that there are no rational claims to knowledge. Theories provide such grounds. But what political theory seeks, as philosophy traditionally has, are metatheoretical transcontextual grounds. It is not that political theory can have nothing to say to and about politics, even something that on some basis might be deemed authoritative. It is just that there is no metatheoretical solution to the contingencies involving the relationship between theory and practice. By the mid-1970s, however, academic political theory had largely constructed a dilemma from which it could not extricate itself on its own terms.

There are few places in which the dilemma, or perceived dilemma, of philosophy and political theory—with their common foundational concerns—has been more clearly illustrated than in the discussions that have surrounded the work of Peter Winch (1958; 1972). The issues are almost exactly the same as in the case of Kuhn, but for political theorists the controversy about Winch tends to cut a bit closer to the bone. There never was much disagreement, on the part of political theorists, with Winch's claim (which in fact was a bit tongue-in-cheek) that social science was really philosophy. Philosophy wanted to see itself as social science, and at least antipositivist social science wanted to aspire to philosophy. Winch was claiming the identity, literally, on the basis that social science was the epistemological investigation of society. He might also be construed, more ironically, as suggesting that "social science" always had been a philosophical "idea." In any event, there was considerably more difficulty with his claim that the philosopher, and by implication the social scientist and political theorist, was not somehow a "master scientist," and master moralist, who could judge and validate scientific and moral claims by reference to transcendent facts and rationality. To clarify Winch's thesis and the issues about relativism that it has raised is in effect to clarify a great deal about the situation of political theory.

One thing that should be made clear at the outset is that Winch did not offer his analysis as a way of doing social science or as a method or approach. It was basically an argument about why social science as a whole was, by the very nature of the phenomena it studied, unlike natural science. When he likened social science to philosophy, it was, despite his contentious and sometimes infelicitous or wry statement of the point, simply because he conceived them as functionally similar. They both were second-order modes of (ultimately) linguistic analysis devoted to charting and giving an account of preconstituted conceptual universes of discourse and practice, the notions of reality and rationality that are embedded in these "forms of life," and the rules or conventions that compose them and in terms of which individuals think and act.

This *idea* of social science and philosophy as a kind of empirical epistemology and conceptual analysis had little to do with what most social scientists did and what they wanted or professed to do. It should be no surprise that Winch's argument had a poor reception among positivist philosophers and behavioral scientists. What is more interesting and significant was the grudging qualified acceptance in the philosophy of social science and political theory. He said what many wanted to say and hear, but clearly he failed to provide what just as many in these realms of discourse really sought—which was something more than autonomy, freedom from positivism, and a revitalized notion of social science as interpretation. To the extent that philosophy, social science, and political theory sought self-validating transcendent standards of judgment, about either what is or what ought to be, Winch's claims were, to say the least, potentially disturbing. Cavell and Rorty may have written longer and more recent works about philosophy and rationality, but in basic force it would be difficult to distinguish their claims from those of Winch—and Kuhn.

There is no need to rehearse the various distorted representations of Winch's argument: that he claimed it was the role of social science simply to "reproduce" the phenomena it encountered, that the language of social science must be identical to the language of its object, and that social scientific interpretations must be validated by the actors who are being interpreted. All Winch ever insisted on in this respect was that social scientific explanation demanded "reference to" the self-understanding of the actors and the conceptual practices that constituted its context. What is important to note is that almost without exception these representations are tied to criticisms that are grounded in a concern about the relativistic implications of Winch's work (e.g., Apel, 1967; Brodbeck, 1968; Gellner, 1973; Hollis and Lukes, 1983; Jarvie, 1972; MacIntyre, 1971; Rudner, 1966; 1973; Trigg, 1973;1980; Wilson, 1970). Although ostensibly the problem is the rational grounding of the practices of knowledge, namely, objectivity in science and validity in morals, the real problem is the challenge to the idea of philosophy and political theory as the arbiter of practical rationality and as holding special authority as a consequence of that position.

Winch did not, and has never, suggested that such second-order enterprises, on a variety of grounds, cannot be judgmental, critical, and normative. His point, often only implicit, is, very much like Kuhn's claim about the philosophy of science, that there is no given way that they can substitute their judgments of fact, value, and rationality for those in the domains of discourse they study or arrive at transcendental bases of comparative judgment. It must be emphasized, once again, that the charge of relativism springs essentially not from any real worry about the status of truth claims in the variety of human practices but rather from a worry about the status of philosophy and political theory and their authority. Although it might not be so ludicrous to suggest that philosophical doubt could endanger politics as it would be to suggest that it could endanger science, the concern about relativism has emanated from a defense of critical rationalism as an external judgmental endeavor as much as from a conservationist position. Those who criticize Winch for residual positivism on the basis that he does not provide a rational foundation for critical judgment, that he does not fuse meaning and truth, are in fact much closer to positivism, in both attitude and argument, than Winch.

Not only is there nothing in Winch's argument that would inhibit the notion of political theory or social science as a critical enterprise, but it would seem that there is much to suggest it. Winch emphasizes the conventional constitution of human practices and, in principle, the almost infinite malleability of human action and institutions and the lack of their natural givenness. But the implication of his argument is that the force of such criticism is contingent and not automatically validated by either the position or the grounds of second-order judgments. Political theory, for example, must engage politics persuasively, rhetorically, educationally, or politically. It can no more rely, at least in good faith, than any ideology on "scientific" rationality as authority. Whether it is social science claiming authority to inform, direct, or serve public policy, which is now, for example, the self-image of much of political science, or whether it is political theory and political philosophy seeking to make sweeping claims about the legitimate order of society, it cannot do so, except rhetorically, on the basis that it is to politics as wisdom or thought is to action. It cannot do so on the assumption that "knowing about" is the basis or precondition of "knowing how," or that it is the theoretical dimension of practice simply because one can speak categorically of the relationship as one of theory and practice. But such Hegelian category "mistakes" continue to dominate the literature of political theory.

It is not that Winch's argument either does or does not "permit" external criticism of a form of life. This is a matter to be settled between political theory and politics and not a unilateral consideration. Winch simply holds to the idea that there is no nonpropositional, transconceptual knowledge of fact or structure of rationality. He is quite willing to grant the existence of functional universals like truth and rationality but not transcontextual criteria (1972:58–62; 1976). The political or moral reformer cannot rise above politics and morality. If we employ notions of "world," "rationality," and "reality" to expose the mistakes of others, it is to offer a contrary argument about their criteria of application; it is to offer a contrary theory. "Reality" is not itself a datum; it is, like "facts," a category of data. No more than Kuhn does Winch either challenge the "truth" of science and politics as such or apologize for it, although positivist philosophers attribute to him the former and "critical" theorists such as Habermas attribute to him the latter.

The problem is clear. The metatheoretical philosophical claims are what are really in danger from his formulation. It is a threatening formulation because its implications serve to undermine most of what the modern philosophy of science, metaethics, and political philosophy have sought to accomplish in terms of either establishing their own authority or seeking a transcendental ground for supporting or condemning the practices that constitute their objects of knowledge. There is nothing wrong with seeking knowledge and the authority of truth. The problem is that much of philosophy and political theory wants it afforded them without argument and action.

Just as in the case of the relationship between the philosophy of science and political science, much of the difficulty, much of the inversion of theory and metatheory, is fostered by the mediational literature. Here, more than anywhere, philosophical doctrines are summarized, reconciled, and retailed as if they were theories, and the search for transcendental judgment is pursued. A paradigm case is Richard Bernstein's *Restructuring of Social and Political Theory* (1976).

This work places itself solidly within the dominant metatheoretical structure of the value/fact fetish and attempts to talk of the "restructuring of social and political theory" in terms of a conceptual synthesis of work in the philosophy of social science that would satisfy the demand that "an adequate, comprehensive political and social theory must be at once empirical, interpretative and critical" (Bernstein, 1976:xiv,235). To the "naturalistic" self-image of social science (represented by claims such as those of Robert Merton), Bernstein juxtaposes the "challenges" of linguistic analysis (e.g., Winch), phenomenology (e.g., Schutz), and the Frankfurt school of critical theory (e.g., Habermas). The purpose is to "integrate what is right and sound in these competing orientations, and reject what is inadequate and false" (xvii). No small task, but in metatheory all things are possible.

What one would do with this analytical product is something Bernstein is singularly unclear about. He claims that as he progressed with this project his "excitement" grew as he found underlying "coherence" among the differing perspectives as well as some implicit "difficulties" inherent in the view of the theorist as "disinterested observer" that was common to both the empiricists and their critics and that demanded the resurrection of the classical idea of "praxis" and the "*critical* function of theory" (1976:xxii). There is little wonder that the book ends with Habermas, for the intellectual path and synthesis that Bernstein relates are, in effect, simply Habermas's argument.

The theme that runs through this work, in addition to the notion of a synthesis of arguments in the philosophy of social science, is the characteristic demand for philosophical rationality. The problem with Winch, Bernstein claims, is that he "never tells us how to decide which among competing interpretations is best" (1976:71)—as if there were some general way to specify metatheoretically how to do this. What Bernstein wants—and what he believes has been the perennial goal "not only in philosophy but in social and political theory, too—[is] to distinguish the true from the false, the apparent from the real and essential [because] it is indeed the business of philosophy and genuine theory to provide the basis for critical evaluation of the forms of life" (74). If this is their job, it is a self-appointed one, and as a character in Tom Stoppard's play *Jumpers* (1964) notes, if academic philosophy's definition of "rationality were the criterion of things being allowed to exist, the world would be one gigantic field of soya beans!"

Bernstein argues that the task of philosophy and political theory is to "indicate in what ways we can gain a rational critical perspective on the quality of social and political life" and that this cannot "be left to the individual to do in his ad hoc ways" (1976:84). It is reasonable to suggest that there is a strain of antidemocratic elitism that runs, left and right, through this kind of literature. It is small wonder that Bernstein reacts in the characteristic manner to Kuhn. Kuhn, he argues, leaves us with only "persuasion" as a criterion of choice, and (despite what Bernstein persists in believing must be his *real* intentions to the contrary, for, after all, Kuhn is a philosopher) he has not been able to come up with the criteria "to distinguish rational from irrational persuasion" and produce "a more comprehensive and subtle understanding of rationality" that would allow us to assess the degree of rationality in human practices (93). What is lacking in Winch and Kuhn is also, according to Bernstein, lacking in Schutz—"any ground for evaluating these very different forms of life, for saying that one form better approximates what political life is or ought to be" (168).

There is in fact no such lack of ground at all. Bernstein is searching in the wrong place. It is simply that such a ground is not the terrain of academic philosophy and political theory but the firmament of conventional practices. And even there it is porous. But (following Habermas) Bernstein decries the "descriptivist" posture he believes is inherent in the work of Winch, Kuhn, and Schutz simply because they do not accept philosophical foundationalism. How, he asks, can they question the fact/value dichotomy and still fail to see that normative and empirical theory cannot be separated? Bernstein's problem is his confusion of such categoricals with actual practices. Just because one might argue that there are various ways in which the fact/value dichotomy was erroneous, this does not mean that political theory is not distinguishable from its subject matter or that philosophy is the standard of scientific truth.

It is not surprising that Bernstein subsequently (1983) had some difficulty grappling with the latest philosophical authorities. How to square his foundationalism with the hermeneutical circle of the new antifoundationalism and synthesize these philosophical perspectives? How to get "beyond objectivism and relativism" and "gain a new understanding of rationality that has important ramifications for both theoretical and practical life" (2)? It may also not be surprising that he dedicated this book to Arendt and Habermas as well as to Rorty and Gadamer. The answer he finds, the new synthesis, is "an underlying common vision" regarding the "tyranny of Method" and the acceptance of the "dialogical character of our human existence" that propels us beyond the "perplexing theoretical quandary" toward the "practical task" of dissolving it in the process of living (xi, xv). It is also little wonder that Bernstein felt that "this book was writing itself through me, and that what is expressed here are the thoughts, insights, and shared vision to which many individuals have contributed" (xiv).

It is basically a critical summary of Gadamer, Habermas, Rorty, and Arendt (along with Winch, Kuhn, Ricoeur, et al.) with the strained claim that the outcome is a "a type of rationality" that is "historically situated" and ungrounded in the traditional sense and yet "does not lead to, or entail, relativism" (1983:xiv). In the end, it is, in effect, a rejection of the main theme of the previous book and an admission that there is no metatheoretical position for adjudicating practical rationality. At one level there are some cogent critical summaries of some complex arguments, but at another level this is mediational metatheory caught in a frenzy of attempting to pull itself up by its own bootstraps. The level of abstraction to which one must move in order to "decode" and synthesize the foundationalism of Habermas and the antifoundationalism of Rorty and come up with a vestige of the Archimedean point that Bernstein initially demanded is impossible—and meaningless.

The final result is another secondary version of critical rationalism based on the injunction not to block the road to inquiry in the practices of life and to build community on openness to one another and the past and future. This may very well be a maxim that can in some general way be extracted from the literature surveyed, but whether it is good practical advice in either politics or science and what it would mean in concrete terms in these domains is another matter. It is basically an injunction that suits academic pluralism and dialogue. If, in the end, this is all that philosophy and political theory have to offer politics, the dream is dead. What it in effect means is that neither the position nor the content of political theory can yield authority. The question that is finally begged is that of the nature of the dialogue between political theory and politics and the terms on which it could be conducted. Bernstein's problem is only typical of the contemporary dilemma of political theory. This kind of work is the end, the last whimper of metatheory and its enslavement to philosophical faddism in search of the transcendental foundations of social and political judgment. Blinded by its belief that philosophy held the key to practical judgment, it ran into the trap laid by antifoundationalism. It has bitten the latest attractive fruit of philosophy only to find itself poisoned and paralyzed.

There is reason to suggest that political theory, in the forms in which it has existed since the early 1950s, is dead or, at least, it has proliferated to the point where it has choked its own garden and where it has become a self-caricature. Many may see the work of Rawls and Habermas as the beginning of a new era in political theory, but though their work is certainly the epitome of the form, it and the kind of literature it has engendered represent a species of academic dinosaur. The last thing we need is another summary of Habermas, and I will refrain from producing one. But in the reticulate corpus of his work the various myths of alienated political theory have been woven together in an epic manner. It is, I would suggest, whatever its various merits and defects might be, the reductio ad absurdum of academic political theory.

Here, first of all, are most of the basic features of the myth of the tradition: a synoptic philosophical meaning attributed to the evolution and devolution of Western civilization and discernible in, and explained by, the path of epic philosophies from Plato to Marx; the claim that this meaning is fully apprehended in the critical but prophetic moment of the present as political theory and politics fall into crisis; the image of a political and social crisis of modernity that demands and makes possible reflective objective thought; the constrast between the classical and modern conceptions of politics and science characteristic of, for example, Aristotle and Hobbes, respectively; and the reconstitution of political theory in the work of the academic analyst who seeks to overcome positivism, historicism, and relativism and recapture transcendental truth as a basis of political judgment that will serve to aid in the reconstitution of modern politics. Here also are the myths of theory and politics—the reification of the idea of theory and its projection into history as the evolution of a distinct activity and career as well as the reification of a classical ideal of politics and the story of its alleged decline and revitalization. Here is the myth that epistemology is the foundation of science and the myth that philosophy can arrive at transcendental foundations of empirical and normative claims. And, finally, there is the myth that the problem of theory and practice or the authority of academic discourse in the arena of politics has a philosophical solution.

If, as I have suggested, much of the alienation of contemporary political theory is rooted in its dependence on various kinds of metatheoretical claims and the inversion of theory and metatheory, then Habermas constitutes the paradigm case. Here is collected and synthesized nearly every conceivable metatheoretical theme in the modern academic philosophical universe. These are collated and offered up as a theory and as a defense of a certain idea of theory. To the extent that Habermas does engage substantive theoretical issues and make theoretical claims, he employs them and tailors them in such a way as to justify various metatheoretical arguments about the character and uses of theory, which in turn are elaborate justifications of attenuated ideological positions long ago detached from any immediate practical context. In a very important sense, the history of the Frankfurt school was the history of alienated intellectuals seeking a rational and authoritative ground of metatheoretical judgment that could undermine or underwrite practice. Their antipathy to logical positivism masks the extent to which they shared similar concerns in a similar setting. Both the Frankfurt school and logical positivism saw themselves as developing a critical philosophy that could transform and purify life.

Critical theory was never a theory but rather an *idea* of theory and one that, in the work of Horkheimer, was both an extension of what was understood as Marx's project and a counterpart to the positivist image of theory. From the beginning, through Habermas, the positivist account of theory was largely assumed to be identical to the practice of natural science. Although not entirely adequate for social analysis, it was something to be transcended more than rejected in the course of developing a critique of modern bourgeois capitalist domination which, after the Enlightenment, employed scientific and instrumental rationality as a mode of political legitimation. Horkheimer's image of what he termed "traditional theory" was basically a notion derived from philosophical apologies for modern science that reflected ideas about technology and the mastery of nature and society. Critique and the separation of appearance and reality, and the postulation of the idea of a rational emancipated society, required a different form of theory than that of traditional theory (science) which no longer, after the Enlightenment, played a critical role (Horkheimer, 1972). Habermas's work has been basically the metatheoretical elaboration of this notion of theory, its role, and its epistemological authority—a notion he did not believe had been adequately developed by his predecessors and contemporaries, including Adorno and Marcuse, and for which Marx's theory was no longer adequate in the conditions of advanced capitalism. But Habermas's project is basically the same project that is in evidence in most of contemporary political theory—overcoming relativism created by positivism in the social sciences and historicism in the cultural sciences.

It is the fact/value, normative/empirical framework in which Habermas situates the problem that he sees manifest in the split (since Weber) between social science and classical political philosophy; that is, how to "redeem" the "promise" of "a practical orientation about what is right and just in a given situation" without sacrificing "the rigor of scientific knowledge" regarding "the social relationships of life" (1973:44). What bothers Habermas is that "epistemology" has, in the contemporary age (after Kant), been reduced to the philosophy of science or positivism and scientism and a description of the methodology identified with natural scientific knowledge. What Habermas wants is to ask once again "how is reliable knowledge possible" and to reconstitute the authority of philosophy and reestablish the position from it which was "dislodged" following the "dissolution of epistemology" (1971:vii, 4). Philosophy destroyed itself, and now it must reestablish itself and its critical, reflective role.

Habermas's project is not one that can be accomplished, and critiques that focus on his failure to bring it off, or quite bring it off, miss the problem. The project is nothing but the old epistemological quest in the form of social theory. Habermas believes that what "defined the tradition of great philosophy since its beginnings"—to Hegel—was the idea that "the *only* knowledge that can truly orient action is knowledge that frees itself from mere human interests and is based on Ideas" (1971:301). To be sure, he rejects what he calls the "illusion of pure theory," which had become exacerbated in the modern age when *theoria* fell under the spell of positivism and broke from its classical and practical role of "orientating human action" (306). But what he attempts to erect is a surrogate form grounded in a transcendental philosophical anthropology, which posits three basic human interests that underlie equally basic modes of knowledge, types of science, and forms of social life.

The empirical analytical sciences, exemplified by natural science and positivistic social science, have been concerned with predictive nomological explanation and reflect a technical interest in the control of objective processes within the realm of work. The hermeneutical and historical or cultural sciences are the manifestation of a practical interest in communication and intersubjective understanding, which is the stuff of language and politics. What is required to reconstitute theory fully is a critical theory and social scientific mode of activity that would serve the fundamental human interest in emancipation and go beyond the objectivist or contemplative stance of the other sciences and penetrate ideological constraints produced by "hypostatized powers" through a kind of Freudian reflection writ large (Habermas, 1971:13).

As with Mannheim, the argument is that, if self-reflection "cannot cancel out interest, it can to a certain extent make up for it" (Habermas, 1971:308–13). Of course, even if one might accept the revelation regarding the human condition that "can be apprehended a priori" and the "standards of reflection" that possess "theoretical certainty," one might still ask who has the position and ability to gain and apply this reflective knowledge. The answer is in effect quite clear. The academic social theorist and the university are to be the vehicle of a rational society. But Habermas does not face up to this practical issue. Instead he has turned his attention toward the thesis that the standards of reflection are in some way self-validating and grounded in the nature of language and discourse— "our first sentence expresses unequivocally the intention of universal and unconstrained consensus" (314).

Habermas's work has for the most part been a very forced synthesis of various metatheoretical claims designed to render an idea of critical theory as an activity and to present an image of the rational authority on which it is allegedly based. What is called for is not so much theorizing as the strategic application of metatheory in defense of privileged knowledge. What Habermas has sought is the rehabilitation of epistemology and philosophical rationalism as substitutes for theory. What is ironic is that in his search for a self-authenticating standard of rationality, Habermas has in recent years been led first to the theory of language (e.g., 1970; 1979) and then, more broadly, to the theory of human action in general (1984). Though one might applaud this shift from methodology to theory (see Gunnell, 1979a), what has marked this venture is the inversion of theory and epistemology. He has manipulated his analyses of the phenomena of human action and language to legitimate his claims about a comprehensive philosophy of rationality cut loose from, and claiming authority over, all actual realms of human practice.

What Habermas has sought in the theory of language is what a number of contemporary philosophers have sought. First, it is a model of social scientific understanding that, by its reliance on the notion of conventional public language, revitalizes the hermeneutical and idealist tradition. Second, it involves a semantic theory of truth that would locate formal universal truth conditions and criteria of validity within the structure of language. Such notions are immediately attractive to those in the social sciences and philosophy of social science (e.g., Macdonald and Pettit, 1981) who want not simply a universal model in terms of which to understand forms of social action and critically assess them on the basis of corrigible reasons and comparisons but a model that provides some philosophically assessable standard of truth and rationality. In an age in which natural law is in poor repute, this becomes the substitute. But the content remains very much the same.

Universal rationality, procedurally, nearly always turns out to be the Western notion of instrumental rationality and scientific logic that puts us in touch with the external objective world. Its substantive moral dimension is always reflection leading to an understanding of the authentic Self as the autonomous subject of action and choice—actions and choices that if fully understood and free would validate a common human nature or condition that in turn demands a social and political world that in fact turns out to be at least liberal democracy or the next step beyond. The idea is to make meaning and truth, rationality and reality, one.

Habermas's basic model is the speech act as explicated in the work of such philosophers as J. L. Austin and John Searle. The ideal speech act and context presuppose consensus and undistorted communication, which in actual cases can be only partially achieved. Habermas suggests that these conditions of communicative competence, both internal to speech acts and involving reference and correspondence to reality, provide universal standards of truth and rationality. It is an attempt to find transcendental standards within the pragmatics of speech, a kind of immanent but nonsubstantive transcendentalism grounded in validity claims at least implicitly raised in any communicative act or form of intersubjective understanding and which function as necessary "oughts" to be redeemed in practical arguments (see also Apel, 1985). Here fact and value will be bridged, because democracy and the classical political ideals of freedom and justice are inherent in language. Those familiar with American pragmatism and Peirce, Dewey, Popper, and even John Stuart Mill might think that they had heard all this before. "Comprehensively critical rationalism" and a procedural notion of rationality may not in some context be bad advice, but here this is hollow rhetoric reverberating down academic corridors.

There is little need to follow Habermas through the tortuous journey from Weber to the present in search of the foundations of rationality in speech and action and the meaning of social evolution (1984). He leaves few thinkers and schools of thought out of his synoptic account and quite systematically distorts both the content and the purpose of most of the material to which he refers (e.g., Winch and Toulmin) in the process of weaving this complex scheme. The conclusion is not as important as the goal, and the goal is never in doubt. It is to find a *philosophical*, epistemological, metatheoretical ground for overcoming relativism and historicism (which he believes are still present in the hermeneutical/interpretative approaches of Gadamer and Winch) that would restore the Kantian and Marxian promise and once again give substance to the critical Enlightenment ideal.

As with Rawls, it is difficult to imagine what could possibly be the significance of such a philosophically contrived solution to these echoes of practical problems. It offers nothing substantive to a person really faced with making a choice about justice or freedom, and arguments about this work are largely arguments confined to the context created by the work itself. Seemingly practical applications are usually in effect only examples for validating the philosophical argument. One might hope that its real purpose were rhetorical, that because it is, even if in some alienated manner, a kind of political argument and commentary it might be brought to bear in a persuasive way on specific issues. But it is neither part of theory nor part of practice. It is metatheory and remains imprisoned within a form of academic discourse, which in its relationship to politics is marked merely by a kind of abstract cognitive dissidence.

Alienated political theory presents itself as speaking about politics and having the authority to do so, but it fails to do the former and lacks the latter. Much like public policy analysis in political science, it attempts to legitimate itself by suggesting that it is to politics as thinking is to doing, but this "intellectualist model" (Gunnell, 1976) is not a cogent one for thinking about human action, to say nothing of the highly contingent relationship between political theory and politics. It is, however, increasingly finding a home in mainstream political science as the evaluative or normative dimension of political inquiry. This is not surprising because the self-understanding of each remains bound within the same basic metatheoretical structure and range of ideology.

Brian Barry and Douglas Rae, for example, writing in the *Handbook of Political Science* (1975), argue that the task of political theory is to produce a formal method for making evaluative choices and to "set up some criteria of evaluation which will enable us to say that one set of consequences is perferable to some other set of consequences" (394). They specify what they claim are *the* three elements of evaluation in general (internal consistency, interpretability of criteria, standards for choosing between criteria), and then they designate *the* requirements of "political" evaluation (recognition of forced choice, risk and uncertainty, relevance of time, and condition of individual human beings). They discuss various pure or single criteria of evaluation (utilitarianism, equality, optimality, maximization, and dominance) and possible responses to conflicts between criteria (e.g., absolutism, trading off, etc.), and they decide that evaluation is indeed complex and difficult but that in the end "human well-being is the only possible foundation of political evaluation" and thus certain "simplifying devices" such as political principles (justice, freedom, equality, etc.) along with factual circumstantial data can be the premises in a practical syllogism for reaching choices (369).

They admit that this scheme is governed by liberal utilitarian and "consequentialist" assumptions (as is nearly all contemporary metaethics), but the ideological bias is secondary to the prodigious irrelevance of attempts to find a metatheoretical and transtheoretical answer to practical questions of judgment, be they scientific or moral. Again, what is involved here is less a mistake than an attempt to find logical and epistemological authority for academic political theory. The questions of whether academic political theorists should, can, or do influence public policy and political judgments are complex and seldom confronted. It is simply assumed that good practice is knowledgeable practice (normatively and empirically), knowledgeable practice is practice informed by theory, theory is the province of political theorists who can discover the essence of rationality, and therefore they should have a role as master policy makers (e.g., Goodin, 1982). In the end, it makes little difference whether it is a German rationalist and critical theorist or an Anglo-American rationalist and public policy analyst. The attitude and results look pretty much the same, and even ideological differences pale in the fire of academic elitism.

Much of the illusion of relevance created by political theory and political philosophy is that it seems to address the great questions of the age—modernity, justice, political obligation, world alienation, and the like. But these turn out to be metaphysical problems that have about as much concrete reference as the problems of knowledge and doubt that traditional epistemology pursued. It is sometimes claimed that today professional workaday political theory is adopting a much more hands-on approach and is dealing with abortion, medical ethics, intergenerational justice, the environment, population problems, animal rights, and so on, but despite what may be some very sound analysis in such areas, much of the discussion is only stipulatively about such matters. It is usually pursued in terms of either the typical hypothetical paradigm-case examples characteristic of philosophical discourse or actual issues so abstracted from their context and the real political claims involved that they might as well be hypothetical.

My point, however, is not to assess how well some aspects of political theory are doing in attempting to be relevant. Neither is it simply to suggest that the main currents in the field move along in profound indifference to the real issues involving the relationship between political theory and politics—both now and in the past. Before there is likely to be much progress in thinking through this complex, contingent, practical relationship, there must be a clearer understanding of, or at least argument about, the cognitive relationship that goes beyond philosophical methodology and transcendentalism. What is required is at least a move in the direction of substantive theoretical claims about politics.

# 6

## Politics and the Theory of the Conventional Object

So I decided that I must have recourse to theories [*logoi*], and use them in trying to discover the truth about things.

PLATO

When reality is depicted, philosophy as an independent branch of knowledge loses its medium of existence.

MARX

THERE IS little doubt that the variety of postpositivist work in the philosophy of social science dealing with language, action, and human understanding, whether inspired by phenomenology, hermeneutics, or linguistic analysis, represents and reflects a distinct substantive theoretical concern (see Dallmayr, 1984). But the concern has become diverted into a range of metatheoretical arguments that in the philosophy of social science have taken on a life of their own detached from the practices toward which they were once directed. In the social sciences, these metatheoretical claims have been designed to distinguish between social and natural science and deal with the question of "man as a subject of science" (cf. Ayer, 1967), defend ideas about the nature of social science and its social role, legitimate ideologies, and justify certain practices of inquiry. To the extent that theoretical claims are explicitly advanced, they tend to be entered in defense of the metatheoretical arguments. In short, there has been an inversion of theory and metatheory or epistemology and ontology. This is hardly simply a recent problem. As suggested earlier, it is tied up with the very origins of the social sciences and their relationship to politics and philosophy. But, whatever the historical roots of the difficulty, it is necessary to clarify the issues involved.

It is important to distinguish, and understand the possible and necessary dimensions of the relationship between, at least nine categories that have been conflated in the current literature: (1) metatheoretical activities (e.g., the philosophy of social science); (2) metatheoretical claims (epistemology, methodology); (3) disciplines or fields; (4) modes or activities of inquiry; (5) theories or the constitutive claims that posit a domain of facticity; (6) claims (explanatory, descriptive, evaluative, etc.) entered in a theoretical context; (7) research norms and goals; (8) methods or technique; and (9) social behavior and practices that constitute the object of inquiry. Many of the problems involved in the alienation of political theory cannot be understood without exploring the manner in which these distinctions have been either purposefully or accidentally blurred and the relationships confused and inverted.

In the case of the discipline of political science (3), for example, I have explored (chapter 2) how epistemological claims (2) derived from the philosophy of science (1) not only have been employed to legitimate behavioralism (4) but have produced inappropriate and misunderstood research goals (7), such as emulating natural science, that led to the poverty of substantive theory (5) and an impoverished notion of theory. This in turn gave rise to a kind of theoretical practice that confused methodology with method (8) and generated claims (6) that not only failed to explain politics (9) but often idolized and distorted it and obscured the problems involved in the relationship between political theory and politics. Similar syndromes, as indicated in the previous two chapters, are the cause of the alienation of political theory in other areas. What is particularly frustrating, however, is when political theory moves to the edge of theoretical issues in its metatheoretical pursuits but retreats and simply uses theoretical claims instrumentally and invertedly. This is, quintessentially, the case with Habermas, but it is also evident in the work of Quentin Skinner and Paul Ricoeur.

There is a definite and significant theoretical component to Skinner's arguments (1969;1970;1971) that is both explicit and embedded in the interpretative claims he advances. As in the case of Habermas, Skinner's arguments are largely extracted from Austin's analysis of speech acts. The difficulty with his claims is that he advances them as a "method," or even technique, of interpretation and in justification of a certain mode of historical practice. Theories have prescriptive implications for methods and norms of inquiry, but the latter, which are highly relative to particular research problems, cannot be simply deduced or logically extrapolated from theories. The relationship between theories and methods is largely contingent. Furthermore, in Skinner's work, the theory of speech acts largely serves, like most similar postpositivist work in the philosophy of social science to which Skinner's arguments are related, to reformulate a traditional epistemological, methodological, or hermeneutical position regarding the interpretation of texts and human action that is in turn used to justify a contextualist idealist, neo-Collingwoodian approach to intellectual history (for an extended discussion, see Gunnell, 1980; 1982). As in the case of much of political theory, the assumption, or claim, is that epistemology is the foundation of inquiry and the criterion of judgment.

In the case of Skinner, metatheory does at least serve to justify a certain practice of inquiry, but in the work of Paul Ricoeur, it is less attached to any definite substantive project and becomes more an autonomous but contextless mode of discourse. Although there are theoretical elements in Ricoeur's argument, it is primarily an attempt to mediate metatheoretically what he conceives to be two opposed hermeneutical positions. While individuals like E. D. Hirsch (1967; 1976) argue, much like Skinner, that textual meaning is an expression of an author's mind and that understanding is a matter of recovering the author's intentions, Gadamer and others stress the autonomy of the text and insist that meaning is a function of language and an encounter between a text and an interpreter. It is at least questionable that the positions of Hirsch and Gadamer are in fact comparable (see Gunnell, 1979*b*:ch.4), but Ricoeur, drawing upon a wide range of authors (including Saussure, Austin, Frege, Husserl, Popper, and Lévi-Strauss), treats them all at the same level of abstraction and weaves arguments ranging from method to metaphysics into a composite metatheoretical image of textual interpretation and the explanation of human action. He seeks to take account of both semantics and semiotics and dialectically to unite subjectivity and objectivity, understanding and explanation, and various other conventional philosophical polarities (1971; 1976*b*).

The purpose that this metatheoretical synthesis is supposed to serve and the audience to which it is addressed are far from clear. In the course of his discussion, Ricoeur distorts the claims of the authors he draws upon both by not sufficiently taking into account the specific projects in which they are engaged and by often infelicitously juxtaposing their work. He claims that he wishes "to initiate a truly reciprocal discussion between philosophical hermeneutics and the methodology of historical inquiry" (1976*a*: 683), but the questions of how and why this is to be done are not directly addressed. He seems, however, to assume that metatheoretical hermeneutics is the foundation of interpretative practice and the authority for its claims.

Habermas now concedes that his early work was primarily "methodological," and he is also sensitive to the charge of falling into the "snares of foundationalism" at a time when "transcendental-philosophical hopes" and "all attempts at discovering ultimate foundations . . . have broken down" (xxxix, xli, 2; on these points, see Gunnell, 1979*a*). He claims that his earlier approach has now "given way to a substantive interest" and that "the theory of communicative action is not a metatheory but the beginning of a social theory." Yet it is one that is designed "to validate its own critical standards" (xxxix). Habermas's concern with the theory of action remains instrumental and subordinate to methodological and other metatheoretical issues. What has changed is that he now (1984) attempts to derive a normative theory of immanent rationality from the structure of action and an evolutionary image of science and society.

When the theory of action is approached, or constructed, in such a way as to produce certain a priori critical standards and provide the validation of those standards, when the real concern is overcoming philosophical relativism and historicism, it is deformed. As theoretical discourse, it is disingenuous, and as rhetorical or practical discourse, it is misplaced. Habermas's goal has always been to integrate political philosophy and social science, and, not surprisingly, he now finds sustenance in derivatives of truth-conditional semantics where meaning, truth, and rationality merge. It is clear, however, that he engages this material only long enough and deeply enough to move forward with his notion that validity is both pragmatic and universal and ultimately the province of "reflective" or "theoretical" (academic, philosophical) discourse.

The aim is to reach philosophical standards that are authoritative and overcome the contingencies of practice and the contingent relationship between theory and practice. As Habermas significantly asks, is not a "higher tolerance for contradiction, a sign of a more irrational conduct of life?" (1984:60). He claims that "the context-dependence of the criteria by which the members of different cultures at different times judge differently the validity of expressions does not, however, mean that the ideas of truth, of normative rightness, of sincerity and authenticity that underlie (only intuitively, to be sure) the choice of criteria are context-dependent in the same degree" (55).

Habermas's work is simply the latest chapter in German rationalism and rationalist philosophy. The "positivist dispute in German sociology" (Adorno et al., 1976) between the positions of individuals like Habermas and Popper is a displaced and rarefied ideological debate carried on among rationalists who ultimately, through their attachment to philosophical certainty, are more alike than different. These kinds of claims reflect, and appeal to, the persistent epistemological quest and transcendental urge in philosophy, and they continue to offer academic political theory what that enterprise has always sought—grounds for authoritative judgment. But the attachment to this literature also condemns political theory to alienation. This is true not only because it confines political theory to a world of metatheoretical images but also because it has neither sensitivity to the actual modes of practical action (including politics) nor a real interest in the phenomena in question—either in their general or particular dimension.

The real theoretical issues involved in claims about human action and speech are largely either sidestepped or selectively chosen and summarily concluded in the work of Skinner, Ricoeur, and Habermas. These issues include questions about: the individuation of actions and the relationship of individuation to description, evaluation, and so on; the components of an action; the status of mental predicates and their relationship to behavior; the relationship between concepts such as intention, purpose, and reason; the relationship of individual actions to social conventions; and a range of other problems. It is only by answering these kinds of questions, or by making claims involving these matters, that a realm of theoretical discourse can be carved out. It is not enough simply to extract some principle affirming that human action is rule-governed, conceptually and linguistically mediated, intentional, purposive, or reflective.

The history of the concept of theory in both science and philosophy is varied and contentious (Gunnell, 1983*a*). Despite all the arguments about what theory really is or was (e.g., Habermas, 1971:301–2) designed to bolster various metatheoretical positions, there is little point in seeking some direction from the etymology of "theory." The concept is employed here to refer to a basic claim about the nature of political phenomena. What political theory is as an activity is not unrelated to political theory as a kind of claim, but they are not identical. The very idea of critical theory, for example, usually involves a systematic conflation of the two. Some of the practical implications of the argument developed here about political reality will be explored later, but the problem with much of contemporary political theory as an activity, the cause of its alienation, is precisely the fact that it lacks an explicit universe of discourse regarding political ontology that advances criteria of validity for assessing claims about politics. These are not the kind of criteria that Habermas has in mind—criteria that tell us deductively what is right and just outside of any context—but rather criteria for specifying what a political object is and under what conditions it exists. But these criteria as well as the explanatory and evaluative judgments we make in light of them are claims and not revelations.

The single most extensive treatment of action as an object of inquiry in contemporary social science was Parsons and Shils's *Toward a General Theory of Action* (1951), but this was largely a series of essays formulated around the methodological behaviorism of E. C. Tolman and justified in terms of the philosophy of logical positivism. Here "action" was simply used as a "more neutral term" for behavior, and the task of social science was presented as one of dealing with the "activity of human beings" as a dependent variable in the relationship between the human "organism" and its environment.

My argument is, in a general way, fundamentally derivative of recent work in the philosophy of action and philosophy of language and particularly of arguments related to and growing out of the work of Austin and Wittgenstein. To indicate this derivation, however, is only to situate the claims in a broad manner. No attempt has been made to document indebtedness, because there are few points of exact correspondence with the constitution and meaning of the works in question or standard renditions of that meaning. In addition, the argument is intended to stand on its own, and I want to emphasize the argument itself and not whether it is faithful to someone's notion of what somebody else said. One immediate objection to this project is obvious.

Is this not exactly the kind of dependence on philosophy that I have been decrying and, particularly, a dependence on the very material that I have singled out for criticism? The answer, simply, is no. Metatheoretical arguments are identified not by the literature and disciplines in which they appear but rather by their content and the functions they perform. Underlying most of the social sciences, humanities, and political theory are implicit and explicit theoretical propositions regarding human action, but these propositions have been poorly explicated. To the extent that philosophy has focused on the phenomena of human action and contributed to an explication of these propositions, it has created a realm of discourse that is theoretically relevant to social science and political theory. Philosophy, as an academic field, is not all of one piece, and I want to distinguish sharply between, on the one hand, metatheoretical claims about such matters as social scientific explanation, which only incidentally and summarily deal with the nature of social phenomena, and, on the other hand, detailed substantive claims about the structure of such phenomena.

What follows is hardly exhaustive. It is part of a continuing attempt (Gunnell, 1968; 1973; 1979a; 1983a) to develop some systematic explication of the basic principles of human action that bear on the analysis of politics and to follow out the theoretical implications of those principles free from metatheoretical entrapment. The principal purpose of this compact, and even truncated discussion in this context is to provide a concrete example of what I have referred to as substantive theory, but there are at least three ancillary purposes. First, it is an attempt to demonstrate that metatheoretical arguments are parasitic and that in the face of theoretical propositions they dissolve, become transparent as the residue of rejected theories, or are reconstituted as explications of an actual theoretical practice. Second, without a theory of political objects, it is impossible to begin to come to grips with the practical question of the relationship between the activity of academic political theory and the activity of politics. Third, this particular theory undermines the transcendental status of politics which is presupposed in so much of contemporary political theory.

The theory of human action or, in a more comprehensive sense, *conventional objects* of the kind advanced here is not the only theory that may be relevant to social science and political theory, and it conflicts with, or is at least incommensurable with, other potential ontologies (e.g., behaviorism, theism, Freudianism, Marxism, sociobiologism). The basic argument is that politics is a species of conventional phenomena, but this is less a premise of the argument than a consequence of it. Two closely related and extremely important implications of this claim must be stated immediately. The first is that *there are no intrinsically political phenomena* and that politics is not a form of life rooted in human nature or the human condition or any other extrapolitical datum. The second is that *there can be no political theory* in the sense of a theory of political phenomena.

Politics is a historical type, token, or configuration of conventional action and has no extraconventional foundation. The application of "political" is predicational. There thus can be no political ontology or political theory per se. Politics is an instantiation of certain conventions of human action; it is a property, attribute, or quality attaching to instances of conventional objects. It is a spatially and temporally delimited form of conventional action and its artifacts (institutions), and there are no generic or universal political objects except as persisting conventional forms (or instances of some stipulated sense of sameness). If politics is at all natural, it is only in the sense that we might speak of a natural language. There can no more (or less) be a theory (ontology) of politics than there can be a theory of English. To ask theoretical questions about politics is to ask about the nature of conventional objects. All other questions about politics are hypothetical and judgmental.

Conventional objects are (1) what people do (act, speak, think) and (2) the artifacts of these doings (institutions, texts, and other products of artifice). One might want to say that conventional objects are a species of human behavior, what people do as opposed to what happens to them or how they, as well as many other creatures, behave phylogenetically. But it is a mistake, or at least misleading, to attempt to solve the issue in terms of a delimitation of human being. What may in fact be the bearer or instantiation of a conventional object is a complex, and somewhat different, issue (educated simians, computers, etc., in the view of some), but whether these objects are *only* produced and instantiated by biological humans is less significant than the fact that they *are* produced and instantiated by humans. Furthermore, where they ultimately come from or what makes them possible (genetic code, transcendental ego, etc.), though interesting, is a different matter from their constitution.

Many of the most contentious and burdensome metatheoretical issues in areas such as political theory, social science, and the philosophy of social science are the product of confusing species of conventional objects with generic factors in their explanation, which are often in turn the vestige of an obsolescent theory of mind or at least a theory very different from that presented here. For example, to ask how, as a general matter, thought causes or otherwise produces, or is produced by, action or institutions is, in terms of this theory, a mistake. Thought, action, and speech are *modes* of conventional objects. An instance of one mode might, as a particular event, in some way be the cause of another instance of that same mode or an instance of another mode, such as a thought giving rise to an action or one action producing another, but there is no general manner in which thinking produces action or in which action and its artifacts produce thinking. Not only does this theory solve the issues attached to the great metatheoretical thought/action dilemma, but it solves the circular problem of ontological priority.

It should be no surprise that people have tried to explicate action in terms of a theory of language or that they have difficulty conceiving of thought as something other than "inner" speech. They are *analogous* because they are theoretically identical and simply represent three modalities of conventional doing just as solid, liquid, and gas are three modes of water. Once this is understood, metatheoretical puzzles, such as that revolving around two concepts of intention, intention as prior to action, and intention in action, disappear.

The structure of conventional objects consists of three basic integral but analytically distinct dimensions or levels. In speaking of these matters, I am employing what might be understood to be some essentially contested concepts, but I am legislating their criteria of application. The concepts and the distinctions are what are important, not the lexical meaning that often attaches to the words. The first dimension is, almost truistically, *extensional* character, which is essentially the criteria or sign of the object that may be manifest in bodily movements or attitudes, vocal sounds, inscriptions, artifacts, and so on. One might ask what is the extensional dimension of thought, but it should not take very long to realize that the idea of thought without criteria of existence is quite meaningless.

Although extension is a necessary condition, it is not sufficient. There are no actions that are simply identical with, for example, bodily movements, and such movements do not, despite all the claims that have been made to the contrary, constitute some stratum of primitive or basic actions. Extensionality must have *significance* within a context of conventions (grammatical, semantic, social) that give it identity as a certain kind of thing and an instance of that kind. In language, this would be understood as sense and reference, but comparable criteria are necessary for any conventional object. Having significance in this sense is, however, not enough to individuate or specify a particular object.

It is this individuation that defines it as a particular object and most essentially and sufficiently determines its *meaning*. This meaning conceivably could be expressed through a variety of significations. Meaning is the dimension of conventionality that identifies the particular conventional object and indicates the intentional force it carries within a particular set of circumstances. Intention is a dimension of a conventional object and thus embedded in it. It is meaning that most essentially governs intelligibility in terms of both expression and understanding. There are unconventional meanings but no nonconventional ones. Once meaning is assigned, the autonomy and identity of the object are established.

Conventional objects have a fourth "dimension" that is not logically or constitutionally an integral aspect of the object or a component of its structure but contributes to situating it in the conventional universe. This is its contingent (but often conventionally grounded) *relation* to other objects, both conventional and otherwise, in terms of what it generates and how it is generated. Conventional objects may be construed in various circumstances as having various outcomes (conventional and nonconventional) and as producing certain effects, consequences, and results (conventional and nonconventional). It is in this respect that we enter the realm of cause, motive, purpose, and reason.

These are the four principal characteristics of conventional objects, but some further points and distinctions must be indicated before we proceed with a more concrete analysis. Conventional objects are not in themselves, any more than any theoretical entity, particulars or particular events that are temporally and spatially bounded. They are universal predicates ascribed to and instantiated, in this case, by actors. Universal here means not metaphysically universal but only universal within a conventional universe, as in the case of linguistic meanings or the force of concepts. And the actor is neither a transcendental subject nor necessarily some individual person. These performed acts, the instantiations according to contextual criteria, are particulars and events that become the subject of descriptions, adverbial attributes, evaluations, and so on. There is thus an important difference between the specification or individuation of a conventional object and, for example, the description of an action. What is it to call an action "political"?

It can certainly be more than one thing, and this is one of the difficulties with the concept as opposed, for example, to the relatively restricted use of a concept such as "religious." Although one might occasionally employ "religious" in its original, more generic sense (scrupulous conformity), its specific sense as designating a particular kind of conventional activity tends to dominate. Even the functional, abstract, and stipulative uses of "political," characteristic of political science, are parasitic on its narrower construal, but the former have become so ubiquitous that reification is a problem. The generic categorical use of "politics" is typically intermixed, both in political theory and in everyday discourse, with its use in designating a particular historical and traditional conventional activity. There is nothing necessarily inappropriate with generic uses, but in the analysis of politics they must be clearly distinguished from (nonarbitrary) claims specifying the substantive preconstituted conventional configuration or activity to which a particular conventional object belongs. The following schematic analysis will, it is hoped, make some of these matters clear.

Let us take Jones voting for Reagan as a "conventional object." This is a *theoretical designation* or claim, which is corrigible in the sense that the theory could be challenged (e.g., by B. F. Skinner) or the object could be misconstrued (e.g., Jones turns out to be one of the Stepford wives). This "action" (theoretically informed specification of the *mode* of object) is specified, individuated, and gains *meaning* as a particular instance of the conventional intentional performance of voting, which must in turn be located in the particular historically and socially constituted and differentiated *symbolic form* of "political activity" where that intention is available. Performing this action requires an *extensional* dimension (such as "moving the arm") that has *significance* (e.g., "pulling the lever") in the social lexicon or conventional context.

This discrete, now identified and internally analyzed, action could then be viewed in terms of its *relational* properties, such as "contributing to Reagan's election." We might hypothetically suggest that the *purpose*, in this case also the anticipated *result* and purposively pursued *consequence*, was to elect Reagan (although the unintended *effect* was to increase the deficit); that the *motive*, based on a *belief* about the efficacy of supply-side economics, was to change the direction of public policy; and that the *reason* was to restore the economy to health. What should be clear from this case is not that concepts such as intention, purpose, motive, and belief are properties of "mind" expressed in language and action but rather that mind is taken largely as a property of language and action.

Thus far we have an analysis of a conventional object, but beyond this analysis, which consists of various corrigible propositions ranging from theoretical to circumstantial, other things might be said about it that must be distinguished from these truth claims. Political scientists might find it useful, for various purposes, to subsume the object under some *category* within the framework of disciplinary discourse (maybe "citizen participation") or speak about it in various ways governed by the conventions of the disciplinary matrix. There is, however, a realm of other claims that fall between the analysis of a conventional object and the number of somewhat arbitrary ways in which one might find it useful to categorize it and talk about it. This is the realm of *description, explanation, and evaluation.* These are, of course, dependent on and in various ways relative to the concerns and problems one brings to inquiry, but at the same time they are dependent on the claims involved in the analysis of the object. To describe Jones as "following the party line," to explain the action in terms of his intention, purpose, and motive, and to evaluate it as an action that is not really in his self-interest would be to assume the correctness of the range of theoretically informed claims in the analysis. To do so is to assume the domain of facticity and the specification of the particular conventional configuration, in this case politics, and the events within it.

Descriptions, evaluations, and explanations do not constitute and discriminate the phenomena but rather presuppose their specification. There are not as many actions as there are descriptions. Conflicts between descriptions may be about the adequacy of the descriptions, but there can be an underlying conflict that is not really about the description at all but about the specification of the phenomena (either theoretically or contextually).

Such a claim is likely to bring the objection that this is a return to the myth of the given and to the positivist notion that facts are independent of description and interpretation. But this would be to mistake theoretical givenness for philosophical or metatheoretical claims about the "world" or the facts as such. As Rorty has observed, this is a "world well lost" (1982)—a world divorced from theory that is only the fading image of past theories. But in terms of the theory of conventional objects, the kinds of facts posited do have a kind of givenness that goes beyond simply being theoretically constituted. It is the character of conventional objects that they are preconstituted by conventions separate from those of the interpreter, describer, and evaluator.

What an action is and what symbolic form it belongs to are not, for example, functions of an investigator's description or categorization of it. It is something of this kind that Wittgenstein meant, I assume, when he noted that the forms of life are given. They are given not in the sense that positivism talked of the facts as given but in the sense that this is an attribute of this kind of fact—that they are conventional and preconstituted. From the perspective of political science, the form of political life (no matter how historically variable and contingent) is given just as from the perspective of the drama critic the play as a form is given, no matter what is said about it and how it is interpreted. The existence of the play is not a function of the interpretation, and the respective interpretations of the actors and the critics are distinct and autonomous and without predetermined relationships of authority.

The issue involved here has become clouded because of the unfortunate mixture of theoretical and metatheoretical arguments that has plagued discussion. In the case of the natural sciences, the facts are, as noted earlier, no more or less "brutish" than in any other theoretically constituted domain of facticity. But at a certain level of generality we can reasonably say that the facts of natural science are of a kind that makes it rather silly to ask what they are independent of the scientist's image of the world. The alternatives are common sense or another scientific theory. In one sense, the same is true of social science when we are talking about such matters as whether the facts are conventional objects. But, within the context of the theory of conventional objects, the very character of facts is that they are constructions that have conventional autonomy quite apart from descriptions (including self-reflective ones) and the like, which are fundamentally parasitic.

These are to be sure rudimentary and densely presented theoretical principles, but the basic purpose in this context is neither to elaborate them fully nor to defend them against either rival theories of a different kind or competing propositions in the theory of action. It is rather to distinguish these claims from metatheoretical claims about the nature of social scientific explanation and understanding and to demonstrate the manner in which the abstract issues in the latter universe of discourse, these ghosts of theoretical arguments, can be exorcised. The hypothetical analysis of action offered above can be extended to texts, speech, institutions, and the activities of groups.

One might ask if it can be extended to thought. The answer is yes, but not to nonconventional, nonextensional thought—whatever that might be. It has already been noted how this analysis solves the persistent meta-theoretical question of how thought is related to action, and it should be clear that it implicitly solves the dilemma about whether the interpretation of speech and text entails a recovery of the author's ideas. If it does, it is in the obvious sense that text and speech *are* the author's ideas. If for some reason one would want to say that they are *only* expressions of authorial ideas, then those ideas must be in a desk drawer or on recording tape or on the tip of the author's tongue. If thoughts precede action, it is in the way a rehearsal of a play precedes a performance. They are two different and contingently related events.

A full explication of a theory of conventional objects would involve a thicker analysis of what might be called "regional" theoretical characteristics and differences such as those relating to the interpretation of texts or historical events. One common metatheoretical argument is that there is something more than a pragmatic difference between understanding the meaning of action and speech in the present and understanding historical artifacts (e.g., Ricoeur, 1976b) that somehow involves the proximity of the former, but there is usually no theoretical grounding for such a claim. The pragmatic difference is great, but the theoretical difference is nonexistent.

One of the mistakes that characterizes much of the literature in the philosophy of social science is the assumption that one can first make a general claim about the nature of social phenomena and then extrapolate some equally general proposition about what constitutes their explanation and the method for achieving it. This may in a way be possible, but not in any very meaningful sense. Part of the difficulty springs from the fact that the real concern is usually the question of the degree of symmetry with natural science or with some other such metatheoretical issue. Social scientific explanation is not one-dimensional. It is relative to theories which in a large sense provide the context of explanation.

To some extent, the problems of explanation within the context of the theory of conventional objects break along the lines of the analysis, but a wide range of questions may be posed, depending on the concerns generated within a disciplinary matrix and the accidental properties of the particular phenomena and events in question. The idea that there is something that can be called *the* explanation of action, or social scientific explanation, is as much a philosophical myth as the idea that there really is any such metatheoretically specifiable unitary thing as natural scientific explanation. The question "What is explanation?" is neither a valid scientific nor a valid philosophical question. To talk, for example, about whether social scientific explanation, outside the context of a theory, is causal or noncausal is merely another example of disembodied meta-theoretical discussion about concepts set free from their criteria of application. Different philosophical accounts of the nature of explanation stand to the practice of inquiry as theories of linguistic meaning stand to the practice of speech. They provide nothing; they change nothing.

Issues like those represented in some of the characteristic dichotomies of the philosophy of social science, such as theory and fact, fact and value, nomological and historical, individualism and collectivism, are neither theoretical issues nor issues of method. They are not really issues at all but only the skimmed philosophical dross of theoretical dispute. Like most dichotomies, as Austin noted, they cry out for elimination, not via synthesis and complementarity but by dissolution. Another metatheoretical issue that disappears in the context of the theory of conventional objects is that regarding the ontological priority of individual and society.

First of all, conventional objects are not distinguished from other kinds of objects in terms of what instantiates them, and this can be groups as well as individuals. Questions about the reality of groups are hypothetical (factual, historical) issues and not theoretical ones. What is ontologically prior is the conventional object. Individualism and collectivism are not *theoretical* choices. Second, because an intention is understood as an instance of a social convention and, as Wittgenstein suggested, is "embedded in its situation, in human customs and institutions" (1968: para. 337), the question of whether the individual is a function of society or whether social forms are reducible to individual choice is not some general problem to be decided prior to particular situated issues regarding the relationship between individuals and groups. Third, because the notion of intention in this theory refers to a dimension of a conventional object and not to some psychological datum in the sense of a prior mentalistic event, the question of priority is only an "empirical" matter. There may be some real theoretical issues revolving around whether intention is, for example, a function of language or whether its place in language is a reflection of a more fundamental human intentionality. But often, and particularly in political theory and the philosophy of social science, these have degenerated into abstract metatheoretical issues that break along traditional dichotomous lines.

The philosophy of social science, and consequently political theory, continues the long tradition, albeit in more sophisticated form, of debating the matter of the "reality" of collectivities. And it can be quite consistently predicted that those in the Anglo-American tradition will ultimately opt for individualism in some form whereas those in the Continental tradition will posit some kind of collective realism. And there are always those who strain for some impossible compromise while retaining the very dichotomy that gave rise to the problem (e.g., Hollis, 1977; Quinton, 1976). All of this is a result of a detachment from substantive theory. Like realism and nominalism, this is a metaphysical, metatheoretical debate severed from a theoretical ground and propelled by its own internally generated momentum. What the theory of conventional objects suggests (argues) is that this problem, apart from its roots in ideology and old theories, is maintained by the search, the futile search, for *the* subject of social action. The great debate about whether deconstructionism in philosophy has destroyed the subject is a quintessential metatheoretical issue. The point is that there are many subjects, because there are many bearers of conventional objects. And we know a subject is a subject when it can be such a bearer—although we may at times be fooled, just as we might be fooled by an "intelligent" machine. If we finally get an ape up to the functional equivalent of a linguistically and conceptually competent human being, we will simply have to find a new way to demarcate our species (if, for example, we want to keep on with animal research). It is, of course, our species that we really are concerned with and not the manifold possibilities regarding the criteria of humanness.

What we need to ask is not whether groups are logical constructions of individuals or whether individuals are designed genes. And the question is not whether a corporation, for example, is a moral (or immoral) individual. If political theory is simply a matter of twisting theoretical claims to suit various ideological, rhetorical, and metatheoretical purposes, it cannot be taken seriously intellectually (except by itself), and as long as it remains academic it cannot be taken seriously politically. At present there is a persistent confusion of theoretical and practical concerns that renders each futile.

Are social facts different from natural facts? What is at issue here are categories, and the categories are too broad to be very meaningful. This metatheoretical question has a long history in social science and philosophy, and to understand it is simply to tell that history. But there is no (theoretical) reason why we should continue to engage it. There can be no such thing as natural facts, because there is no theory of nature. There are the facts of motion, the facts of evolution, the facts of atoms, and so on. Do we mean that if we take all the theories that are present in the various natural sciences we can see a certain sameness about the facts they posit that might lead us to reasonably suggest they are of a different kind than the domains of facticity associated with the social sciences and humanities? Maybe, such as in the sense discussed above, but not in the manner the question is usually answered.

There are many kinds of sameness. What makes the facts of natural science the same is not, for example, theoretical sameness, numerical sameness, functional sameness, or historical sameness. It might be understood as generic sameness or as family-resemblance sameness, at least in a negative sense. Natural facts are not, or not recently, conventional in the sense of being conventionally preconstituted. What they *are* in some more generic sense is more difficult to say. We might, as indicated earlier, suggest that the character of natural scientific inquiry is such that there is no point in asking what facts are as opposed to theories. The only challenge to a theory is another one. This is the case in social science also, but, in the context of the theory of conventional objects presented here, one of the attributes of social phenomena is their conventional and thus preconstituted character.

What distinguishes natural facts cannot be their "brutish" character (except in biology), because all facts are equally brute in the sense of given. That is, after all, what we mean when we call them facts. There probably is no really satisfactory answer to such generic categorical questions, because there is no real problem in question. There may be some reasons for wanting to make a generic distinction between the facts of natural and social science, but most of the reasons have been a function of metatheoretical controversies. The matter only *seems* to be important because it has been incorrectly elevated to the status of a theoretical issue. And this is, above all, the case with the value/fact fetish, which has set the whole framework for discourse for all parties in political theory and whose dissolution is the ultimate key to rethinking and reconstituting political theory. But the only answer to this metatheoretical dilemma is a theoretical one.

Once we understand the metatheoretical, rhetorical, and ideological roots of the fact/value dichotomy in the work of Weber and others, it should be apparent that there is no need to be saddled with this as if it were an ontological or theoretical problem. And the extent to which it is rooted in later versions of the *Methodenstreit* and reflects various kinds of intradisciplinary interests is also clear. The dichotomy may reflect some reasonable distinctions that arguments for denying the split fail to recognize, but for the most part it is a misleading distinction growing out of metatheoretical claims about the ability of philosophy to specify transcendental domains of factual and evaluative givenness. What is required is a theoretical analysis of this problem in terms of the theory of conventional objects.

On the positive side, it must be noted that, whatever the metatheoretical accretions attaching to it, the dichotomy reflects, however remotely, a theoretical distinction and the practical importance of differentiating between the specification or individuation of a conventional object (action, speech act, etc.) and saying various things (descriptively, categorically, evaluatively, etc.) about it. In this sense, there is also a practical significance in the distinction, for example, between empirical and normative inquiry. The criteria of talking about a conventional object, cogently and adequately, are predicated on a logically distinct claim about its existence and kind. But the relation of this to the fact/value dichotomy as commonly employed is distant. The dichotomy is the metatheorized residue and transcendentalization of this practical distinction, and the denial of the dichotomy is a metatheoretical recognition of a practical interdependence between a class of phenomena and the various modes of talking about it. When the issue is taken out of a theoretical practice and considered in a contextless manner, it degenerates into such questions as whether, a priori, one can describe without evaluating. Maybe more than anything, however, the problems associated with the fact/value dichotomy are the residue of an obsolete theory of linguistic meaning—a residue that has gained a life of its own.

At best, fact and value might be construed (although not very successfully) as generic categories of linguistic meaning, but they do not represent, and could hardly be exhaustive of, specific conventions of intentional meaning (describing, evaluating, explaining, recommending, stating, etc.). They do not represent specific types of linguistic performance. They are not things one does with words. When someone like Hare suggests that evaluative propositions have descriptive meaning, this reflects only the fact that they must be employed according to conventions of sense and reference in order to have significance and not, as he suggests, that there can be two simultaneous meanings. The latter would indicate ambiguity on the part of either the speaker or the interpreter. The idea of descriptive meaning is a carry-over from the verificationist theory of language in which conventions of sense and reference (significance) and extension were identified with meaning and cognitive status.

Meanings are coextensive with the conventional intentions in any natural language and are hardly reducible to the categories of fact and value. Although certain words, expressions, and grammatical and syntactical forms might be characteristically associated with certain kinds of meaning, the conventions of intentionality are what specify and individuate meaning. Words and expressions, such as "justice," to the extent that they have independent or lexical meaning, are the residue of their use in various speech acts. And even then it is largely the force of the concept that is retained in meaning and not the criteria of application or sense and reference. There is, first of all, no substantive language that belongs to the performances of explaining, evaluating, describing, and so on, and, second, there is no class of meanings that is coextensive with activities such as morals, politics, or science. The existence of normative political theory, for example, is not a matter of linguistic possibilities. It is not a matter of redeeming the evaluative potential of language.

The difficulties are further exacerbated when the so-called fact/value problem is tied to the question of objectivity. Nagel and numerous other philosophers and social scientists attempt to suggest not only that the unity of science is a matter of its empirical language or its descriptive speech acts but that objectivity and bias are matters of linguistic purity. But the notion of purely factual content is not intelligible—not because it is impossible to achieve but because the notion is incoherent on the basis of anything other than a verificationist theory of meaning and the assumption that words rather than propositions are the basic vehicle of meaning. We would indeed be in trouble if we could not, for example, describe without evaluating and be understood as doing so, but this has little to do with individual words and even less to do with the question of objectivity. Finally, bias, interest, concern, perspective, and other such factors are not matters of linguistic meaning. The familiar claim that they either can or cannot be divorced from, for example, descriptive claims involves a confusion between what one is doing with words and various contextual criteria regarding the validity of propositions.

Often what is really at stake in discussion of fact and value is a distinction between claims that are on some basis resolvable in terms of their truth and falsity and those that are merely matters of choice, decision, and taste. But these are categories of claims that will differ in content between contexts, depending on substantive criteria of adjudication if such criteria are available and agreed upon. These are practical matters and not matters of linguistic form and meaning. If it were not possible, for example, in principle and practice to explain without prescribing we would never be able to speak without ambiguity, but this has little directly to do with the truth conditions of the explanatory claim. In fine, the fact/value gap is not a problem to be solved by either bridging the gap, maintaining it, or claiming that the gap is an illusion. It is a problem to be *forgotten* along with such epistemological open questions as "How can we *really* know the *world*?" The problem and the solutions are, in the first instance, inappropriately formulated, and, second, to the extent that they reflect real issues they cannot be solved transcendentally and metatheoretically.

It is, however, very difficult to slough off the idea that the conditions and constitution of political theory are situated within this complex of metatheoretical problems dealing with such matters as how one can gain reliable knowledge; how political theory is possible; how objectivity is possible; what rationality is; what the difference is between natural and social phenomena; what the relationship is between theory and practice;

what the nature of explanation is; and the like. And the question that is likely to be posed when we are confronted with a substantive theory is something on the order of how it is to be applied or used. The instrumentalist perspective continues to dominate. Theories can dissolve metatheoretical problems, but they do not underwrite the practice of political theory and social science or give them some sort of blanket legitimacy and authority. And theories are corrigible even if what much of political theory seeks is the transcendence of corrigibility.

A theory of conventional objects offers only a theory for indicating the universe to which political objects belong. It does not provide a program for political theory as an activity. It does not explain anything. Theories do not explain, because they provide the context in which explanatory claims are made. It does not constitute a method. Neither does it provide a warrant of success in undertaking various explanatory, descriptive, evaluative, prescriptive, and critical endeavors. It does not solve, in any ultimate way, the practical question of the relationship between political theory, as an academic field, and politics. It provides no automatic answers to the practical questions within politics of what is just and right. In short, it can never do what most of alienated political theory has sought. That goal has been some ground, whether methodological, epistemological, or meta-ethical, that would release political theory from the responsibility for its claims to truth and relieve it of the burden of judgment and the defense of that judgment. The pervasive and often conceptually incoherent problem of relativism is only the anxiety caused by the lack of guarantees and universal certainty.

At this time in this place, political theory and politics are two symbolic forms that stand in an ambiguous relationship to one another. Political theory, despite its reference to the myth of the tradition, is not invested with any world-historical mission, and it is not the mouthpiece of prophetic truth. As Hobbes noted long ago, the age of miracles is over. And it is an equally exaggerated notion of politics, and also part of the myth of the tradition, that suggests that it is necessarily the realm of human fulfillment and redemption. What academic political theory has in various ways believed is that it could, through the avenues of certainty that philosophy professed to possess, gain a point of purchase by which it could with the hammer of knowledge persuade and coerce an intractable political reality. Whatever the wisdom of that belief, it found itself trapped within the dilemmas of philosophy and particularly within the circle of ideas that suggested that epistemology was theory. It has not been able, even after Kuhn, to face up to the real problem. Philosophy, as metatheory, cannot solve the problem of practical judgment.

The foundations of knowledge, if we must think in terms of this distorting metaphor, are rooted in the practices of life and the theories that orient and inform them. There are no foundations of the foundations, but, again, the image of foundations only leads to justificational regress. Even when foundationalism is rejected in principle, the question is usually "What is the alternative?" which characteristically means a substitute for foundations. But it is not so much that there is no substitute as that looking for one is, as Austin suggested, "barking up the wrong gum tree." Rorty's idea of edification is, as noted earlier, a kind of weak foundationalism, and the "consequences of pragmatism" in his case are much like any version of pragmatism whether in Dewey or in Peirce.

Pragmatism, like epistemology (it is epistemology!), is either a critical instrument for attacking consensus or an apology that assumes that we have consensus on basic principles. Rorty would seem to suggest the latter. He claims, for example, that "the relations between academic politics and real politics . . . are not tight enough to justify carrying the passions of the latter over into the former" (1982:229). Despite his protestations to the contrary, he cannot really give up the idea of "keeping philosophy pure" (19–36). But before we worry about whether Rorty gives us a way out, as Bernstein implies, whether there is a promise of redemption in pragmatic tolerance that demonstrates that dialogue is its own reward, we should remember that academic philosophy is not a likely place to look for practical and theoretical answers. For the most part, it is only social science that does so—only the insecure seek out the arrogant in the hope that truth will make them free.

The end of philosophical foundationalism is only a threat if one thinks that philosophy holds the kind of answers that it promised. It is really only Kuhn and Winch who are unrelenting in the denial of the ability of second-order inquiry to legislate for practice and to seek the resolution of the relationship between metatheory and practice. Epistemology as a mode of inquiry can find a role in the exploration of what constitutes the criteria of knowing in the practices of knowledge, and, as the reflective dimension of practice, it can think about its own activity. But it cannot play the role of theory. This is not to say that epistemology, as either reflection or reflective practice, is sealed off from its object, but the relationship is a matter to be settled in practice and not by the putative authority of reflection. Reflexivity is not self-validating. Yet in one way or another political theory seeks solace in philosophy—in metaphysics, metaethics, epistemology, and the philosophy of history. Even when individuals such as Heidegger and Foucault would seem to suggest in some respects that the game is over, political theory seems to say "You don't really mean it." But all that antifoundationalism promises is the freedom of political theory.

Theories do, nevertheless, have consequences. A theory does not yield a deductive answer to the practical role of political theory as an academic activity, but it does suggest something about the practice of knowledge in the sense of what kind of questions can and might be asked and what inquiry involves. The theory of conventional objects suggests that political theory is, as most might agree, a form of symbolic or interpretative analysis. In this sense, it stands, epistemologically, to politics in much the same way that philosophy, history, literary criticism, and similar fields stand to their respective objects to the extent that those objects are conventions and conventional artifacts. It is not possible to go much further. Such a theory does not entail many of the attributes often suggested in the philosophy of social science regarding the demands of explanation in interpretative inquiry. It does not necessarily entail using the same language as the object, practical immersion in cultural forms, reproduction of the phenomena, testing the intelligibility of claims against the authority of the actors' self-conscious understanding, intuitional apprehension, or penetration of other minds in some deep psychological or biological sense.

The theory of conventional objects does not yield the kind of revealed truth and therapeutic authority that political theory has sought, but it has critical implications—not the least of which is the denial not only of the transcendental character of any political configuration but of the political form itself. If the history of political theory, the classic texts, can offer us any wisdom, it is surely the knowledge that by its very nature politics is a form of life grounded in varying degrees of lie and illusion. Thus an exploration of the world of political meaning and its "ontology" and "epistemology" is potentially, and maybe almost automatically, a critical activity. It is almost by necessity a claim to understand politics better than it understands itself. But neither the truth of that claim nor its practical consequences are self-validating.

One can make the argument, as do Popper, Habermas, Strauss, and other substantive and procedural foundationalists, that criticism requires philosophical certainty that transcends the context of practice, but this kind of triumph over "relativism" is hollow and irrelevant. The "political" differences between these individuals pale in the face of their common rationalist posture. The claim, common to their arguments, that the positions of Nietzsche, Winch, Kuhn, Gadamer, or Foucault entail practical quiescence because they eschew metatheoretical authority is weak, if not fatuous. Rationalism *in* politics or science might be the source of effective dogma, but as a philosophical claim on practice, it is futile and both an antitheoretical and antidemocratic stance. Criticism and foundationalism may be compatible in practical contexts, but they are intrinsically antinomous and ultimately debilitating when joined to create and sustain a vision of politically relevant critical theory. It is just such an attempt at conjunction that is responsible for much of the alienation of political theory, and that alienation cannot be overcome until we can accept the idea of political theory without foundations.

There are, to be sure, strains of political theory and eccentric works that, within the limits of academic discourse, escape some of the more extreme forms of alienation. My concern is not to catalogue the work that tends to exist outside the dominant trends and structures of the political theory establishment that I have attempted to analyze in this book. I would single out, as an example, what might be called feminist political theory as a case in point. This is a mode of discourse that is about something, that is defined by an existential problem rather than by a philosophical category, and that speaks to and for an actual audience. Yet here also, already, the dangers of alienation are apparent. Much of the literature is being drawn within the orbit of the usual academic authorities, and the problems addressed are increasingly defined within the modes of philosophical discourse, which distance them both theoretically and rhetorically from the world about which they purport to speak. The problems are being transformed into conceptual objects, and the practical question of the relationship of academic to public discourse is relegated to a metatheoretical issue. This seems to be the fate of all academic political theory, and although that fate may not be justifiable, I have been concerned to demonstrate that it has a cause.

There is, finally, a certain poignancy attaching to the condition of political theory, and there is pathos in the literature and activity. These qualities may be somewhat faint in the post-1960s world of professional political theory, which in many respects looks very little different from any other professional academic pursuit. But at least in the work of individuals like Strauss, Arendt, and Wolin, who have somewhat unwittingly contributed to the present situation, there is a passion for and sensitivity to politics that have been tragically and paradoxically tied to a search for the sublime. The sublime and the political are ultimately incompatible, but in the contemporary attempt to conjoin them, there is a least a sentimental bond with the classic canon. In the end, in both cases, but maybe for different reasons, the attachment to the sublime triumphed. As a consequence, political theory became at once little more than a ritual plea, an entreaty, unheard, except fortuitously and indirectly, in the world of politics and a curiosity in the world of academe.

# References

Achinstein, Peter. 1971. *Law and explanation*. Oxford: Clarendon Press.

Achinstein, Peter, and Barker, Stephen F., eds. 1969. *The legacy of logical positivism*. Baltimore: Johns Hopkins University Press.

Ackerman, Bruce. 1980. *Social justice in the liberal state*. New Haven: Yale University Press.

Adorno, Theodor W., et al. 1976. *The positivist dispute in German sociology*. New York: Harper and Row.

Alker, Hayward R., Jr. 1965. *Mathematics and politics*. New York: Macmillan.

Almond, Gabriel A. 1966. Political theory and political science. *American Political Science Review* 60:869–79.

Almond, Gabriel A., and Genco, Stephen J. 1977. Clouds, clocks, and the study of politics. *World Politics* 29:489–522.

Almond, Gabriel A., and Verba, Sidney S. 1963. *The civic culture*. Princeton, N. J.: Princeton University Press.

Apel, Karl-Otto. 1967. *Analytic philosophy of language and the Geisteswissenschaften*. New York: Humanities Press.

———. 1985. *Understanding and Explanation*. Cambridge: MIT Press.

Arendt, Hannah. 1958. *The human condition*. New York: Doubleday.

———. 1961. *Between past and future*. New York: Viking.

———. 1978. Martin Heidegger at eighty. In Michael Murray, ed., *Heidegger and modern philosophy*. New Haven: Yale University Press.

Austin, J. L. 1962. *How to do things with words*. Cambridge: Harvard University Press.

Ayer, A. J. 1967. Man as a subject of science. In Peter Laslett and W. G. Runciman, eds., *Philosophy, politics, and society*, 3d ser. New York: Barnes and Noble.

Barber, Benjamin. 1981. Political theory in the 1980s: Prospects and topics. *Political Theory* 9:291.

———. 1982. *Political Theory* 10:491.

———. 1984. *Strong democracy*. Berkeley: University of California Press.

Barry, Brian. 1980. The strange death of political theory. *Government and Opposition* 15:276–88.

Barry, Brian, and Rae, Douglas. 1975. Political evaluation. In Fred I. Greenstein and Nelson W. Polsby, eds., *Handbook of political science*, vol. 1. Reading, Mass.: Addison-Wesley.

Baumgold, Deborah. 1981. Political commentary on the history of political theory. *American Political Science Review* 75:928–40.

Berlin, Isaiah. 1962. Does political theory still exist? In Peter Laslett and W. G. Runciman, eds., *Philosophy, politics, and society*, 2d ser. New York: Barnes and Noble.

Bernstein, Richard. 1976. *The restructuring of social and political theory*. New York: Harcourt Brace Jovanovich.

———. 1983. *Beyond objectivism and relativism*. Philadelphia: University of Pennsylvania Press.

Blalock, Hubert M. 1961. *Causal inference in nonexperimental research*. Chapel Hill: University of North Carolina Press.

Bluhm, William T., ed. 1982. *The paradigm problem in political science*. Durham, N.C.: Carolina Academic Press.

Braybrooke, David. 1958. Relevance of norms to political description. *American Political Science Review* 52:989–1006.

Braybrooke, David, ed. 1965. *Philosophical problems of the social sciences*. New York: Macmillan.

Brecht, Arnold. 1959. *Political theory*. Princeton, N.J.: Princeton University Press.

Brodbeck, May, ed. 1968. *Readings in the philosophy of the social sciences*. New York: Macmillan.

Burger, Thomas. 1976. *Max Weber's theory of concept formation*. Durham, N.C.: Duke University Press.

Cavell, Stanley. 1979. *The claim of reason*. New York: Oxford University Press.

———. 1984. *Themes out of school*. Berkeley, Calif.: North Point Press.

Cobban, Alfred. 1953. The decline of political theory. *Political Science Quarterly* 68. Reprinted in James A. Gould and Vincent V. Thursby, eds., *Contemporary political thought*, pp. 289–303. New York: Holt, Rinehart and Winston, 1969.

Connolly, William. 1981. *Appearance and reality*. Cambridge: Cambridge University Press.

Crews, Frederick C. 1963. *The Pooh perplex*. New York: Dutton.

Dahl, Robert. 1963. *Modern political analysis*. Englewood Cliffs, N.J.: Prentice-Hall.

———. 1969. The behavioral approach in political science: Epitaph for a monument to a successful protest. In Heinz Eulau, ed., *Behavioralism in political science*. New York: Atherton Press.

Dallmayr, Fred. 1984. *Language and politics*. Notre Dame, Ind.: Notre Dame University Press.

Deutsch, Karl W. 1963. *The nerves of government*. New York: Free Press.

———. 1971. On political theory and political action. *American Political Science Review* 65:11–27.

Deutsch, Karl W., and Rieselbach, Leroy N. 1965. Recent trends in political theory and political philosophy. *Annals of the American Academy of Political and Social Science* 360:139–62.

Dunning, William A. 1902, 1905, 1920. *A history of political theories.* 3 vols. New York: Macmillan.

Dworkin, Ronald. 1977. *Taking rights seriously.* Cambridge: Harvard University Press.

Easton, David. 1951. The decline of modern political theory. *Journal of Politics* 1953. 13:36–58.

———. 1953. *The political system.* Chicago: University of Chicago Press.

———. 1965a. *A framework for political analysis.* Englewood Cliffs, N.J.: Prentice-Hall.

———. 1965b. *A systems analysis of political life.* New York: Wiley.

———. 1966. Alternative strategies in theoretical research. In David Easton, ed., *Varieties of political theory.* Englewood Cliffs, N.J.: Prentice-Hall.

———. 1969. The new revolution in political science. *American Political Science Review* 63:1051–61.

Eulau, Heinz. 1967. Segments of political science most susceptible to behavioristic treatment. In James Charlesworth, ed., *Contemporary political analysis.* New York: Free Press.

———. 1969. Quo vadimus. *P.S.: Newsletter of the American Political Science Association* 2:12–13.

———. 1973. The skill revolution and consultative commonwealth. *American Political Science Review* 67:169–91.

———. 1977. The drift of a discipline. *American Behavioral Scientist* 21:3–10.

Feigl, Herbert. 1969. The origin and spirit of logical positivism. In Peter Achinstein and Stephen F. Barker, eds., *The legacy of logical positivism.* Baltimore: Johns Hopkins University Press.

———. 1970. The "orthodox" view of theories: Remarks in defense as well as critique. In Michael Radner and Stephen Winokur, eds., *Minnesota Studies in the Philosophy of Science*, vol. 4. Minneapolis: University of Minnesota Press.

Feyerabend, Paul K. 1964. Realism and instrumentalism: Comments on the logic of factual support. In Mario Bunge, ed., *The critical approach to the philosophy of science.* Glencoe, Ill.: Free Press.

———. 1965. Problems of empiricism. In Robert Colodny, ed., *Beyond the edge of certainty.* Englewood Cliffs, N.J.: Prentice-Hall.

———. 1970. Against method: Outline of an anarchistic theory of knowledge. In Michael Radner and Stephen Winokur, eds., *Minnesota Studies in the Philosophy of Science*, vol. 4. Minneapolis: University of Minnesota Press.

Flathman, Richard. 1966. *The public interest.* New York: Wiley.

Freeman, Robert and Robertson, David, eds. 1980. *The frontiers of political theory.* New York: St. Martin's Press.

Friedman, Milton. 1953. *Essays in positive economics*. Chicago: University of Chicago Press.

Gadamer, Hans-Georg, 1975. *Truth and method*. New York: Seabury Press.

———. 1976. *Philosophical hermeneutics*. Berkeley: University of California Press.

Gellner, Ernest. 1973. The new idealism: Cause and meaning in the social sciences. In Imre Lakatos and Alan Musgrave, eds., *Problems in the philosophy of science*. Amsterdam: North Holland.

Germino, Dante. 1967. *Beyond ideology*. New York: Harper and Row.

Goodin, Robert. 1982. *Political theory and public policy*. Chicago: University of Chicago Press.

Goodman, Nelson. 1978. *Ways of worldmaking*. Indianapolis: Hackett.

Gregor, James A. 1971. *An introduction to metapolitics*. New York: Free Press.

Gunnell, John G. 1968. Social science and political reality: The problem of explanation. *Social Research* 34:159–201.

———. 1969. Deduction, explanation, and social scientific inquiry. *American Political Science Review* 63:1233–46.

———. 1973. Political inquiry and the concept of action: A phenomenological analysis. In Maurice Natanson, ed. *Phenomenology and the social sciences*. Vol. 2. Evanston, Ill.: Northwestern University Press.

———. 1975. *Philosophy, science, and political inquiry*. Morristown, N.J.: General Learning Press.

———. 1976. Social scientific knowledge and policy decisions: A critique of the intellectualist model. In Phillip M. Gregg, ed. *Problems of theory in policy analysis*. Lexington, Mass.: Heath.

———. 1978. The myth of the tradition. *American Political Science Review* 72:122–34.

———. 1979a. Political science and the theory of action: Prolegomena. *Political Theory* 7:75–100.

———. 1979b. *Political theory: Tradition and interpretation*. Cambridge, Mass.: Little, Brown (Winthrop).

———. 1980. Method, methodology, and the search for traditions in the history of political theory. *Annals of Scholarship* 1:26–56.

———. 1981. Political theory and the theory of action. *Western Political Quarterly* 34:341–58.

———. 1982. Interpretation and the history of political theory: Apology and epistemology. *American Political Science Review* 76:317–27.

———. 1983a. In search of the political object: Beyond methodology and transcendentalism. In John S. Nelson, ed. *What should political theory be now?* Albany: State University of New York Press.

———. 1983b. Political theory: The evolution of a sub-field. In Ada Finifter, ed. *Political science: The state of the discipline*. Washington, D.C.: American Political Science Association.

———. 1985. Political theory and politics: The case of Leo Strauss. *Political Theory* 13.

Habermas, Jürgen. 1970. Towards a theory of communicative competence. *Inquiry* 13:360–75.

———. 1971. *Knowledge and human interest.* Boston: Beacon Press.

———. 1973. *Theory and practice.* Boston: Beacon Press.

———. 1979. *Communication and the evolution of society.* Boston: Beacon Press.

———. 1984. *The theory of communicative action.* Vol. 1, *Reason and the rationalization of society.* Boston: Beacon Press.

Hallowell, John H. 1950. *Main currents in modern political thought.* New York: Henry Holt.

Hanson, Norwood Russell. 1958. *Patterns of discovery.* Cambridge: Cambridge University Press.

———. 1969. Logical positivism and the interpretation of scientific theories. In Peter Achinstein and Stephen F. Barker, eds., *The legacy of logical positivism.* Baltimore: Johns Hopkins University Press.

———. 1971. *Observation and explanation.* New York: Harper and Row.

Hare, R. M. 1952. *The language of morals.* Oxford: Oxford University Press.

———. 1963. *Freedom and reason.* Oxford: Oxford University Press.

Harré, Rom. 1970. *The principles of scientific thinking.* Chicago: University of Chicago Press.

Hempel, Carl G. 1965. *Aspects of scientific explanation.* New York: Free Press.

———. 1969. Logical positivism in the social sciences. In Peter Achinstein and Stephen F. Barker, eds., *The legacy of logical positivism.* Baltimore: Johns Hopkins University Press.

Hesse, Mary. 1980. *Revolution and reconstruction in the philosophy of science.* Bloomington: Indiana University Press.

Hirsch, E. D. 1967. *Validity in interpretation.* New Haven: Yale University Press.

———. 1976. *The aims of interpretation.* Chicago: University of Chicago Press.

Hollis, Martin. 1977. *Models of man.* Cambridge: Cambridge University Press.

Holt, Robert T., and Richardson, John M., Jr. 1970. Competing paradigms in comparative politics. In Robert T. Holt and John Turner, eds., *The methodology of comparative research.* New York: Free Press.

Hollis, Martin, and Lukes, Steven, eds. 1983. *Rationality and relativism.* Cambridge: MIT Press.

Horkheimer, Max. 1972. *Critical theory.* New York: Herder and Herder.

Jacobson, Norman. 1958. The unity of political theory. In Roland Young, ed., *Approaches to the study of political theory.* Evanston, Ill.: Northwestern University Press.

Jarvie, I. C. 1972: *Concepts and society.* London: Routledge and Kegan Paul.

Kaplan, Abraham. 1964. *The conduct of inquiry.* San Francisco: Chandler.

Kateb, George. 1968. *Political theory: Its nature and uses.* New York: St. Martin's Press.

———. 1977. The condition of political theory. *American Behavioral Scientist* 21:135–59.

Kemeny, John G. 1960. A philosopher looks at political science. *Journal of Conflict Resolution* 4:292–302.

Keohane, Robert O. 1983. Theory of world politics: Structural realism and beyond. In Ada Finifter, ed., *Political science: The state of the discipline*. Washington, D.C.: American Political Science Association.

Kettler, David. 1967. Political science and rationality. In David Spitz, ed., *Political theory and social change*. New York: Atherton.

Kirkpatrick, Evron M. 1962. The impact of the behavioral approach on traditional political science. In Austin Ranney, ed., *Essays on the behavioral study of politics*. Urbana: University of Illinois Press.

Kress, Paul. 1979. Against epistemology. *Journal of Politics* 41 : 526–42.

Kuhn, Thomas S. 1970a. Logic of discovery or psychology of research? In Imre Lakatos and Alan Musgrave, eds., *Criticism and the growth of knowledge*. Cambridge: Cambridge University Press.

———. 1970b. Reflections on my critics. In Imre Lakatos and Alan Musgrave, eds., *Criticism and the growth of knowledge*. Cambridge: Cambridge University Press.

———. 1970c. *The structure of scientific revolutions*. Chicago: University of Chicago Press.

———. 1977. *The essential tension*. Chicago: University of Chicago Press.

Lakatos, Imre. 1970. Falsification and the methodology of scientific research programmes. In Imre Lakatos and Alan Musgrave, eds., *Criticism and the growth of knowledge*. Cambridge: Cambridge University Press.

Lakatos, Imre, and Musgrave, Alan, eds. 1970. *Criticism and the growth of knowledge*. Cambridge: Cambridge University Press.

Landau, Martin. 1972. *Political theory and political science*. New York: Macmillan.

Laudan, Larry. 1977. *Progress and its problems*. London: Routledge and Kegan Paul.

Laslett, Peter, ed. 1956. *Philosophy, politics, and society*. 1st ser. New York: Barnes and Noble.

Laslett, Peter, and Fishkin, James, eds. 1979. *Philosophy, politics, and society*. 5th ser. New Haven: Yale University Press.

Laslett, Peter, and Runciman, W. G., eds. 1962. *Philosophy, politics, and society*. 2d ser. New York: Barnes and Noble.

———. 1967. *Philosophy, politics, and society*. 3d ser. New York: Barnes and Noble.

Lasswell, Harold, and Kaplan, Abraham. 1950. *Power and society*. New Haven: Yale University Press.

Leiserson, Avery. 1975. Charles Merriam, Max Weber, and the search for synthesis in political science. *American Political Science Review* 69 : 175–85.

Lenin, V. I. 1950. *Materialism and empirio-criticism*. London: Laurence and Wishart.

Lindblom, Charles E. 1982. Another state of mind. *American Political Science Review* 76 : 9–21.

Louch, A. R. 1966. *Explanation and human action*. Berkeley: University of California Press.

Macdonald, Graham, and Pettit, Phillip. 1981. *Semantics and social science*. London: Routledge and Kegan Paul.

MacIntyre, Alasdair. 1971. *Against the self-images of the age.* Notre Dame, Ind.: Notre Dame University Press.

———. 1982. *After virtue.* Notre Dame, Ind.: Notre Dame University Press.

Marcuse, Herbert. 1941. *Reason and revolution.* New York: Oxford University Press.

———. 1964. *One-dimensional man.* Boston: Beacon Press.

McDonald, Neil A., and Rosenau, James N. 1968. Political theory as an academic field and intellectual activity. *Journal of Politics* 30:311–44.

Meehan, Eugene J. 1965. *The theory and method of political analysis.* Homewood, Ill.: Dorsey Press.

Merriam, Charles. 1925. *New aspects of politics.* Chicago: University of Chicago Press.

Merton, Robert K. 1957. *Social theory and social structure.* Glencoe, Ill.: Free Press.

Miller, David, and Siedentop, Larry, eds. 1983. *The nature of political theory.* Oxford: Clarendon Press.

Miller, Eugene F. 1972. Positivism, historicism, and political inquiry. *American Political Science Review* 66:796–873.

Miller, Warren E. 1981. The role of research in the unification of a discipline. *American Political Science Review* 75:9–16.

Moon, J. Donald. 1975. The logic of political inquiry. In Fred I. Greenstein and Nelson W. Polsby, eds., *Handbook of political science,* vol. 1. Reading, Mass.: Addison-Wesley.

———. 1982. Interpretation, theory, and human emancipation. In Elinor Ostrom, ed., *Strategies of political inquiry.* Beverly Hills, Calif.: Sage.

Nagel, Ernest. 1961. *The structure of science.* New York: Harcourt Brace and World.

———. 1971. Theory and observation. In Ernest Nagel et al., eds., *Observation and theory in science.* Baltimore: Johns Hopkins University Press.

Nelson, John S., ed. 1983. *What should political theory be now?* Albany: State University of New York Press.

Nozick, Robert. 1974. *Anarchy, state, and utopia.* New York: Basic Books.

Oakes, Guy. 1977. The Verstehen thesis and the foundations of Max Weber's methodology. *History and Theory* 16:11–29.

Ostrom, Elinor. 1982. Beyond positivism. In Elinor Ostrom, ed., *Strategies of political inquiry.* Beverly Hills, Calif.: Sage.

Parsons, Talcott. 1949. *The structure of social action.* Glencoe, Ill.: Free Press.

———. 1954. *Essays in sociological theory.* Glencoe, Ill.: Free Press.

———. 1970*a*. On building social systems theory: A research history. *Daedalus* 99:826–82.

———. 1970*b*. Theory in the humanities and sociology. *Daedalus* 99:495–523.

Parsons, Talcott, and Ackerman, Charles. 1966. The concept of "social system" as a theoretical device. In Gordon J. Di Renzo, ed., *Concepts, theory, and explanation in the behavioral sciences.* New York: Random House.

Parsons, Talcott, and Shils, Edward A., eds. 1951. *Toward a general theory of action.* Cambridge: Harvard University Press.

Pitkin, Hanna F. 1967. *The concept of representation.* Berkeley: University of California Press.

———. 1972. *Wittgenstein and justice.* Berkeley: University of California Press.

Pocock, J. G. A. 1971. *Politics, language, and time.* New York: Atheneum.

Popper, Karl. 1961. *The logic of scientific discovery.* New York: Science Editions.

———. 1962. *Conjectures and refutations.* New York: Basic Books.

———. 1970. Normal science and its dangers. In Imre Lakatos and Alan Musgrave, eds., *Criticism and the growth of knowledge.* Cambridge: Cambridge University Press.

———. 1972. *Objective knowledge.* Oxford: Clarendon Press.

Poschman, Eugene. 1982. Emerging American social science and political relevance: Extractions from a less than classic American literature. Washington, D.C.: American Political Science Association.

Quinton, Anthony. 1976. Social objects. *Proceedings of the Aristotelian Society.* 76:1–27.

Ranney, Austin. 1976. The divine science of politics: Political engineering in American culture. *American Political Science Review* 70:140–48.

Rapaport, Anatol. 1966. The use of theory in the study of politics. In Edward Buehrig, ed., *Essays in political science.* Bloomington: Indiana University Press.

Rawls, John. 1971. *A theory of justice.* Cambridge: Harvard University Press.

Ricci, David M. 1984. *The tragedy of political science.* New Haven: Yale University Press.

Richter, Melvin. 1980. Introduction to Melvin Richter, ed., *Political theory and political education.* Princeton, N.J.: Princeton University Press.

Ricoeur, Paul. 1971. The model of the text. *Social Research* 38:529–55.

———. 1976a. History and hermeneutics. *Journal of Philosophy* 73:683–95.

———1976b. *Interpretation theory, discourse, and the surplus of meaning.* Fort Worth: Texas Christian University Press.

Riggs, Fred. 1964. *Administration in developing countries.* Boston: Houghton Mifflin.

Riker, William H. 1962. *The theory of political coalitions.* New Haven: Yale University Press.

———. 1977. The future of a science of politics. *American Behavioral Scientist* 21:11–38.

———. 1982a. *Liberalism against populism: A confrontation between the theory of democracy and the theory of social choice.* San Francisco: Freeman.

———. 1982b. The two-party system and Duverger's law: An essay on the history of political science. *American Political Science Review* 82:753–66.

———. 1983. Political theory and the art of heresthetics. In Ada Finifter, ed., *Political science: The state of the discipline.* Washington, D.C.: American Political Science Association.

Riker, William H., and Ordeshook, Peter C. 1973. *An introduction to positive political theory.* Englewood Cliffs, N.J.: Prentice-Hall.

Rorty, Richard. 1979. *The mirror of nature.* Princeton, N.J.: Princeton University Press.

————. 1982. *The consequences of pragmatism*. Minneapolis: University of Minnesota Press.

Rudner, Richard. 1966. *Philosophy of social science*. Englewood Cliffs, N.J.: Prentice-Hall.

————. 1973. Some essays at objectivity. *Philosophic Exchange* 1:115–35.

Runciman, W. G. 1963. *Social science and political theory*. Cambridge: Cambridge University Press.

Sabia, Daniel R., Jr. 1984. Political education and the history of political thought. *American Political Science Review* 78:985–99.

Sabine, George. 1937. *A history of political theory*. New York: Holt, Rinehart and Winston.

————. 1939. Political theory. *Journal of Politics* 1:1–16.

Schaar, John H., and Wolin, Sheldon S. 1963. Essays on the scientific study of politics: A critique. *American Political Science Review* 57:125–50.

Scheffler, Israel. 1967. *Science and subjectivity*. Indianapolis, Ind.: Bobbs-Merrill.

Schutz, Alfred. 1967. *The phenomenology of the social world*. Evanston, Ill.: Northwestern University Press.

Scriven, Michael. 1958. Definitions, explanations, and theories. In Herbert Feigl, Michael Scriven, and Grover Maxwell, eds., *Minnesota studies in the philosophy of science*, vol. 2. Minneapolis: University of Minnesota Press.

————. 1959. Truisms as the grounds for historical explanation. In Patrick Gardner, ed., *Theories of history*. Glencoe, Ill.: Free Press.

————. 1962. Explanations, predictions, and laws. In Herbert Feigl and Grover Maxwell, eds., *Minnesota studies in the philosophy of science*, vol. 3. Minneapolis: University of Minnesota Press.

Searle, John. 1969. *Speech acts*. Cambridge: Cambridge University Press.

Seidelman, Raymond. 1985. *Disenchanted realists*. Albany: State University of New York Press.

Sellars, Wilfrid. 1963. *Science, perception and reality*. New York: Humanities Press.

Shapere, Dudley. 1966. Meaning and scientific change. In Robert Colodny, ed., *Mind and cosmos*. Pittsburgh: University of Pittsburgh Press.

————. 1984. *Reason and the search for knowledge*. Boston: Reidel.

Sheldon, Richard C. 1951. Some observations on theory in social science. In Talcott Parsons and Edward A. Shils, eds., *Toward a general theory of action*. Cambridge: Harvard University Press.

Simon, Herbert A. 1947. *Administrative behavior*. New York: Macmillan.

Skinner, Quentin. 1969. Meaning and understanding in the history of ideas. *History and Theory* 8:3–53.

————. 1970. Conventions and the understanding of speech acts. *Philosophical Quarterly* 20:118–38.

————. 1971. On performing and explaining linguistic actions. *Philosophical Quarterly* 21:1–21.

Smith, James Ward. 1957. *Theme for reason*. Princeton, N.J.: Princeton University Press.

Spragens, Thomas A., Jr. 1973. *The dilemma of contemporary political theory.* New York: Dunellen.

Stevenson, C. L. 1945. *Ethics and language.* New Haven: Yale University Press.

Stoppard, Tom. 1964. *Jumpers.* New York: Grove Press.

Storing, Herbert J., ed. 1962. *Essays on the scientific study of politics.* New York: Free Press.

Strauss, Leo. 1953. *Natural right and history.* Chicago: University of Chicago Press.

————. 1959. *What is political philosophy?* Glencoe, Ill.: Free Press.

————. 1962. Epilogue. In Herbert J. Storing, ed., *Essays on the scientific study of politics.* New York: Free Press.

————. 1963a. Introduction to Leo Strauss and Joseph Cropsey, eds., *History of political philosophy.* Chicago: Rand McNally.

————. 1963b. *On tyranny.* Glencoe, Ill.: Free Press.

————. 1964a. *The city and man.* Chicago: Rand McNally.

————. 1964b. The crisis of our time: The crisis of political philosophy. In Herbert Spaeth, ed., *The predicament of modern politics.* Detroit: University of Detroit Press.

————. 1972. Political philosophy and the crisis of our time. In George J. Graham, Jr., and George W. Carey, eds., *The post-behavioral era.* New York: McKay.

————. 1975. The three waves of modernity. In Hilail Gildin, ed., *Political philosophy: Six essays by Leo Strauss.* Indianapolis, Ind.: Bobbs-Merrill.

Suppe, Frederick, ed. 1977. *The structure of scientific theories.* Urbana: University of Illinois Press.

Taylor, Charles. 1964. *The explanation of behaviour.* New York: Humanities Press.

————. 1967. Neutrality in political science. In Peter Laslett and W. G. Runciman, eds., *Philosophy, politics, and society.* 3d ser. New York: Barnes and Noble.

————. 1970a. Explaining action. *Inquiry* 13:54–89.

————. 1970b. The explanation of purposive behavior. In Robert Borger and Frank Cioffi, eds., *Explanation in the behavioral sciences.* Cambridge: Cambridge University Press.

————. 1971. Interpretation and the sciences of man. *Review of Metaphysics* 25. Reprinted in Fred R. Dallmayr and Thomas A. McCarthy, eds., *Understanding and social inquiry,* pp. 101–31. Notre Dame, Ind.: University of Notre Dame Press, 1977.

————. 1980. The philosophy of the social sciences. In Melvin Richter, ed., *Political theory and political education.* Princeton, N.J.: Princeton University Press.

————. 1983. Political theory and practice. In Christopher Lloyd, ed., *Social theory and political practice.* Oxford: Clarendon Press.

————. 1984. Foucault on freedom and truth. *Political Theory* 12:152–83.

Thorson, Thomas Landon. 1962. *The logic of democracy.* New York: Holt, Rinehart and Winston.

Toulmin, Stephen. 1950. *An examination of the place of reason in ethics.* Cambridge: Cambridge University Press.

————. 1953. *The philosophy of science.* London: Hutchinson.

————. 1958. *The uses of argument*. Cambridge: Cambridge University Press.

————. 1961. *Foresight and understanding*. Bloomington: Indiana University Press.

————. 1968. Conceptual revolutions in science. In Robert S. Cohen and Marx W. Wartofsky, eds., *Boston studies in the philosophy of science*, vol. 3. New York: Humanities Press.

————. 1969. From logical analysis to conceptual history. In Peter Achinstein and Stephen F. Barker, eds., *The legacy of logical positivism*. Baltimore: Johns Hopkins University Press.

————. 1972. *Human understanding*. Vol. 1. Princeton, N.J.: Princeton University Press.

Trigg, Roger. 1973. *Reason and commitment*. Cambridge: Cambridge University Press.

————. 1980. *Reality at risk*. New York: Barnes and Noble.

Truman, David B. 1965. Disillusion and regeneration: The search for a discipline. *American Political Science Review* 59:865–73.

Van Dyke, Vernon. 1960. *Political science: A philosophical analysis*. Stanford, Calif.: Stanford University Press.

Voegelin, Eric. 1952. *The new science of politics*. Chicago: University of Chicago Press.

————. 1956. *Order and history*. Vol. 1, *Israel and revelation*. Baton Rouge: Louisiana State University Press.

————. 1957. *Order and History*. Vol. 3, *Plato and Aristotle*. Baton Rouge: Louisiana State University Press.

————. 1968. *Science, politics, and gnosticism*. Chicago: Regnery.

————. 1975. *From enlightenment to revolution*. Durham, N.C.: Duke University Press.

Von Wright, Georg Henrik. 1971. *Explanation and understanding*. Ithaca, N.Y.: Cornell University Press.

Wahlke, John C. 1979. Pre-behavioralism in political science. *American Political Science Review* 73:68–77.

Walzer, Michael. 1983. Philosophy and democracy. In John S. Nelson, ed., *What should political theory be now?* Albany: State University of New York.

Weber, Max. 1948. *The methodology of the social sciences*. Edited by Edward A. Shils and Henry A. Finch. Glencoe, Ill.: Free Press.

————. 1975. *Roscher and Knies: The logical problems of historical economics*. Edited by Guy Oakes. New York: Free Press.

Weldon, T. D. 1953. *The vocabulary of politics*. Harmondsworth: Penguin Books.

————. 1956. Political principles. In Peter Laslett, ed., *Philosophy, politics, and society*, 1st ser. New York: Barnes and Noble.

Wildavsky, Aaron. 1979. *Speaking truth to power: The art and craft of policy analysis*. Boston: Little, Brown.

Wilson, Bryan R., ed. 1970. *Rationality*. Oxford: Blackwell Publisher.

Winch, Peter. 1958. *The idea of a social science and its relation to philosophy*. London: Routledge and Kegan Paul.

———. 1970. Comment. In Robert Borger and Frank Cioffi, eds., *Explanation in the behavioral sciences*. Cambridge: Cambridge University Press.

———. 1972. *Ethics and action*. London: Routledge and Kegan Paul.

———. 1976. Language, belief, and relativism. In H. D. Lewis, ed., *Contemporary British Philosophy*. London: Muirhead Library of Philosophy.

Wittgenstein, Ludwig. 1968. *Philosophical investigations*. New York: Macmillan.

Wolff, Robert Paul. 1969. *The poverty of liberalism*. Boston: Beacon Press.

Wolin, Sheldon S. 1960. *Politics and vision*. Boston: Little, Brown.

———. 1968a. Paradigms and political theories. In Preston King and B. C. Parekh, eds., *Politics and experience*. Cambridge: Cambridge University Press.

———. 1968b. Political theory: Trends and goals. In David L. Sills, ed., *International encyclopedia of the social sciences*, vol. 12. New York: Macmillan.

———. 1969. Political theory as a vocation. *American Political Science Review* 63:1062–82.

———. 1970a. Communication. *American Political Science Review* 64:592.

———. 1970b. *Hobbes and the epic tradition of political theory*. Los Angeles: William Andrews Clark Memorial Library.

———. 1973. The politics of the study of revolution. *Comparative Politics* 5: 343–58.

———. 1977. Hannah Arendt and the ordinance of time. *Social Research* 44: 91–405.

———. 1980. Political theory and political commentary. In Melvin Richter, ed., *Political theory and political education*. Princeton, N.J.: Princeton University Press.

———. 1981. Max Weber: Legitimation, method, and the politics of theory. *Political Theory* 9:401–42.

———. 1983a. Hannah Arendt: Democracy and the political. *Salmagundi* 60: 3–19.

———. 1983b. On reading Marx politically. In J. Roland Pennock and John W. Chapman, eds., *Marxism. Nomos* 26. New York: New York University Press.

# Index